MERCEDES-BENZ

A History

*The fascinating story of automotive development,
begun nearly a hundred years ago by Daimler and Benz*

by W. Robert Nitske

Motorbooks International
Publishers & Wholesalers Inc
Osceola, Wisconsin 54020, USA

Books by W. Robert Nitske

The Complete Mercedes Story (Macmillan, New York, 1955)

The Amazing Porsche and Volkswagen Story (Comet Press, New York, 1958)

Rudolf Diesel, Pioneer of the Age of Power (with Charles Wilson) (University of Oklahoma Press, Norman, 1965)

The Life of Wilhelm Conrad Röntgen, Discoverer of the X-Ray (University of Arizona Press, Tucson, 1971)

Travels in North America, 1822-1824 (translation of exploration diary of Duke Paul Wilhelm of Württemberg) (University of Oklahoma Press, Norman, 1973)

Mercedes-Benz 300 SL (Motorbooks International, Minneapolis, 1974)

The Zeppelin Story (A. S. Barnes & Company, Cranbury, 1977)

Mercedes-Benz Production Models 1946-1975 (Motorbooks International, Osceola, 1977)

First Printing

*All illustrations are from the archives
of Daimler-Benz A. G.*

Designed by Ad/Graphics, Inc.
Printed by Shandling Lithographing Co., Inc.
Tucson, Arizona 85705

Library of Congress Cataloging in Publication Data

Nitske, W. Robert
Mercedes-Benz: a history.

1. Mercedes automobile.   2. Daimler-Benz Aktiengesellschaft.
I. Title.
TL215.M4N515   629.22'22   78-9044
ISBN 0-87938-055-1

World-wide distributors:

Motorbooks International
Osceola, Wisconsin, U.S.A.

Contents

Preface to This Book 4

Acknowledgments. 4

Preface 5

Gottlieb Daimler (1834-1900) 6

Karl Benz (1844-1929). 20

The Automobile Conquers the World (1894-1914) 34

The Blizten Benz (1909). 46

Racing and Sports Cars (1921-1933) 52

The 750-Kilogram Formula (1934-1937) 62

The 3-Liter Formula (1938-1940). 72

The 1.5-Liter Racer (1939) 80

World Speed Record Cars (1901-1939) 86

Mercedes-Benz Drivers (1894-1955) 94

Grand Prix Statistics (1934-1939 and 1954-55). 112

Allied Automotive Products (1884-1977). 120

Daimler and Benz Production Models (1885-1939). 146

Postwar Production Models (1949-1965) 166

The Sports- and Racing-Car Program (1952-1965) 176

Production Models (1966-1973) 200

Production Models (1973-1978) 216

Model Details 225

Preface to this Book

The Mercedes-Benz History is a greatly expanded version of the successful earlier book, *The Complete Mercedes Story, The Thrilling Seventy-Year History of Daimler and Benz*.

First published in 1955 by the Macmillan Company, subsequent enlarged editions appeared over the years until it seemed advisable to publish a new book now. The text is almost entirely that of the previous work with few alterations but many additions. The current book is completely redesigned and contains many more pictures. It is, of course, up-to-date as of the time of publication, and includes details of the 1978 line of cars.

The title of the first book appeared rather presumptuous to me, for the Mercedes Story was not yet complete, and the contributions by Benz seemed ignored. However, the early history of the men and the company — Daimler and Benz — was definitive, but new technological advances are continually incorporated into new models and the entire story is not yet completed.

It is the desire of the author to bring this edition up-to-date periodically by adding new chapters whenever the need arises and sales of the book allow, so that the interested owner of a fine Mercedes-Benz automobile can readily find the truly remarkable history behind the creation of his car.

W. Robert Nitske

Tucson, Arizona
March 1, 1978

Acknowledgments

I owe the greatest appreciation to Albrecht Fürst von Urach of the Press Division of Daimler-Benz A.G., Stuttgart, for invaluable assistance in assembling many pertinent facts of the Mercedes story.

The monumental biographies of Gottlieb Daimler and Karl Benz by Paul Siebertz, upon which I have relied in the early chapters, were most helpful.

The excellent photographic illustrations are from the archives of Daimler-Benz A.G.

The quotations from the catalog of the Museum of Modern Art, New York, written by Arthur Drexler, are used by permission of the Museum.

I also wish to thank my wife Betty, who has read faithfully these pages and made necessary corrections — incidentally, it pleases me to think, becoming as familiar with such great names as Daimler, Benz, Mercedes, and Caracciola, as she is with those of Bach, Beethoven, and Brahms.

W. Robert Nitske

Preface

This book is respectfully submitted to the untold many automobile enthusiasts to whom Mercedes-Benz is a fabulous, but legendary name. I hope that it may bring a better appreciation of the invaluable pioneering work of the great men of vision, Gottlieb Daimler and Karl Benz, who founded the industry and guided it in the first toddling steps toward its phenomenal growth.

This book is dedicated to the multitude of unknown, ingenious workers who have worked diligently to improve the first practical motor vehicles and bring into existence the present superb automobiles.

As will be evident, the writer is not a technician. I have never driven a Grand Prix Mercedes-Benz; but I have admired many. My only personal experience on the speedway occurred when, as a motorcycle side-car rider in a well padded crash helmet, I once bounced on the bumpy racing circuit. I thought that I had already done my utmost when my driver shouted "Farther" or the equivalent as we roared into the next, steeply banked turn at absolutely terrifying speed. I pulled my head in, instead, not caring to lose it. In the safety of the pits, I removed the scarred helmet quickly, put it into the austere side car, and, from a safe distance, shouted over the staccato noise of the stripped-down, hopped-up racing cycles, "Auf Wiedersehen." What I really meant was "Good-bye."

The Complete Mercedes Story is not a technical treatise. It is written from the heart, out of an admiration which began many years ago. As a young man I was strolling on a sunny afternoon along Unter den Linden. At the curb in front of the fashionable Adlon Hotel stood, in dazzling brilliance, a dream car: an immaculately kept, highly polished, white Mercedes-Benz SS model. The bright red leather upholstery, the flashing silver pipes that protruded from under the long, racy hood, and the spare tires attached to the rear deck of the low-slung sports car made it the most exquisite thing I had ever seen. It was out of this world.

The sumptuous Adlon of that day is rubble, the beautiful and majestic Unter den Linden is torn apart, and over the once dignified and stately metropolis hangs an ominous cloud. But, perhaps, the beautiful Mercedes-Benz may come to life in these pages.

W. Robert Nitske

Santa Barbara, California
March 29, 1955

Gottlieb Daimler (1834-1900)

The Mercedes story begins, like the entire history of automobiles, with Gottlieb Daimler. More than any other man, Daimler was undoubtedly responsible for bringing the motor age to the world. He was rightly called "father of the automobile."

Significantly, perhaps, in 1834, the year in which Gottlieb Daimler was born, the Berlin chemist Eilhard Mitscherlich named a recently developed refined petroleum product "benzine" (gasoline). He experimented to find other, more useful, purposes than cleaning, and he thought that gasoline offered promising possibilities as a fuel.

Interestingly, Daimler was born in an age when steam was king. In 1827 the first European-built steamship, the *Curacao,* had made a successful Atlantic crossing from Antwerp to Paramaribo, Dutch Guiana. And the *Royal William,* launched in Montreal, had crossed to Europe in twenty-five days, completely independent of the unreliable winds. She used no other power than steam. All this happened twenty years after Robert Fulton had made the first practical steamboat trip up the Hudson River.

Steam locomotives appeared on the scene. Progress was rapid. The scientific world teemed with anxiety.

By 1838 the *Great Western,* a steamer of 450 horsepower and 1,340 gross tons, had crossed the Atlantic in the unbelievably short time of fifteen days. Gottlieb Daimler was then four years old.

Born in the small town of Schorndorf, in Württemberg, Gottlieb was the second son of a master baker, Johannes Daimler. Like all the children of the community, he attended the public school. Then came the *Realschule* (high school), where he made good grades and was an eager student according to his final report card. Turning away from his father's trade, he went to a tinsmith shop for the usual four-year apprentice period.

What influenced the young Daimler to choose the trade of tinsmith is uncertain. He may have been swayed by such stirring events as the completion of the first telegraph line, on which the inventor, S. F. B. Morse, tapped out the question, "What hath God wrought?"

Or other inventions, promising a glorious future in the technical and mechanical fields, may have affected his choice. It was a golden age of invention, a period of bold imagination and eager anticipation of extraordinary, revolutionary things.

Finishing the apprenticeship at the age of eighteen, Gottlieb Daimler went to near-by Stuttgart to the state trade school to broaden his theoretical and practical knowledge.

It was his good fortune to have the instruction of the learned Ferdinand Steinbeis, who later earned the affectionate title of "father of Württemberg industry." The teacher was able to inspire the student, who followed the wise man wholeheartedly and most keenly.

There followed a busy but happy period in the workroom, in the smithy, and in the machine shop. Under Jakob Friedrich Messmer came study courses in the Grafenstadener Werkstätten, mostly on locomotive building. Daimler became an excellent mechanic here, but left in 1857 to broaden and advance his studies in the Polytechnic Institute at Stuttgart.

During two years at this institution, Daimler became fascinated and engrossed in the study of the little-understood "benzine." He felt that this petroleum product had great possibilities for driving machines, and thought it illogical to use it only as a cleaning agent. Although it was highly inflammable, he thought that it could be harnessed.

The young engineer left the institute and, as promised, returned to Messmer and his locomotive works. Here was a good opportunity to convince Messmer that the building of a gasoline-powered small and portable motor was feasible. However, Messmer was perfectly content to continue to build reliable and tested steam engines, instead of spending valuable time and money on new experiments in an unknown and, perhaps, extremely dangerous field.

So, Daimler kept on building steam locomotives until he read in a French publication that a mechanical engineer named Lenoir had suggested that fluid fuel, mixed with air, could be used to power engines.

Daimler went to Paris and talked with Lenoir, but soon convinced himself that the Frenchman did not have a practical engine in mind; and he told him so in no uncertain terms. Afterward he went to England and worked two years in the steam-engine plant of Smith, Peacock & Tannet, at Leeds.

Gottlieb Daimler, 1834-1900

In the meantime Heinrich Straub, an old friend of the Polytechnic Institute days in Stuttgart, asked Daimler to come and run his Metallwaren Fabrik, which was badly in need of a good manager. He accepted the post and, during the two years at Geislingen, tried to interest Straub in the development of a gasoline motor. But again he failed to win an ally.

Then Emil Kessler asked Daimler to take over the management of his Reutlingen machine shop, and he accepted gladly. He soon found, however, that he had no time at all for experimentation, and he left the post after two years to become works director of the Maschinenbaugesellschaft at Karlsruhe. Here he met again the young Wilhelm Maybach, whom he had known at Reutlingen, and hired him. It was the beginning of a close cooperation and friendship. Daimler now had free time to spend at the Technical University, working in the laboratory on his process to preheat gasoline by combustion and ignite it.

Through a recommendation, Gottlieb Daimler came to an executive position at the Deutz Gasmotorenfabrik, the leading manufacturer of illuminating-gas engines based on the Nicolaus August Otto invention. The management soon realized his ability and made him technical director in charge of development and manufacture.

Otto had exhibited his first practical atmospheric gas engine in the 1867 Exposition de Paris (world's fair), where its decided economy over other engines caused much excitement. He perfected his four-cycle internal combustion engine in 1876, still using regular illuminating gas as fuel. A year after the German patent was issued, he secured an American patent. His process still forms the basic engine principle.

Daimler contributed greatly to the technical improvement of the atmospheric engine. In 1876 he devised a mechanism which improved the manner of preparing the explosive mixture of fuel and air. This early-type carburetor and other developments soon made the Otto engine the outstanding gas motor of the time. Daimler, seeking to improve it further, adapted it to gasoline as a fuel. He wished to create a smaller, easily portable engine which, using fuel that it could itself transport, would cease to be dependent on the gas works. However, his fellow workers were satisfied with the cumbersome gas engines and showed no interest whatever in his experimentation. After ten years he left Deutz.

Wilhelm Maybach was reluctant to leave his secure position at the Deutz works, but eventually was persuaded to rejoin his friend.

In the spacious garden of a newly purchased villa at Cannstatt, near Stuttgart, Daimler had a roomy workshop constructed, with a huge concrete cellar to store large gasoline drums. This could be considered as the first gasoline filling station.

Now, the various still unresolved problems of the proposed gasoline engine were systematically attacked. The greatest, of course, was to devise a satisfactory way of igniting the fuel that would allow high engine revolutions. Another was to build a light engine which would be useful for all imaginable types of transportation.

News from America startled the world in 1879. Thomas Alva Edison had perfected an incandescent light which had burned continuously for forty hours at a demonstration. Inventors were working feverishly on many astonishing and highly imaginative innovations. The scientific world was on the march.

Daimler and Maybach diligently attacked the problems before them. For a whole year they calculated, drew plans, and built models. Eventually, they were successful, and on December 16, 1883, the Reichspatentamt issued patent number 28022 to Gottlieb Daimler for his compression-ignition, called "hot tube ignition." By regulating the heat of the tube he controlled the point at which ignition took place. Engine speeds of 700 to 750 revolutions per minute were achieved. Another patent, number 28243, was issued six days later, covering some improvements over the earlier process.

Daimler had Wilhelm Kurtz, the Stuttgart fire equipment manufacturer, build three engines for him. The first, completed on August 15, 1883, was a small engine with a horizontal cylinder and a large flywheel, mounted on a wooden block. A slightly larger engine, mounted on a stand, was built in November 1883; and the third engine, in a round housing, was finished in January 1884.

These were the first Daimler engines. They were the first light, high-turning gasoline-powered engines ever built, anywhere. They operated at 900 revolutions per minute and weighed but 88 pounds per horsepower output. The Otto gas engines, on the other hand, turned over at

Patent document of December 16, 1883

First high-speed, four-cycle gasoline Daimler engine
in 1883

a maximum of 180 revolutions per minute and weighed 725 pounds. In addition, their fuel supply limited them to the gasworks. The Daimler invention was unquestionably an event of great magnitude, and a most important step in the development of motorized transportation.

In far-off America, 1883 was a year of progress in many fields, especially in transportation. The great Northern Pacific Railway completed its main line, crossing mountains and rivers, and drove the customary golden spike to commemorate the event. A tremendous bridge was built to link the city of Brooklyn with New York. At the dedication ceremony, the huge crowd became unruly and, perhaps, frightened, and twelve people were trampled to death. And in the nation's capital a plain granite shaft, reaching like a silent finger straight into the sky, was nearing completion as memorial to George Washington, the father of his country. 1883 was a great year.

In Germany, Gottlieb Daimler offered his newly invented gasoline engine to the Deutz company for manufacture. When the directors failed to see any future for it and turned down the offer, he undertook again to develop his own invention and adapt it for transportation. He decided to make a gasoline-powered bicycle. Motorized transportation, he thought, would benefit the most people. However, he was not satisfied with the high front wheel and the small rear wheel of the contemporary velocipede, and so he designed and made a sturdy bicycle with wheels of equal size.

Upon submission of twelve precise, detailed drawings and diagrams of his motorcycle, the Kaiserliche Patentamt issued patent number 36423 to Gottlieb Daimler on August 29, 1885. The vehicle was built of wood, and the wheels were covered with protective steel rims. The engine was cooled by a small ventilator, and featured two different speeds and a neutral.

When all the "teething troubles" had been overcome on numerous test runs about the dignified Cannstatt neighborhood, Daimler's oldest son, Paul, finished successfully what was considered as a *kolossal* trip to near-by Untertürkheim — a distance of no less than two miles. But the useful motorcycle did not find ready acceptance.

After many tests in the factory grounds of the Esslinger Maschinenfabrik, a slightly altered horse carriage with a 1.5-horsepower Daimler engine appeared on the streets. (A short time before, Karl Benz had tested elsewhere his three-wheeled motorcar.)

Daimler now used water to cool his engine, diverted otherwise useless exhaust gases to heat the gasoline mixture as well as provide comfortable heat for the vehicle's two passengers, and used rubber blocks to reduce the vibration of the engine.

As expected, neighbors and gendarmes were rather disdainful of this unusual and frightening conveyance. As the belligerent, influential local press was protectively pointing out, this devilish vehicle endangered the entire community with its highly inflammable fuel and its unwarranted, galloping speed. The police concurred heartily, and refused to allow the diabolical contrivance on the city streets under any conditions.

Rather than fight the apparently unsurmountable opposition, Daimler turned to a different field. He installed a gasoline engine in a boat and rode up and down the beautiful Neckar River.

"The boat carried eight passengers, upstream, at great speeds," the hostile but decently fair *Cannstatter Zeitung* reported on November 5, 1886. The motorboat had begun to operate in early August of that year, but many people thought it a menace on the river. So Daimler quit the river until late fall, when the many summer vacationers had left and excursion and pleasure boats had all but disappeared from the stream.

He had a special boat built, eighteen feet long with room for eleven passengers, under his patent number 39367 of October 1, 1886. Its 1.5-horsepower engine enabled it to cruise, fully loaded, at a steady speed of six miles per hour.

For the new series of boat trips, Daimler strung wires around the boat and connected them to the dock by means of porcelain insulators. Attitudes once reluctant changed completely now. People believed the boat was driven by electricity and was safe from explosions.

Success of the gasoline-powered boat was thus assured. Its fame spread quickly, and Gottlieb Daimler began to make boats in July 1887 in the

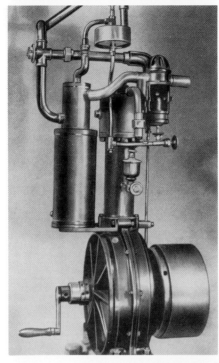

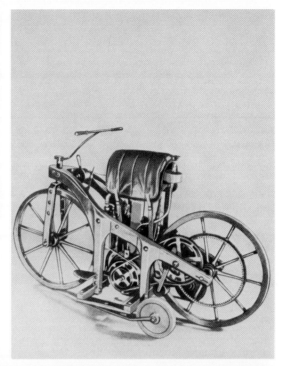

Single-cylinder Daimler engine of 1885

Daimler motorcycle of 1885

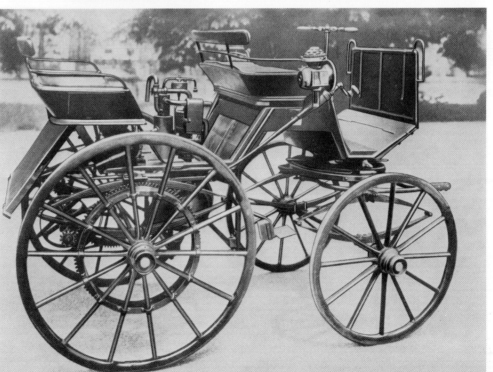

First Daimler motor carriage, 1886

former plant of a nickel-plating concern, purchased exclusively for that purpose.

About the same time Daimler developed a means of transmitting gasoline power to a streetcar. This new horseless "Pferdeeisenbahnwagen" caused a considerable stir. The now friendly local press speculated enthusiastically that it might no longer be necessary to import the costly steam engines from far-off America for the forty-three-year-old Cannstatt-Untertürkheim railway.

Huge gasoline engines were now manufactured on a regular schedule, and soon similar, narrow-gauge cars appeared in Bremen, and eventually as far away as Paris and Vienna, Holland and Italy. Even railroad cars were pulled by Daimler-powered engines in Württemberg.

Fire engines and ambulances were built in 1888, driven by Daimler's gasoline engines. A year later, his boats were seen in many harbors. Daimler boats carried crowds on lakes and rivers all over the world. On a serene, deep blue Mediterranean Sea, a Daimler motorboat circumnavigated Sicily in a rousing demonstration. Firms around the world clamored to sell Daimler's boats and engines, and he soon had an excellent world-wide sales representation.

In 1888 he developed a one-cylinder motor for use in an airship which the Leipzig book dealer Wölfert tested. Eleven years later, Graf Zeppelin took delivery of a four-cylinder Daimler motor for his first airship.

And Gottlieb Daimler kept working on improvements. After satisfactory tests of a new-type engine consisting of two regular, upright cylinders joined at a twenty-degree angle, he received a patent on June 9, 1889. This was soon produced in large numbers and proved to be well suited for practically all purposes where greater power output was desirable.

Earlier in the year, he had completed the first entirely new-design four-wheel motor vehicle. The "steel-wheel carriage," as he called it, had a strong frame of steel tubing. Some of the tubes served also as a cooling system for the water used to cool the motor. A pump circulated the water. The bench-type seat for two passengers, higher than that in a conventional horse carriage, was above the engine, which was just ahead of the rear axle. The engine was the newest V type. The power was transmitted to the wire wheels through several cog wheels. Four speeds were possible: four, six, eight, and twelve miles per hour. A tiller was used for steering.

Exhibited in the pavilion of the fashionable Paris Exposition of 1889, the Daimler all-steel automobile competed strongly for public attention with the Benz Patent-Motorwagen and the new, sensational 984-foot steel tower, built for the fair by Alexandre Gustave Eiffel.

Despite the enthusiastic acceptance of the new vehicle, Daimler postponed production in order to improve it further. On the wall of his workshop hung a plainly framed motto, "Das Beste oder nichts," and he meant to produce nothing but the best. He kept working on the steel automobile: took it apart, tested the various components, and made such changes as he deemed advisable.

Perhaps the first luxury custom-built automobile was delivered to the Sultan of Morocco in 1892. It was sumptuously furnished in silk upholstery with a tassel-studded fringe suggestive of a throne canopy, and with curtains on the sides. The outside was painted in a combination of gold and gay pastel colors. The coach was a product of the Stuttgart master coachbuilder Otto Nagele.

Some capitalists realized the possibilities for profits in the new industry and approached Gottlieb Daimler with a proposal for the building of a large plant to produce his engines and vehicles; and on November 28, 1890, the Daimler Motoren Gesellschaft, A.G., was founded with a capital of 600,000 marks. Daimler brought his debt-free Cannstatt factory and all his patent rights into the new corporation. As compensation he received stock equal to 200,000 marks outright, plus 5 percent interest on the 200,000 and dividends on 100,000 marks' worth of company stock.

Soon after the contract was signed, Daimler realized that his new partners were interested only in the manufacture and sale of the engines and vehicles, and would allow no time or money for research. His repeated requests for research facilities were voted down by his fellow directors, who reasoned that there was an easy sale for all the engines, boats, and vehicles the young company could produce, for a long time to come.

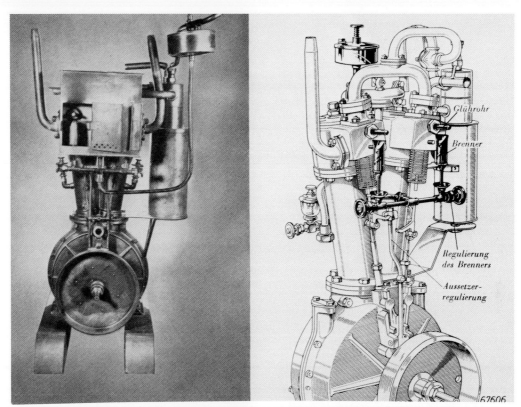

Twin-cylinder V-type engine and
Diagram with burner housing

Glührohr

Brenner

*Regulierung
des Brenners*

*Aussetzer-
regulierung*

67606

Daimler wire-wheel car of 1889

13

Once again, Daimler went to work alone. At his own expense, he changed the spacious garden room of a Cannstatt hotel into a laboratory and workshop. Together with Wilhelm Maybach and other capable assistants, he started a new business. It seemed indeed like old times.

In the meantime Daimler's Paris friend Edouard Sarazin, who with Emile Levassor, owner of the Panhard-Levassor woodworking plant in Paris, had built various vehicles, acquired the French rights to build and distribute the inventor's engines, boats, and vehicles. Other French manufacturers also were building the engines, but without permission. When the German reproached one of them the offender admitted readily: "Of course we build them. You don't build that type any more, yourself." Although the "hot-tube ignition" engines were obsolete by Daimler's standards, they constituted, for the unauthorized manufacturers, a solid foundation of a thriving business.

Several important improvements were made on the current engine design at that time. The newest type, the N-Model ("N" standing for new), which was assigned to Panhard-Levassor for licensed manufacture in 1895, became known as the "Moteur Daimler-Phénix." The greatest improvement over the former types was the new carburetor, patented under Maybach's name, which controlled the fuel and air mixture automatically. It was a float-feed type and replaced the vaporizing type which had been in use since 1885. The Phénix motor was slightly different and featured a smoother regulating mechanism, cooling improvements, easier and more effective lubrication, and a considerable reduction in exhaust noise.

Soon after winning acceptance in France, Daimler products found their way to the United States. William Steinway, long renowned for his pianos, had obtained a license during a visit to his native Germany a year before to build the Daimler vehicles in the United States. In 1891 the Steinway Motor Company advertised three Daimler motor vehicles: the motor quadricycle (Daimler's steel-wheel carriage); a motor carriage; and the motorcycle.

Under the first illustration was the statement:

> The drawing represents the 1 HP Daimler Steel Quadricycle to carry 2 persons, with 4 different speeds, 4, 6, 8, and 12 miles per hour, and will take grades up to 10%; weight complete about 400 pounds.
>
> As will be seen from [the] illustration, the motor is located under the seat and the machinery is so arranged that by moving a small lever the speeds can be changed without stopping. By drawing the lever, which is on the left side, backward, the gearing is connected with the motor and the quadricycle brought into motion. By placing it in the central position, the machinery is thrown out of gear, and by pressing it forward the brake is brought into operation, bringing the quadricycle instantaneously to a standstill, [with] the motor still running.
>
> Sufficient petroleum can comfortably be carried for a whole day's use, as only about 1¾ gallons are required for 12 hours, thus bringing the cost per mile to a mere nothing.

Under the next drawing was the explanation:

> This represents the Daimler Motor Carriage. Seats 4 persons. Motor, 2 HP (indicated). The general arrangements of this carriage are similar to those of the quadricycle; it runs at the general carriage speed and takes the usual occurring grades.
>
> These vehicles have been in successful use since 1887, in and about Stuttgart, Germany, and experience shows that horses do not shy either at this or any of our street conveyances, propelled by a Daimler Motor.
>
> Our motors can also be attached to ordinary buggies and coaches of every description.
>
> The other illustration represents a German "Fahrrad" (bicycle) fitted up with 1 HP Daimler Motor.

Six Daimler products of various types were exhibited at the World's Columbian Exposition in Chicago in 1893, and at the Sportsman Exhibition in New York in 1896.

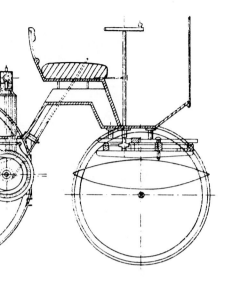

Construction drawing of first Daimler carriage

Gondola of Wölfert airship with 4-horsepower engine, 1888

Daimler riding in carriage, with son Paul
at steering tiller, 1886

Daimler motorboat for Fürst Bismark, 1888

A British syndicate approached Daimler for the purchase of the patent rights in the British Isles and Dominions. The directors of the German corporation then saw the error of their ways, and toward the end of 1895 the inventor returned actively to the company which bore his name. He now had full rein in making policy. The British syndicate acquired the rights requested for 350,000 marks.

In the same year, Rudolf Diesel perfected an internal combustion gasoline engine, operating with pulverized fuel and air compression; and the German physicist Wilhelm Conrad Röntgen discovered the remarkably penetrating X rays. The highly controversial Dreyfus case had just ended in France with the condemnation of Captain Alfred Dreyfus to Devils Island and the acquittal of Major Esterhazy. A Parisian, Henri Becquerel, had discovered that uranium contained radioactivity; but more Frenchmen were interested in the "first international race for automobiles," from Paris to Bordeaux and return, a distance of 730 miles.

The four leaders, and the cars in sixth place and seventh, were Daimler-powered. Emile Levassor drove the winning Panhard-Levassor racer the distance in less than forty-nine hours, at an average speed of 15.2 miles per hour. The three Peugeots, also Daimler-powered, took sixty hours to complete the run. The fifth- and eighth-place cars were of German Benz manufacture.

Actually, the first automobile race on the Continent, sponsored by the *Petit Journal*, had been held on July 22, 1894, on the dusty road from Paris to Rouen. While more than a hundred stalwart pioneers were eager to participate, only twenty-one machines reached the starting line, and only thirteen completed the run. The four leading automobiles had Daimler engines, and the winner's average speed was over twelve miles per hour for the seventy-eight-mile distance. The two-cylinder, V-shaped Daimler engines developed 3.5 horsepower.

France took to the motor vehicles much more enthusiastically than Germany. The Gallic temperament adapted itself more readily than the Teutonic to this radically new but promising means of transportation.

Several German manufacturers had now undertaken to build gasoline engines of Daimler's design and invention, without a license. The com-

pany brought suit against some of them, and when it won the suit others volunteered to pay for the privilege to manufacture the engines. The Daimler company realized some 677,000 marks from such sources within the next few years.

Instead of resting on the reliable performance record of his successful and widely accepted engines, Daimler developed new, improved types. In 1898 he built a four-cylinder engine and a special 6-horsepower racing car. But he was reluctant to build such a powerful machine and felt that similar abundant power would allow excessive and dangerous speeds in a regular road vehicle. He suggested that there was no need to use six horsepower if four would reach the destination as well. People and horses should get used to the fuming and sputtering monsters gradually. Also, greater speeds meant greater responsibility for the inexperienced drivers, many of whom were unprepared for sudden emergencies.

That year, a Daimler automobile reached a steady speed of thirty miles per hour on level ground. Other Daimler vehicles traveled over difficult mountain passes and hazardous roads in the Alps. They had now proved their reliability.

Since 1896 the thirteen-mile-long railroad from Saulgau to Riedlingen had used cars with Daimler engines. The company had also furnished the the first buses for a line maintaining a regular schedule between Künzelsau and Mergentheim, in Württemberg, in August 1898. And it had built delivery trucks, ambulances, fire engines, and farm tractors.

In the late nineties Gottlieb Daimler relinquished active participation in the company. His sons Paul and Adolf took over the management.

When in the fall of 1899 Emperor William II asked to see all types of Daimler-produced vehicles, a long procession of models, including magnificent limousines, passenger vehicles of various sizes, buses, trucks, and racing cars set off past the Cannstatt home of the ailing Gottlieb Daimler, who sat watching, propped up in a chair.

It was a well deserved last tribute to the great man who had made the automobile possible. Gottlieb Daimler died on March 6, 1900.

Daimler draisine of 1887

Daimler-engined Stuttgart-Canstatt streetcar, 1888

Canstatt Exhibition streetcar, 1887

Details of first motor carriage: Engine position

The drive wheel arrangement and

The springing and turning arrangement

Karl Benz (1844-1929)

Historians have often compared the two pioneering giants in the German automobile industry, Gottlieb Daimler and Karl Benz, with Goethe and Schiller in literature. The two in each field were outstanding, worked independently of each other about the same time, and left an indelible imprint on their age and on time to come.

If Gottlieb Daimler chose his profession with well considered deliberation, Karl Benz had his mechanical ability through heredity. His father became a locomotive engineer in 1843 for the just established Grossherzogliche Badische Eisenbahn, on the Karlsruhe-Heidelberg run, and died in a railroad accident less than two years after the birth of Karl on November 25, 1844.

When the young Karl in play only drew prophetic pictures of locomotives, usually embellished with heavy curly smoke billowing from a tall, thin stack, his worrying mother tried to guide his thoughts into other channels. At the age of nine he progressed from the public school to the Karlsruhe Gymnasium, where she hoped his mind would be directed into higher fields than mechanics and railroading.

At the Gymnasium, Homer and the other luminaries of Greece and Rome failed to captivate the boy. Railroads were then making their bold mark in many parts of the world, and his thoughts dwelt in the present. One afternoon a week he assisted in the "Physics Cabinet" with unofficial and informal experiments carried out by faculty members.

From such activities it was but a step to the Polytechnic University, whose director, Ferdinand Redtenbacher, was one of the great scholars of his time. Benz enjoyed his lectures, and laboratory work under him, for more than two years. Then he died, and Benz, with other grief-stricken students, accompanied his body to the final resting place. Under the new director, Franz Grashof, the boy continued his theoretical and practical studies. Hydraulics and heat theories fascinated him, and promised to yield answers to some perplexing questions connected with the Lenoir gas-engine tests of 1860.

When Karl Benz finished his studies in July 1864, he looked for employment that would provide more than a mere subsistence. His widowed mother, meanwhile, had been working as a cook and had rented rooms to augment her meager railroad compensation.

At the age of twenty he became a locksmith in the Karlsruhe Maschinenbaugesellschaft, the first locomotive manufacturing plant in Germany, where Gottlieb Daimler was later to be works director. After two years he obtained a better position as draftsman and construction engineer with the Johann Schweizer Machine Works in Mannheim.

In the three years that followed he held high hope for an opportunity to work on some technical phase of planning new machines or improving old ones. But the company was engaged in a comprehensive expansion program, and he was kept busy in the erection of buildings.

At last Karl Benz left his position and went to work for the Gebrüder Benckiser, bridge builders at Pforzheim. The year was 1870, and the Franco-Prussian War had begun. Planning to get married, he felt that he could better himself in the Vienna branch of the concern. After transferring to the Austrian capital, however, he realized that the opportunities were considerably less, and he soon returned to Pforzheim — staying this time only long enough to convince his fiancée that prosperous industrial Mannheim would be a good substitute for Vienna.

In the city at the junction of the Neckar and the Rhine, Benz's search for employment became desperate as the post-war depression deepened. Then he decided courageously to open a machine shop of his own. Lacking the necessary capital, he took in a partner and acquired a parcel of land with a building where the Carl Benz & August Ritter Mechanische Werkstätte was founded on August 9, 1871.

The partnership did not work out, as hoped, and Benz was able to buy Ritter's share the next year; but business was bad, and the newly established machine shop had an especially hard row to hoe. One of its first large contracts was ironwork in the fortification of Metz. The Treaty of Frankfurt had now ended the war formally.

During spare moments, Karl Benz recalled some of the problems which had challenged him at the Polytechnic University: how, for instance, to apply machine power to the transportation of persons. He became interested in a bicycle and in means to power it. In his shop he developed an improved hydraulic press for baling tobacco. Although he expected great sales, few buyers were interested in it. However, the infant gas-engine industry offered tremendous promise for the future. Benz realized that

Karl Benz, 1844-1929

he could not successfully compete with the large, well established Deutz factory, where Daimler was technical director; but he thought he could improve the Deutz product, or create an engine based on an entirely new principle.

In 1873 the new German Reich under Emperor William I underwent a severe financial crisis, and all German industry had an uneasy time.

The year 1878 was especially difficult for Karl Benz. In the exacting work of engine development, there were no windfalls, no accidental stumblings on solutions of difficult problems. Every action was painstakingly planned, minutely diagrammed, carefully executed, and hopefully tested; and the tedious, detailed work went on for year after year.

Eventually, a two-cycle gas engine appeared to be workable. Just as the year 1880 was about to make its entry, the prototype engine turned over and coughed. Then, having caught its breath, it ran successfully and smoothly. The first gas engine to use electricity for ignition had been perfected.

In Mannheim on October 1, 1883, Karl Benz founded Benz & Cie., Rheinische Gasmotorenfabrik. On December 1, the name of the new company was registered. The following year the factory was in production and delivered gas engines which would, as advertised, "be completely odorless and start immediately without a gas flame, consequently, without danger of fire."

In 1884 the French government issued to him patent number 161209 for the new ignition-type gas engine; and in 1885 he received the American patent number 316868 for it.

The building of a motor vehicle was not then considered as worthy of report in a dignified newspaper. It was regarded as the work of a crank. In Cannstatt, about sixty miles away, Gottlieb Daimler had built a motorcycle and was working on an engine-powered carriage. Yet neither man knew that the other was working on a similar problem, or that the other even existed.

By the late fall of 1885 Karl Benz had completed his "Patent-Motorwagen Benz." The following July, the Mannheim *Zeitung* noted that the vehicle had been driven, quite successfully, on the Ring, the city's main thoroughfare.

The "Patent-Motorwagen" was a rather unusual vehicle. Benz had planned to use a conventional carriage; but he could not solve the complicated steering problem to his satisfaction. Therefore he built a completely new, three-wheeled steel vehicle. The one front wheel presented no steering problem. The small engine developed 0.75 horsepower and weighed less than 200 pounds; it was capable of 450 revolutions per minute and developed 0.88 horsepower according to tests made, but he claimed only 250 to 300 revolutions per minute. The engine and gas tank were above the rear axle, and the seat for two passengers was just ahead of them. A large lever on the left side of the driver regulated the gas engine. Tiller steering was used. The single front wheel was considerably smaller than the rear steel-spoke wheels. And it was the first motor vehicle built which had a differential.

On January 29, 1886, the Deutsche Reichspatent number 37435 was issued to Karl Benz for his motor vehicle. Now the inventor was ready to take orders for his "Patent-Motorwagen-Benz" and begin manufacturing.

Instead of orders, however, Benz, like most of the daring pioneers before and after him, received ridicule and abuse. Many people pitied the apparently sane man who had spent considerable effort and not a little money on an entirely useless, sputtering and smoking horseless carriage. Some astute observers pointed out that, as long as there were enough horses in the country, it was ridiculous to buy a motor vehicle.

Fortunately for Benz and his partners, their gas-engine business developed to such an extent that their quarters became inadequate. The factory was turning out ten large stationary engines monthly and had an urgent need for more space. A larger tract was purchased outside the city, on which a factory was built, and a home for the Benz family.

In August 1888 Frau Benz and her two sons, without the knowledge of her husband, made a trip in the Motorwagen to Pforzheim and back. This was a considerable distance, and the undertaking was unheard of, especially for a woman. The news created quite a stir in the community, but had little effect in furthering the sale of the vehicle.

Prospectus of Benz gas engine, 1883

Benz, spurred on by his wife's daring trip, drove the Motorwagen two hundred miles to the important trade and industry fair at Munich. There he met an overwhelming reception. The judges bestowed the gold medal of the fair on his automobile, and the press gave it bountiful praise. However, only one prospective customer appeared.

As Karl Benz later told the story, the prospective buyer unfortunately was committed to a mental institution before the vehicle could be delivered. When this became known, people suggested mockingly that a similar fate would befall any and all buyers of a Motorwagen.

The fact that motor vehicles were barred from the roads may have contributed to the reluctance of purchasers. After prolonged insistence, the Duchy of Baden authorized the use of the roads by Benz motor vehicles. However, the license had many qualifying clauses, so that the ultimate permission rested still with the local, often unreasonable, gendarmes.

The partners in the Benz company were greatly discouraged by the apparent impossibility of selling the motor vehicles, in which the inventor had now made several slight improvements. However, they decided to postpone until after the 1889 world's fair at Paris any decisions on future relations with the Rheinische Gasmotorenfabrik.

The Benz-built gas engines had been distributed in France by Emile Roger for several years. One day Roger had appeared at the Mannheim factory and purchased a Benz motor vehicle. Back in Paris he demonstrated it to René Panhard and Emile Levassor, who were already building engines licensed by Daimler. They showed extraordinary interest and bought the Benz vehicle at once. However, they kept their Daimler franchise.

Roger now acquired the distribution rights in France for the Benz motor vehicles. He proposed to import them in parts in order to circumvent the higher rate of duty on a completed vehicle. Also, he suggested that they would sell more readily under the French name, Roger — a proposal that Karl Benz turned down promptly.

The otherwise aggressive Roger did not, for some reason, take advantage of the outstanding acceptance of the Benz Motorwagen at the 1889 fair. It and the Daimler vehicle shared the honor of being the first automobiles to be exhibited internationally. They stood, in superbly polished luster, in the flower-filled grand pavilion. Wildly excited exhibitors shouted and gesticulated explanations over the noise of the fast-running motors. However, the exhibition did not result in any immediate sales.

After this disappointment the original partners left the Benz company. New partners, more sympathetic toward the building of the still unprofitable and apparently highly dubious motor vehicles, were found.

By 1890 the company gave steady employment to fifty men in the building of engines and motorboats that sold readily.

In the spring of 1891 Benz solved the steering problem to his satisfaction. He received patent number 73515 in February 1893 for his device. Then he built a four-wheeled vehicle and called it, quite appropriately, "Victoria." It had the appearance of a conventional carriage. The one-cylinder engine, which turned 400 revolutions per minute and developed three horsepower, was housed in a box at the rear. The top speed of the 1,430-pound vehicle was twelve miles per hour.

In Chicago, at the wondrous World's Columbian Exposition of 1893, one great attraction was the hurriedly completed Benz "Velo" model, which stood in the sprawling Transportation Building, along with the Daimler exhibits. The German displays had many serious admirers and sparked the automobile industry in the United States.

Many of the American automobiles which soon appeared bore a remarkable resemblance to this Benz product. Ingenious automotive mechanics modified the design, and some, perhaps, improved on the Benz vehicle; but as many corrupted its features horribly.

The Rochester attorney George Selden had filed a patent application in 1879 for a road vehicle powered by a gasoline engine. He did not, however, construct such a vehicle at that time. By filing revisions from time to time he cleverly delayed the granting of a patent until 1895, when a functioning vehicle was finally built. Other early American inventors who built motor vehicles during that time were forced to pay royalties to Selden, although they did not copy the principle of the Brayton engine which was the basis of his patent claim.

Engine of the first Benz vehicle

Benz "Patent Motorwagen" of 1886

The Benz Motor Company of New York was organized in 1894 to sell Benz vehicles in the United States.

The "Velo" model, built from 1893 to 1900, resembled a horse carriage only slightly. The wire-spoke steel wheels had pneumatic tires. The steering tiller rose straight up, in the center, in front of the two-passenger seat. The regulating lever was at the left. The engine, completely covered, was mounted under the comfortable bench seat. The 1.5-horsepower engine allowed the 600-pound vehicle a reasonable speed of more than twelve miles per hour.

In 1894 Baron von Liebig drove his Victoria from the Bohemian town of Reichenberg to Mannheim on the Rhine and Trier, and thence to Paris, a distance of some 600 miles. The "Benz Baron," as he was soon called, made many trips and participated frequently in rallies and reliability runs with his sturdy vehicle. He did much to further the acceptance of the motor vehicle, and especially of the Benz name. The vehicle earned a well deserved reputation for reliability. Benz automobiles had now crossed high and difficult Alpine passes repeatedly and were guaranteed to climb 20 percent mountain grades.

In the 730-mile cross-country race from Paris to Bordeaux and return in 1895, the two Benz vehicles entered made a good showing. Outclassed by the more powerful Daimlers — which took the first four places and the sixth and seventh — the one-cylinder, 3-horsepower Benz Vis-à-Vis vehicles took fifth and eighth places.

That same year, the resourceful and energetic Emile Roger, who had the distribution rights in France for the Benz vehicles, took three cars to New York. He placed them shrewdly with the leading department stores there. R. H. Macy & Company, Gimbel Brothers, and Hilton, Hughes & Company (later taken over by Wanamaker's), all featured the Benz vehicles in their advertisements and created quite a sensation in the metropolis.

Hilton, Hughes & Company proclaimed emphatically:

> Now for the Horseless Wagons. Paris is going wild over them. All the world is watching. Up hill, down hill, twist, turn — at a snail's pace or up to 15 miles an hour, they say.

> No steam, no electricity, just a little petroleum air-engine — simple, cheap, almost noiseless. Have they solved the run-about wagon problem? Judge for yourselves.

> We have the first Horseless Wagon ever brought to America — just landed from La Champagne. At 11 a.m. today it shall have a trial on the streets of New York.

Thousands of eager New Yorkers accepted the invitation and turned out to see for themselves. Washington Square was a mass of pushing humanity long before the appointed time, and the police had tremendous difficulty in controlling the huge crowd.

The enterprising Roger also organized a manufacturing company in New York, the Roger Mechanical Carriage Company; but no vehicles were ever built.

New Yorkers were speed-conscious that year. The first Empire State Express had established a new record. Four years before, the New York Central crack train had covered the 436 miles between Buffalo and New York in 8 hours and 42 minutes for what promised to be a long-standing mark. Now, however, the same train had cut the running time to 6 hours, 54 minutes, and 27 seconds, an average of 64.34 miles per hour.

The brothers Charles and Frank Duryea had studied the design and construction of the Benz automobile diligently and had fashioned their vehicle, the first successful gasoline automobile built in the United States, after the German car.

The *Scientific American* stated on December 14, 1895, that "the paternity of the motor vehicle of Charles Duryea is admittedly that of Karl Benz." The Frenchman Louis Bonneville, a canny observer, wrote that the Winton vehicle was "a Benz copy," and that the first Detroit-built King vehicles were "a variation of the Benz machine."

Chicagoans were thrilled in 1895 when in the battle of ever increasing railroad speeds a Lake Shore & Michigan Southern Railroad engine beat the New York Central's recent record. The engineer made the 510-mile run to Buffalo in 8 hours, 1 minute, and 7 seconds, at an average of 64.98 miles per hour. And the Chicago *Times Herald* offered five thousand dollars in prizes to the winners of a race for horseless carriages or motor vehicles from Chicago to Waukegan and return, to be held on

Front page of Benz prospectus of 1888

November 2. The fact that few men were working at a practical motorized vehicle did not seem to bother the publisher. In fact, he intended to encourage the construction of "practicable, selfpropelled road carriages by American inventors."

Although eighty-four enthusiastic builders entered vehicles, the list of competitors shrank before race time to thirty-four: twenty-one gasoline-engined vehicles, seven electric machines, four steam-powered cars, one with compressed air, and one with a steel-spring mechanism.

At starting time for the practice runs, on October 31, only four vehicles appeared under their own power. A Daimler and a Benz, en route from New York, had bogged down on muddy roads and did not arrive. The promotors were greatly embarrassed by the limited line-up.

On November 2 only two cars were ready to start: a Benz, imported by H. Mueller & Co. of Decatur, Illinois, and a Duryea, built in Springfield, Massachusetts. The race was postponed until Thanksgiving Day. It seemed ridiculous that there should be but two vehicles prepared to compete in the race. Twenty-two vehicles had started at Versailles for the *Petit Journal* race four months before, in France. Surely, there would be a larger field of contestants in the first automobile race in America.

A consolation race was suggested. The "special" prize was to be five hundred dollars, and one condition was that the entire distance had to be covered. The Duryea started first. Ten minutes later the Benz, with Mueller driving, was flagged on its way. The Duryea vehicle broke its drive chain, and a replacement could not be found. The Benz performed smoothly and, in Waukegan, took on several cans of ice to assist in cooling the engine on the unusually warm November day. Mueller returned before seven o'clock, well within the specified thirteen hours allowed for the 160 miles. This was the first official automobile race held in the United States.

In the Thanksgiving Day race, shortened to 85 miles, six automobiles competed: two electrics, the Duryea, and three Benz cars. The Duryea won. Mueller's Benz broke its drive belt but placed second, and O'Connor, who had just arrived from New York for the race in the Macy car with no opportunity to familiarize himself with the race course, took third place.

The Mueller-owned Benz was taken on a triumphant tour the following spring from Decatur, Illinois, to Indianapolis. "The people were wild with enthusiasm," Oscar B. Mueller reported. In most places several thousand interested spectators battled for a choice spot to see the winning car. The final torchlight parade in Indianapolis was described by a local newspaper reporter as "a comet on its path, with its long fiery tail of bicycle lamps."

Later this Benz vehicle, in which William Jennings Bryan rode through Illinois during the 1896 presidential campaign, created as much interest as the golden-tongued oratory.

In 1897 the automobile was still so uncommon that it was one of the featured attractions, along with ferocious jungle beasts, of the Barnum & Bailey Circus.

In 1896 the Bon Marché department store caused a sensation and much favorable comment in Paris with its five-horsepower Benz delivery truck. It was smart advertising, and chagrined the wailing, outwitted competitors who used horse-drawn delivery wagons. The first Benz taxi was enthusiastically welcomed on the Paris boulevards. Commentators speculated that this new mode of transportation would quickly replace the horse-drawn vehicles and would therefore eliminate the "present awful congestion on the streets."

Under the British Railroad and Highway Act horseless vehicles which traveled at speeds as great as four miles per hour had to be preceded at a distance of fifteen feet by a man with a red flag. The repeal of this law in 1896 opened the way for the automobile in the British Isles. A syndicate took over the sales of Benz vehicles. Motor vehicle owners celebrated their newly acquired freedom with an emancipation run from London to Brighton. Nine Daimler and six Benz automobiles, with eighteen other participants, made the run, which eventually turned into a regular race.

In 1897 Karl Benz began to build multiple cylinder engines. He preferred, however, opposed cylinders to parallel-lying ones. Called "Kontra-Motor," the earliest two-cylinder engine developed up to 8 horsepower. Soon engines of 16 horsepower were constructed. Speeds increased accordingly.

Benz 6-horsepower "Victoria" of 1893

Benz "Vis-a-Vis" of 1895

When Julius Ganss, one of the new partners in the company, announced in 1898 that he had sold 200 automobiles to the French distributor, Benz was rather reluctant to build them. However, the factory facilities were enlarged, and the order was duly delivered. Soon after that, Ganss brought another order for 200 from England. Now, Benz automobiles were sold as far away as Moscow, Buenos Aires, Singapore, and Capetown. Thanks to the aggressive Ganss, they were seen in many world capitals.

The Velo model enjoyed special popularity. It was steadily improved over the years, and by 1898 Benz & Cie. announced proudly that more than 1,200 Velos had been delivered to satisfied customers. The attractive price of 2,000 marks (about $475) probably went far to bring this about.

A large model, the "Phaeton," that would accommodate four passengers comfortably, was built and equipped with a 5-horsepower engine. A luxurious "Landauer," in the finest tradition of master carriage builders, was produced for wealthy customers.

Of 1898 vintage also was the "Comfortable," a rather luxurious two-seater with a 3-horsepower engine. The "Ideal," considerably roomier, also dated from that year.

A Benz "Comfortable" won great honors in the hundred-mile reliability run from London to Oxford and return, sponsored by the *Daily Mail*. Carrying four persons, it traveled the extremely bad roads at an average speed of 13.5 miles per hour, and covered the entire distance with no difficulties whatever. The *Daily Mail* commented that "the Benz wagon, although built in Germany, and cheap, functioned excellently."

When in 1899 the "Tonneau," with a 9-horsepower opposed-cylinder engine, developed a speed exceeding thirty miles per hour, Karl Benz suggested the advisability of constructing adequate roads before any further increase in the engine output. However, the Benz racer of that year reached a speed of almost 50 miles per hour, with an engine of 16-horsepower output. It was priced at 15,000 marks (about $3,600). Fritz Held and Hans Thun in their special Benz won the Distanzfahrt Frankfurt-

Cologne that year against strong opposition; and they scored many other impressive victories in the following years.

The Benz automobile of 1900 had a two-cylinder engine with an unusually low speed of 600 revolutions per minute. Magnetic electric ignition and a water-cooling system were provided. Speeds up to 50 miles per hour were possible, and no grades were too steep.

By the end of 1901 Benz & Cie. had produced, and sold, 2,702 vehicles. Production had reached 603 units in 1900, but had fallen off to 385 the following year. The astonishing success of the revolutionary Mercedes automobile, produced by Daimler, had swept the world. It made all other makes and models suddenly obsolete. In 1902 the Benz factory built only 226 automobiles. The next two years many models were built, and eventually the company got out of its difficulty.

Karl Benz remained active in the company until 1903. From the age of sixty, he passed more and more time in his beautiful home at Ladenburg on the Neckar. In 1906 his sons Eugen and Richard founded their own motor and motor vehicle manufacturing plant at Ladenburg under the name, "C. Benz Söhne."

In 1925 Karl and Berta Benz rode again in their first vehicle at the head of a long and colorful parade through the streets of Munich, and were greeted with thunderous cheers instead of the derision and abuse received in Mannheim forty years before.

When in 1929 the Rheinischer Automobil Klub sponsored a nation-wide "honor run" for the eighty-four-year-old "Father Benz," he lay critically ill in his home. He did not hear the sounds of the exhausts of the multitude of automobiles that came great distances to drive past his villa. Many hundreds of drivers paid a well earned last tribute to the man who had done so much for the development of the automobile.

Karl Benz died three days later, on April 4.

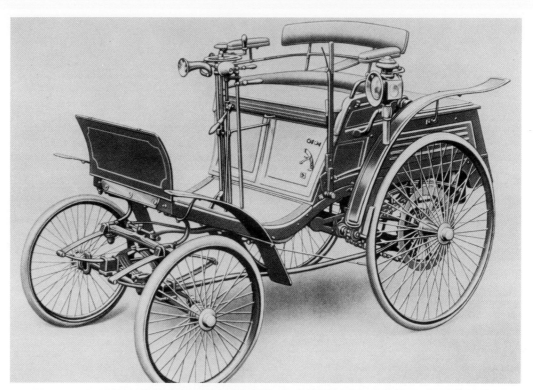

Benz "Velo" of 1894

First Benz omnibus, 1895

Clara Benz driving the "Velo," 1893

An outing in the stylish Mercedes, 1901

Steering mechanism of the Benz "Patent Motorwagen" of 1885

Engine arrangement with electric sparking device

The differential and rear wheel drive

The Automobile Conquers the World (1894-1914)

Before the end of the nineteenth century the gasoline-powered automobile was an accomplished fact. And the entire civilized world knew about it.

Newspapers and periodicals printed detailed information about the new-type vehicles and offered simple explanations of the apparently complicated mechanisms. Although pictures showed ladies driving immaculately clean horseless carriages, it was generally realized that driving one was still a man's job. Automobiles had not yet got beyond the status of interesting playthings for wealthy sportsmen.

People everywhere flocked to exhibitions of automobiles and enjoyed tremendously an occasional race at speeds even greater than that of a runaway horse; but the attitude of most people toward the automobile combined apprehension with that great interest.

Manufacturers realized that the automobile had to establish itself as a legitimate and greatly superior means of transportation before the infant industry could consider itself as secure. An excellent way to convince people of the reliability and safety of the automobile was through races on open roads, and reliability runs over difficult terrain and under conditions of greater severity than the average driver would ever encounter.

When Karl Benz observed in 1899 that existing roads were inadequate for the great speed of thirty miles per hour which his 9-horsepower automobile had achieved, he voiced a chronic complaint of officials and editors of trade journals since his time. It seems that roads have never kept up with the speeds of the vehicles which use them. But in spite of danger, or perhaps because of it, thousands of enthusiastic spectators lined the roads whenever automobiles raced. The early races made a tremendous impression upon the spectators and played a great part in establishing the automobile as a necessity in life. The vehicles that competed were from the regular stock of the makers and were not modified in any way for racing. Consequently, the winning of a race usually meant a generous increase in sale of the victorious model.

Recognizing that superiority in a competitive event was better advertising than printed laudation in a newspaper, Daimler and Benz constantly and rapidly improved their automobiles.

The Daimler-engined Peugeot vehicle of 1894, which averaged more than 12 miles per hour in the Paris-to-Rouen race, had a two-cylinder V-type engine of 75-millimeter bore and 140-millimeter stroke which developed 3.5 horsepower. The Benz vehicle in that race had a one-cylinder engine which developed 3 horsepower. The Daimler Vis-à-Vis of 1894, with opposite facing seats, was powered like the other Daimler of that year; among the events in which it participated was the 1896 London-to-Brighton reliability run. Those vehicles had the outward appearance of conventionally styled carriages.

The Benz Velo of 1894 was, as mentioned earlier, an unorthodox automobile by the prevailing standards. It weighed but 600 pounds, and its one-cylinder engine developed 1.5 horsepower, enough for it to speed along at twelve miles per hour on its pneumatic tires. The Daimler Victoria of 1897, a considerably larger vehicle, was successful in the first of the numerous Austrian Alpine rallies. The two-cylinder engine developed 7.5 horsepower, which afforded welcome reserve energy for the steep mountain grades on that particular run.

The Benz Dos-à-Dos of 1898, with a two-cylinder, 8-horsepower engine, won in the 1899 Berlin-to-Leipzig run. It was the first vehicle equipped with inflated tires of a larger size, insuring a more comfortable ride. This short-wheelbase vehicle developed into the 1899 Benz racer. The bench facing to the rear was left off, perhaps because its passengers had been too much exposed to an overtaking dust cloud. While the engine remained under the seats in the rear, a cowl was built over the front end; and the enlarged front wheels gave the vehicle a well balanced profile. This type of car was victorious in the 1900 road race from Mannheim to Pforzheim and back.

The Daimler Phoenix racer of 1899 was completely redesigned and had many improvements. The frame was short. The pneumatic-tired wood-spoke wheels, front and rear, were of equal size. A steering wheel was used instead of the now antiquated tiller. A substantial cowl added greatly to the general appearance the 3,650-pound vehicle, which had a four-cylinder, 28-horsepower engine.

Peugeot carriage with Daimler engine of 1894

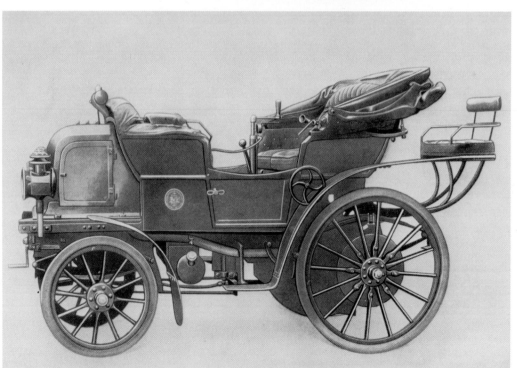

Daimler "Phoenix" with front-mounted engine, 1897

The 1899 Daimler, like the Benz of the same year, looked radically different from the earlier carriagelike vehicles. They heralded a new, revolutionary, and unprecedented automobile style.

For many years, social leaders of the world had passed their leisure time basking in the pleasantly warm sun and splashing in the jewellike Mediterranean Sea at Nice. A new attraction had recently been added. During the celebrated "Week of Nice" automobiles now raced to Salon and back, 243 miles. And a difficult hill climb, the hazardous La Turbie, became popular.

Among the many sportsmen who were impressed by the Daimler performances at those events was the wealthy Austro-Hungarian consul Emil Jellinek, from Vienna. Interested in the sale of Daimler automobiles in France, he invested heavily in the German corporation and was influential in having the new models named Mercedes, after his daughter. He was of the opinion that this name would be more acceptable to the French people than Daimler. When later the cars were offered for sale in Austria by the Oesterreichische Daimler Motoren Gesellschaft, Jellinek suggested that the name of Mercedes' sister, Maja, be used there.

The first Mercedes racer, built under the guidance of Wilhelm Maybach, had only a slight resemblance to the previous Daimler model. The radiator was square instead of sloping, and the low chassis had a longer wheelbase. The steering wheel was set at a better angle, and the four-cylinder engine was improved to develop 35 horsepower. The total weight of the new car was 460 pounds, and the top speed was 55 miles per hour.

Daimler's vehicles had improved considerably through the years. The first Mercedes automobile had the four-cylinder engine in the front, had a honeycomb-type radiator, a multiple gear box, a spring-actuated clutch, a foot throttle, and a magnetic electric ignition system. And its roadability was sensational. The price was 15,275 marks (about $3,650).

As usual, the touring car was practically the same as the racing model car, except that it had a second seat and a folding top instead of the racer's smooth, sloping, rear deck.

First shown in 1901, at the "Week of Nice," the elegant white Mercedes automobiles were an instantaneous success. Adding laurels, Wilhelm

Werner won the Salon race in his new 1901 model, at an average speed of 36 miles per hour. The first Mercedes was a sturdy, dependable, and speedy automobile.

Mercedes models showed constant improvements from then on. The inevitable evolution to superior machines, however, was gradual. The power plant underwent modification and showed steady advancements. While the four-cylinder engine of 1901 developed 35 horsepower, the 1903 enlarged engine developed 60 horsepower. The 1906 Mercedes had a six-cylinder engine of 100 horsepower. Two years later, however, the company engineers returned to the reliable four-cylinder power unit. The large engine of the 1908 automobile racer boasted of a tremendous 140-horsepower output.

The hood of the car became progressively larger. This was necessary in order to accommodate the ever-increasing engine. There was little, if indeed any, wasted space under the hood of the automobile in those days.

In addition to winning the Riviera race in 1901, a Mercedes that year set a new speed record for the one-mile distance. Lorraine Barrow drove his 35-horsepower Mercedes the mile at 49.4 miles per hour, from a standing start. A year later, when the horsepower output had been increased to 40, Degrais bettered this record on the same fashionable Promenade des Anglais in Nice to 51.6.

Also in 1902 the wealthy William K. Vanderbilt in his Mercedes speedster at Achères, France, beat the 66-miles-per-hour record of famed Camille Jenatzy for the flying kilometer. In 1903 Jenatzy won the hotly contested Gordon Bennett race, in Ireland, with his new 60-horsepower Mercedes, averaging 55.3 miles per hour over the 367.5 miles. The racers originally built for this important event had been destroyed by fire. In record time the factory modified several touring cars offered to them by the eager owners. The Jenatzy modified touring car was owned by Clarence G. Dinsmore. The four-cylinder engine had a bore of 140 millimeters and a stroke of 150.

William K. Vanderbilt, in establishing seven new American records in the celebrated "Speed Carnival" in 1904 on the twenty miles of solid

Benz two-cylinder, 16-horsepower racing-touring car of 1900

Daimler "Phoenix" 23-horsepower racing car, 1899

beach at Daytona, Florida, used his 90-horsepower Mercedes racer. Mercedes automobiles were victorious in no fewer than twenty-three events that year.

The next year, 1905, Mercedes racers had another great year at Daytona Beach. Of six victories, three were new world records; and the other three were new American records. The inventive Herbert L. Bowden had built an exceptionally powerful machine. He placed two regular 60-horsepower Mercedes engines end to end on an extralong chassis, so that he had not only the longest racer at the meet, but the fastest. The straight eight-cylinder monster fumed and sputtered, then thundered along the hard-packed sand. After the observers recovered their equilibrium, they found that he had set a new world's record for the mile with flying start at a phenomenal 109.6 miles per hour.

About this time competing racing cars became progressively larger. More speed required more horsepower, and more horsepower suggested larger engines as the simplest solution. Before conditions got out of hand, the representatives of various automobile organizations formed a policy-making board. The A.I.A.C.R. (Association Internationale des Automobile Clubs Reconnus) was empowered to impose limits on the racing machines and regulate the mushrooming, unorganized international competition.

In 1908, the first international formula year, several important races were run according to the limiting formula. In 1904 Vanderbilt had already recognized the problem and imposed a 2,000-pound limit on racers for his cup in the Long Island events.

The 1908 Mercedes, with a four-cylinder, 140-horsepower engine, was much smaller than the gigantic, 11-liter, six-cylinder, 100-horsepower machine of the previous year. The French Grand Prix, a direct result of the earlier Gordon Bennett races which had been put on by the French Automobile Club, was the most important road circuit race on the Continent. The 477-mile course was near Dieppe. Lautenschlager's winning Mercedes, ahead of Hémèry's Benz, averaged 68.9 miles per hour. The track record, set by Salzer's Mercedes, was 10 miles per hour faster. The race was a strenuous one for men and machines. The winner changed tires ten times, and had to do all the work himself under the rules. Built

on a 107-inch-wheelbase chassis, the 12.8-liter engine of the Mercedes was of the F-head type. It had dual ports and used high-tension magneto ignition for the first time.

This 140-horsepower Mercedes was outstandingly successful. The 1908 Grand Prix model distinguished itself greatly with such illustrious drivers as Lautenschlager, Salzer, Spencer Wishart, and Ralph De Palma.

It is interesting to note how the various speeds in the same racing event, and the power of the competing cars, have increased over the years. A good example is the Austrian Semmering Race. From Vienna the course wound through beautifully forested woods across the mountains. The race was held yearly from 1899 on, and was annually won by two Daimler and then nine Mercedes cars. The first year, the 16-horsepower Daimler of Jellinek averaged 14.6 miles per hour. In 1904 the winning Mercedes engine developed 90 horsepower, and the winning speed was 45.5 miles per hour. It seemed to be impossible to improve on that excellent performance by Braun and his car; but when Salzer won the same event in 1909 his 150-horsepower Mercedes maintained an average of 52.3 miles per hour. That record stood unbroken for fifteen years.

The 1910 Mercedes was an entirely new type. The radiator was now pointed, and the hood sloped backward. The smaller four-cylinder engine had two exhaust valves and one large inlet valve, operated by push rods, per cylinder. The 140-millimeter-bore and 175-millimeter-stroke engine had four main bearings and developed 75 horsepower. Two years later a six-cylinder engine developing 75 horsepower was used in the Mercedes cars.

Before the First World War the Daimler engineers perfected a new 4.5-liter four-cylinder engine with a 93-millimeter bore and a 165-millimeter stroke. Despite the relatively small displacement, the output was 115 horsepower at 3,600 revolutions per minute. The valve pockets, cylinder heads, and water jackets were welded in an unusual way. Each cylinder had four spark plugs. The overhead camshaft operated the sixteen valves. Two double-spark Bosch magnetos provided the ignition. The Daimler development was an outstanding engineering feat. While the famous Blitzen Benz of 1909 developed 200 horsepower, that engine had an equally astonishing displacement of 21.5 liters.

Wilhelm Werner in the Mercedes at Nice in 1901

Chart of "Week of Nice," March 1901

25th to 29th March, 1901   "Nice Week"

Event	Distance of course	Driving time Hrs. min.sec.	Average km/h	m.p.h.	Category Position and make	Driver	Remarks
					Cars over 400 kg (880 lbs.) – carrying more than 2 persons		Owned by Rothschild, entered by Dr. Pascal
25th March 1901 Race Nice–Aix–Sénas– Salon–Nice	392 km (244 miles)	6 : 45 : 48	58.1	36.1	1st Mercedes 35 h. p.	Wilhelm Werner, Cannstatt	
		7 : 24 : 40	52.8	32.8	5th Mercedes 35 h. p.	Lorraine Barrow, Paris	Works driver
					Unplaced: Mercedes 35 h. p.	George Lemaître, Paris	Works driver
					Racing cars above 1,000 kg (2,200 lbs.)		Owned by Rothschild
28th March 1901 Mile race of Nice	1 mile st. start	1 : 16.6	75.4	46.8	1st Mercedes 35 h. p.	Wilhelm Werner	
		1 : 17.4	74.8	46.5	2nd Mercedes 35 h. p.	Lorraine Barrow	
	1 km fly-ing start	41.6	86.1	53.5	1st Mercedes 35 h. p.	Wilhelm Werner	
		42	85.7	53.2	2nd Mercedes 35 h. p.	Lorraine Barrow	
25th March 1901 Race Nice–Aix–Sénas– Salon–Nice	1 km fly-ing start	41.8	86.1	53.5	2nd Mercedes 35 h. p.	Wilhelm Werner	
		41.8	86.1	53.5	3rd Mercedes 35 h. p.	Dr. Richard Ritter von Stern, Vienna	Owned by Prince Lubecki
		42.6	84.5	52.5	4th Mercedes 35 h. p.	Lorraine Barrow	
		42.8	84.1	52.2	5th Mercedes 35 h. p.	S. Knapp	
		44.2	81.4	50.6	7th Mercedes 35 h. p.	Henry de Rothschild, Paris	
		44.8	80.4	49.9	8th Mercedes 35 h. p.	Georges	
		51.6	69.8	43.4	10th Daimler 28 h. p.	Prince Lubecki	
28th March 1901 Mile race of Nice	1 mile standing start	1 : 16.8	75.4	46.8	2nd Mercedes 35 h. p.	Lorraine Barrow	
		1 : 18.2	74	45.9	3rd Mercedes 35 h. p.	Wilhelm Werner	
		1 : 19.2	73.1	45.4	4th Mercedes 35 h. p.	S. Knapp	
		1 : 21	71.5	44.4	5th Mercedes 35 h. p.	Dr. Richard Ritter von Stern	
		1 : 22.8	69.9	43.4	6th Mercedes 35 h. p.	Georges	
		1 : 25.8	67.5	41.9	8th Mercedes 35 h. p.	Henry de Rothschild	
		1 : 36.8	59.8	37.1	9th Daimler 28 h. p.	Prince Lubecki	
28th March 1901 Record attempts during the "Nice Week"	1 mile standing start	1 : 12.6	79.7	49.5	Mercedes 35 h. p.	Lorraine Barrow	Was recognised as a world mile record
		1 : 38.3	58.6	36.4	Mercedes 35 h. p.	Henry de Rothschild	
	1 km fly-ing start	42.4	84.9	52.7	Mercedes 35 h. p.	Lorraine Barrow	
		46.8	76.9	47.7	Mercedes 35 h. p.	Henry de Rothschild	
28th March 1901 Tourist race Nice– Draguignan–Nice	132 km (82 miles)	3 : 40 : 10	35.9	22.3	*Six seater cars above 1,000 kg (2,200 lbs.)* 1st Daimler 28 h. p.	S. Knapp	
29th March 1901 Hill-climb Nice–La Turbie	15.5 km (9.5 miles)	18 : 6.8	51.4	31.9	*Twin seater racing cars* 1st Mercedes 35 h. p.	Wilhelm Werner	
		18 : 49.6	49.4	30.6	2nd Mercedes 35 h. p.	George Lemaître	
		42 : 45.2	21.7	13.5	7th Mercedes 35 h. p.	Lorraine Barrow	
		21 : 46	42.7	26.5	*Six seater cars* 1st Mercedes 35 h. p.	Thorn	

The new 1914 Grand Prix model Mercedes distinguished itself in the 466.6-mile French Grand Prix, which was run on July 4 of that year on the fast twenty-four-mile circuit near Lyons. Four new Mercedes racers were entered. The international formula limited engine displacement to 4.5 liters and specified that the weight of the vehicle should not exceed 2,425 pounds. Fourteen manufacturers were represented by thirty-eight cars. The competitors were sent off in pairs, at intervals of half a minute.

Soon it became apparent to the 300,000 partisans that the Mercedes entries were vastly superior to their favorite machines. Max Sailer covered the first lap in record time, nearly 20 seconds faster than the esteemed ace and previous winner George Boillot in his Peugeot. Sailer drove a spectacular race, far ahead of the field, and set many new lap records. However, his engine blew up in the sixth lap, after 120 miles of rapid pacing.

Then the Mercedes cars of Lautenschlager, Wagner, and Salzer pressed the leader. Pushing Boillot hard during the rest of the race, Lautenschlager passed him in the eighteenth lap. Then the Peugeot's engine blew up, and Boillot was finished. The Mercedes cars completed the course, winning first, second, and third places, less than five minutes apart. It was a spectacular victory in which the winner's average speed was 65.5 miles per hour. By the end of the month the First World War was on.

One of the winning cars found its way to Great Britain, where the radical features of the engine were studied for possible adaptation to the Allies' aero engines. Another appeared in the United States. The 1915 Packard racing engine seems to have been remarkably similar to the six-cylinder Mercedes power plant. The Liberty motor also bore unusually close resemblance to the Daimler-designed engine.

Owned by E. C. Patterson, the 1914 Grand Prix Mercedes brought considerable glory to Ralph De Palma when, driving it in the Elgin Road races late in August, he won the two 300-mile races at average speeds of 73.9 and 73.5 miles per hour against many strong competitors. He drove the same car in 1915 in the 500-mile race at Indianapolis, and won with a record of 89.4 miles per hour that was not bettered until 1922.

The early Benz vehicles are described in the preceding chapter. In 1899 the 8-horsepower Benz racer of Fritz Held made an outstanding showing against 20-horsepower machines. Usually the Benz-built racers developed considerably less horsepower than the Daimlers.

The 1900-model Benz racer was much shorter than the Mercedes of that year. Although the engine was in the rear, a large, honeycomb-type radiator graced the front of the vehicle. The slanting steering wheel column was supported by a sturdy upright post. By Mercedes standards, the 20 horsepower which the four-cylinder engine developed was low. Yet, in competition, this much lighter vehicle gave a good account of itself and won, among other events, the 1900 Frankfurt track race.

In building the 1903 Benz-Parsifal racer, factory engineers again created a new style. It was low, with a long wheelbase. The hood had long rows of louvers that gave the car a pleasant, racy appearance and helped to cool the four-cylinder 60-horsepower engine. This Parsifal, a definite departure from the current style of high, square radiators and extremely heavy machines, was created mainly to compete in sales appeal with the popular Mercedes cars. It partook in the Paris-to-Madrid race of 1903.

The Mannheim company decided to reenter automobile racing in 1908, when the Benz engineers joined the prevailing school that advocated more powerful engines and the resulting larger machines. For several years two hostile groups of engineers at the Benz factory had supported basically opposed designs of automobiles. One group, influenced by French designers, had been responsible for the light Parsifal type. The 1907 sports car, built on the long, low lines of the 1903 style, did excellently in the Herkomer Competition against many rivals that had greater power. However, sales of these types did not come to expectations, and now the German school of thought had its way.

The Benz of 1908, even larger than the Mercedes, did not approach its engine in output by 20 horsepower. The large four-cylinder Benz engine developed 120 horsepower. That year a racer, loaded down with many spare tires, set a new distance record in the torturous 426-mile race from St. Petersburg to Moscow; and in the 1908 French Grand Prix Benz cars took second and third places. In the 1909 reliability run from St. Petersburg to Riga and return, the three Benz cars took the first three places. In the 1909 Indianapolis race meet, Barney Oldfield drove a 150-horsepower Benz to a new one-mile world's record of 83.8 miles per hour, from a standing start.

Emil Jellinek and daughter Mercedes — the family name was changed later to Jellinek-Mercedes

The first Mercedes at Nice in 1901

The 1909 Benz engine developed 200 horsepower, and with it the American drivers Bruce-Brown and Robertson established three new world's records at the Daytona, Florida, speed week. The speed of 114 miles per hour was a great achievement. In the Brussels automobile race Héméry drove the 200-horsepower car to a new world's record for the kilometer of 71.5 miles per hour. Many other international successes followed these accomplishments. By adapting the highly streamlined body style of their 1910 sports car, Benz engineers built the outstanding racer which rose to astronomical fame as the Blitzen Benz. The following chapter will recall some of the details.

Several world's records were set in 1913 by a new 200-horsepower Benz racer. Hörner drove the machine to a new European road record when he exceeded 125 miles per hour in the verst race near St. Petersburg; and in the record trials held in England at the Brooklands track Hornsted established a new record for the kilometer of 73.7 miles per hour, from a standing start. He also made a new record for the half-mile distance of 70.6 miles per hour.

In the twenty years preceding the First World War the motor vehicle had made great strides. Engines had increased more than 250 times in horsepower, and speeds had increased more than tenfold. Now much of this technical knowledge was used in implements of war for man's destruction.

Mercedes racing car of 35-horsepower, 1901

The four-cylinder engine of the first Mercedes

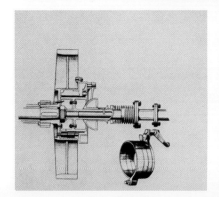
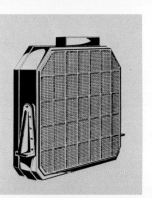
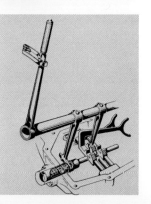

Coil spring clutch, honeycomb radiator, and gear lock

The Benz "Ideal" of 1899

The Benz "Tonneau" of 1899

The Mercedes-Simplex touring car, 1901-1902

The Benz Vis-a-Vis on 1901

The Blitzen Benz (1909)

In the brilliant galaxy of early speedsters, the Blitzen Benz stands out. This racing car was remarkably successful during its long and colorful career and was far ahead of its time in many ways.

Greatly encouraged by the victory in 1908 in the grueling race from St. Petersburg to Moscow, the Benz organization decided to construct an even more powerful racer. The ace driver Victor Héméry in the 120-horsepower machine had made an amazing new distance record across the difficult Russian terrain with an average of more than 50 miles per hour.

The Benz designers, led by the able Max Wagner, reasoned simply, and correctly, that by increasing the engine size they would increase the power output; and at that time there was no restrictive formula to hamper their efforts. The 1908 racer had been equipped with a huge 12.5-liter engine. The new, four-cylinder engine was further increased to 185-millimeter bore and 200-millimeter stroke, giving it a whopping displacement of 21.5 liters (1,312 cubic inches). Huge rocker arms and push rods actuated the immense overhead valves of the rather slow-turning engine, which reached a maximum of 1,650 revolutions per minute. This was one of the largest automobile engines ever conceived. For comparison, the 1939 Mercedes-Benz engine, developing 278 brake horsepower, had a displacement of but 1.495 liters. In other words, the displacement of the Blitzen Benz engine was nearly fifteen times as great as that of the M 165.

With a four-speed gear box, power was transmitted to the rear wheels by heavy chains and huge sprocket wheels. The motor was geared to give a calculated speed of 140 miles per hour at 1,400 revolutions per minute. Despite its mammoth engine, the 112-inch-wheelbase racer weighed only 3,600 pounds.

Not only was the engine unusual, but the frame and body departed from the former, rather standardized, design. To eliminate excess weight, the frame was profusely drilled, clearly visible to observers. The body shell was well rounded, not square and cumbersome like that of earlier models. A most unusual eagle beak, part of the cooling system, protruded over the radiator. The pointed tail of the metal body fitted well into the overall streamlined design.

The entire racer was painted a gleaming white. The beak was of shining brass, as were the oversized hub caps on the silvery, steel wire wheels. And in the best 1909 Benz tradition, four enormous brass pipes projected gracefully from the left side of the hood in a parallel, flowing line to the exhaust below. The Blitzen Benz was a stunning, strikingly beautiful creation. The slim, streamlined racer appeared to be traveling at high speed even when standing still.

At the testing of the new Benz racing machine someone suggested, "Der Wagen geht wirklich wie der Blitz." The phenomenal speed seemed indeed like a lightning flash, and the name "Blitzen Benz" stuck firmly to the new model.

The car was taken for high-speed runs to the Brooklands course in England, where its acceleration was terrific. After a few trial runs, Victor Héméry established a new kilometer record of 125.9 miles per hour, and a new mile record of 115.9. But the short, banked track did not seem to allow the Blitzen Benz its fullest potentialities. The car was shipped to the United States to try for a still higher record on the straight, solid, and smooth beach at Daytona.

The beautiful white and gold streamlined machine, with a large black eagle painted on its side as the symbol of the German Empire, created tremendous interest wherever it was shown. It was acquired by cigar-smoking Barney Oldfield, who drove it in 1910 on the speedy Florida course, roaring from Daytona to Ormond Beach like a streak of lightning. The howling, flaming spectacle fascinated the multitude who eagerly lined the beaches to witness it. A new speed mark of 131.7 miles per hour was established for the flying mile. From a standing start, the racer reached a speed of 88.8 for the mile. Observers believed that such remarkable records would stand a long time.

A barnstorming tour took the famous car and driver across the entire country. Usually a new track record was set at each appearance at a new town. Then, at the next track the following day, that record was broken. The Blitzen Benz performed miraculously, and the thousands of enthusiastic fans were hysterically happy. After the tour, Barney Oldfield sold the racing car.

The 200-horsepower engine of the Blitzen Benz

World record Blitzen Benz, 1911

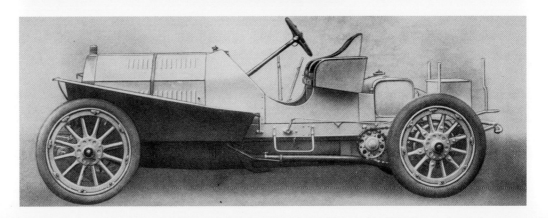

Benz 60-horsepower racing car, 1907

Then, in 1911, when many felt that the racer had seen its greatest glory, the young, audacious Bob Burman took the Blitzen Benz and established many more records. On the straight Daytona to Ormond Beach track, he drove the mile in little more than 25 seconds, at an amazing 141.7 miles per hour. This world automobile speed record remained unbroken for thirteen years.

Crowned speed king by Harvey Firestone that year, Burman hoped to win the Indianapolis 500-miler. However, he used nearly as much time in the pits changing tires as on the brick oval driving, so that he did not finish among the first ten.

Again the famous racer, not quite so white and shiny as before but still amazingly reliable and fast, took the country by storm. Wild Bob Burman established many records on the many tracks where he appeared. A heavy balance weight was attached to the rear of the car, apparently improving its performance. On the circular one-mile dirt track at Brighton Beach, Burman established a record of 74 miles per hour on Labor Day, 1911. New appearances brought, almost automatically, new records. Yet the racer had not been designed for level dirt-track, or banked-circuit, racing. It was at its best in sprinting events.

The Blitzen Benz seemed indestructible in its day. With the care given the Mercedes-Benz Grand Prix machines during the fabulous 1934-1939 racing period, the Blitzen Benz might still set new speed records.

The huge 21.5-liter engine of the "Blitzen Benz," 1909

Mercedes 120-horsepower racing car, 1906

Mercedes Grand Prix racing car of 1908

Benz 150-horsepower racing car, 1908

The Mercedes racing car of 1914

The four-cylinder, 115-horsepower engine

Racing and Sports Cars (1921-1933)

Three years after the First World War international automobile racing began again, spasmodically. The deep wounds of war were extremely slow in healing. Most countries, Germany included, were desperately ill; and, worsening the difficult situation, the racing-car formula underwent frequent changes, which sometimes prevented participation by Mercedes and Benz racers in formula events.

It was almost impossible to construct and enter well tested racing cars in an event and still meet the current formula requirements. To design and produce an entirely new power plant every other year during a difficult period of economic reconstruction was a task which taxed resources to the limit. However, to compensate for the lack of Mercedes or Benz cars, many magnificent sports cars appeared. The fabulous Mercedes-Benz S models and their superb descendants fit into the latter part of the era.

In 1921 Mercedes and Benz machines competed in various international events in Europe.

The maximum engine displacement, according to the A.I.A.C.R. 1921 formula, was 3 liters. In outward appearance the postwar Mercedes car was similar to the prewar model. Wheels of knock-off type were used, to facilitate tire changes. The new six-cylinder engine developed 95 horsepower. Max Sailer, who had burned up the Lyons circuit at the French Grand Prix seven years before, won the Coppa Florio in 1921 at an average speed of 35.9 miles per hour.

However, the distinguished 1914 Grand Prix model with the large 4.5-liter, four-cylinder engine, which developed 115 horsepower, was still the most successful contender in many racing events. In it Count Giulio Masetti won the 1921 Italian Grand Prix and the 1922 Targa Florio.

This Sicilian mountain race was run on one of the most difficult courses anywhere. Established in 1906 by the wealthy Italian, Vincenzo Florio, the circuit twisted through the rugged Madonie mountains from sea level to an altitude of more than a thousand feet. There were a thousand wicked turns on the 93 miles of the course. A competing driver had absolutely no time to admire the exquisite Mediterranean. All his faculties were constantly engaged in keeping to the narrow, seldom straight, road.

A new, small 1.5-liter, four-cylinder engine was developed and installed in a new-model Mercedes sports car in 1922. Daimler engineers also perfected a satisfactory supercharger, and this unit boosted the regular 25-horsepower output to 40 horsepower. A supercharged model, utilizing a 28/95 horsepower engine and driven by Sailer, appeared first in competition for the Sicilian Targa Florio in 1922 and won in the production model class for more than 4.5 liters.

The following year the 1.5-liter engine was used in a lighter car, and the output was increased to 65 horsepower. Rudolf Caracciola made his first appearance in the winner's lane with this model sports car after winning the tricky 1924 Klausenpass hill climb in Switzerland. When the supercharged Mercedes models first appeared in 1922 the exhaust pipes were relocated and left the hood at the right side to lessen the heat under the hood. In the minds of many enthusiasts, the external exhaust pipes became synonymous with supercharger. But already in 1908 a Mercedes had large exhaust pipes coming out of the side of the hood. The 140-horsepower 1908 Grand Prix model for which Spencer Wishart was supposed to have spent some sixty thousand dollars had this feature. Many other models, however, did not have external exhausts. The visible, shiny pipes did not always indicate a supercharged engine, but they added greatly in cooling the engine.

The international racing formula allowed 2-liter displacement engines for the years 1922 to 1925. Daimler engineers used a 2-liter, four-cylinder supercharged engine of 120 horsepower in the 1923 Mercedes racer. Christian Werner won in the 1924 Targa Florio event with this car, driving it at an average speed of 41 miles per hour. Three years before, Sailer won at an average of 35.9 per hour, in a 95-horsepower machine.

For the year 1924 a considerably more streamlined Mercedes racing car was constructed, using the same engine. It did well in the hill-climb event at Prague. And a 2-liter, eight-cylinder engine was built that year which developed 160 horsepower, supercharged. Caracciola drove a racer of this type to victory in the 1926 German Grand Prix on the old Avus track at Berlin — a considerably slower circuit than the highly banked one of 1932 — with an average of 83.8 miles per hour.

Benz 10/30-horsepower sports car of 1921

Benz rear-engined 80-horsepower racing car of 1923

Chassis of Benz rear-engined car, 1923

The beginning of large engines was in 1925. The international formula limited engine displacement to 1.5 liters in 1926 and 1927, but many events were formula libre. There was then no displacement limit.

The 6-liter Mercedes sports car of 1925 was huge and heavy, with a whining supercharger that boosted the output of the 100-horsepower engine to 140 horsepower. Caracciola piloted it successfully in the Baden-Baden automobile tournament and the Austrian Alpine run that year.

When the two oldest automobile manufacturers, the Daimler Motorengesellschaft and Benz & Cie., merged in 1926, the combined engineering staffs focused their efforts on the 1925 Mercedes model. The now classic S series was the happy result.

The Benz engineers had produced some unusually interesting model types in the company's separate forty-year history. In 1921 a 1.5-liter, four-cylinder engine, developing 18 horsepower, was installed in a smooth, cleanly designed racing car reminiscent of the Blitzen Benz of 1909. Aided considerably by extreme lightness, the car did well on the Avus track and in the Baden-Baden tournament.

To comply with the 1922 to 1925 formula, Benz engineers, directed by Max Wagner and the famous airplane designer Rumpler, built a rear-engined, 2-liter, six-cylinder racer in 1922. Four cantilever springs were used for independent suspension. Entered in several events that year, the "Tropfenrennwagen" never distinguished itself greatly in competition. Perhaps the time for a rear-engined racing car had not yet come. Undoubtedly many unusual and unforeseen problems presented themselves at the practical road tests of actual competition which had not been anticipated in the design laboratories or in earlier tests. When the Porsche-designed rear-engined Auto Union racers appeared on the Grand Prix circuits of the Continent twelve years later, it almost seemed like a continuation and successful culmination of the earlier extremely daring and highly unorthodox Benz experiment. The rear-engined Benz appeared on the fast Monza track in 1923. The cars took fourth and fifth places in the 472-mile Grand Prix of Europe — and were ably driven by Minoia and Franz Hörner. During 1924 and 1925 Adolf Rosenberger drove the racer and won in some events. Unfortunately no other information is available from the bombed-out archives of the factory.

The 1924 Benz sports car was a large six-cylinder, 50-horsepower machine with rakish, pleasing lines. It competed in the Baden-Baden automobile tournament, and Fritz Nallinger won the 897-mile Swiss Alpine rally with it.

The postwar years, the early twenties, were difficult for the German automobile manufacturers. Many long-established builders of motorcars had stopped production and closed their factories. Daimler and Benz combined their resources as the Daimler-Benz Aktiengesellschaft and were wedded by a hyphen.

One consequence of the merger was a consolidation of existing facilities. The former Daimler factories at Untertürkheim and Sindelfingen were used to produce the passenger automobiles. The former Benz Mannheim plant was changed over to manufacture only light trucks, and the former Benz Gaggenau factory turned out the combined line of heavy trucks. The former Daimler Berlin Marienfelde manufacturing plant was set aside for the production of specialized vehicles.

The extensive line of passenger cars produced by both firms was concentrated greatly, and the types of models reduced sharply. The Mercedes-Benz K-model was built. K stood for *Kompressor* (supercharger). The six-cylinder engine was similar to that of the previous Mercedes, but it developed 110 horsepower, supercharged to 160 horsepower. The body style of the new model was along the Mercedes more than the Benz lines, although features of both were retained and skillfully combined. The chassis of the 1926 Mercedes-Benz model was considerably shorter than that of the 1925 Mercedes, and many observers were of the opinion that the K stood for *kurz* (short).

The combined engineering staffs, now under the direction of Max Wagner and Ferdinand Porsche, were responsible for the 1927 S model. Outwardly the 1926 K model underwent some changes. The hood was lowered and lengthened. The spare tires were taken out of the fender wells and placed in a slanting position on the rear deck. By lowering the chassis still more, a much sportier and faster-looking car was created. The wheelbase was 134 inches, and the chassis alone weighed a formidable 3,600 pounds. The huge six-cylinder engine developed 120 horsepower, stepped up to 180 by the supercharger.

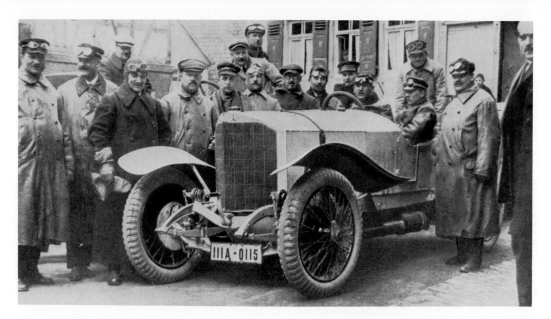

Mercedes 28/95-horsepower sports car of 1921-1922

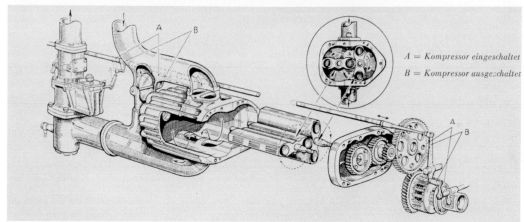

Roots supercharger with multiple disc clutch, drive and pressure carburetor

A = Kompressor eingeschaltet

B = Kompressor ausgeschaltet

Supercharged Mercedes 120-horsepower sports car, 1924

When in 1927 the Nürburg Ring circuit was officially opened for automobile racing, these Mercedes-Benz sports cars proved themselves to be outstanding. Twisting through the picturesque Eifel mountains, the Nürburg Ring had been constructed as a model automobile racing circuit during the economic depression, furnishing employment to many men who were out of work.

One of the most scenic of all the especially planned road-racing circuits on the Continent, it is also one of the most difficult. The extremely well designed and excellently built 14-mile north loop has 172 turns and curves and rises 1,250 feet through heavy forests and mountains. The historic Nürburg castle overlooks the modern proving grounds. The Ring is laid out to test severely car and driver alike. A victory on it is proof of outstanding superiority in both.

It was fitting that both the 1927 Mercedes-Benz S model and Rudolf Caracciola took part at the dedication ceremonies that year. As the crowd of nearly half a million enthusiasts expected, the model S and Caracciola won the opening race. In the German Grand Prix race that followed, Mercedes-Benz cars came in first, second, and third, driven respectively by Merz, Werner, and Walb.

When the improved SS (Super Sports) model appeared on the Nürburg Ring the next year, Mercedes-Benz cars again finished in the first three places. Their superiority was evident. Caracciola won, Merz took second place, and Walb was tied for third with Werner. The average speed of the winner had increased by two miles per hour over the previous year. It was 64.4 miles per hour in 1928.

The Mercedes-Benz SS model of 1928 was large. The 7-liter (7,022 cubic centimeters, or 428 cubic inches), six-cylinder engine had a bore of 100 millimeters (3.94 inches) and a stroke of 150 millimeters (5.91 inches). The engine cylinders were in line, with a single overhead camshaft. The block was built of magnesium and had wet sleeves. The compression ratio was 5 to 1, and at 3,200 revolutions per minute the engine developed 160 brake horsepower. At speeds in excess of 60 miles per hour it practically idled at 1,600 revolutions per minute. With the supercharger engaged, the output was an even 200 horsepower. The Roots supercharger unit was ahead of the carburetors and could be engaged by pressing the accelerator strongly past the point of full throttle. The wheelbase was 134 inches, and the Rudge-type wire wheels had 7.00 x 20 tires.

The Grand Prix events of two decades ago were gay affairs. The stands, decorated with bunting, the long row of flags of all participating nations fluttering in the breeze, the band playing to drown out the tumult of the racing-car engines nearby, and the feverishly expectant holiday crowd made an international race a most festive occasion.

A number of gleaming-white Mercedes-Benz super sports models were lined up in the first starting rows on the concrete track, and their highly polished radiators and splendid exhaust pipes reflected the early afternoon sun. It was a magnificent sight. The idling engines emitted a steady, deep-toned sound. Then their revolutions sped up (your own heartbeats increasing to keep time), and at the starter's signal the cars roared away in a crescendo surge of power. The very atmosphere thrilled, and your throat choked with emotion. Then in the stillness, faintly audible long before the powerful machines could be seen on the opposite side of the smooth track, came the shrill, spine-tingling whine of the superchargers. The sound grew louder and louder as the cars approached and quickly howled past the stand with an earsplitting noise. The great white cars looked like tailless comets, and their bright red upholstery was visible but an instant. As the enthusiastic multitude responded with thunderous cheers they disappeared from view and the tumult died away, only to begin again.

The Mercedes-Benz SS models were the finest automobiles of the time. They stirred the pride of the princes who owned them and the love of the poor who could only watch them. To experience the exhilaration of a Grand Prix race, to feel the acrid exhaust odors burn in your nostrils, and to make the race vicariously with the skillful drivers, was a thrill to last any young man a long lifetime.

Spurred on by the successes of the SS model, the Daimler-Benz engineers developed the SSK (K for *kurz*, meaning short) in 1928. The wheelbase was shortened to 116 inches, and the engine output increased to 170 horsepower. With the supercharger engaged, the output was 225 horsepower. Shortening the car added greatly to its beauty and increased considerably its excellent performance record. A radiantly white Mercedes-

Mercedes eight-cylinder, 2-liter racing car with Alfred Neubauer at wheel, 1924

Mercedes 15/70/100-horsepower engine with transmission

Chassis of supercharged car

Benz with silvery exhaust pipes protruding from the side of the hood and red leather upholstery was exquisitely beautiful. And to hear the shrieking howl of the engaged supercharger was equally pleasant.

With the new SSK model, Caracciola set a new record for the Austrian Semmering race in 1928. Driving the old SS model, he won the International Tourist Trophy at Belfast, Ireland, and established a new track and distance record for the race. The following year, he set a new record for the Prague hill climb. In 1930 he also won the 300-mile Irish Grand Prix at an average speed of 86.2 miles per hour. And he set new records for the Schauinsland hill climb near Freiburg, the Klausenpass hill climb in Switzerland, and the Austrian Semmering race. He became European hill-climb champion for 1930.

The development of the now so successful type sports car reached its climax in 1931. Retaining the superb lines of the winning machines, the engineers lightened the car by drilling a multitude of holes into the chassis. Thus, the letter L (for *leicht,* meaning light) was attached to the others, making the newest model the SSKL. The few machines built for international competition were also equipped with an extralarge blower, boosting the peak engine output to an astonishing 300 horsepower.

Caracciola, together with Sebastian, won the 1931 Mille Miglia driving a Mercedes-Benz SSKL against formidable Italian and French opponents who competed in highly developed road racing machines. He also won the Prague hill climb, setting a new record for the event. He won the Eifel race on the Nürburg Ring and later the German Grand Prix, when he also established a new course record. The 183-mile Avus track race, at Berlin, he won with an average exceeding 115 miles per hour. The SSKL also helped the dashing Caracciola to win again in 1931 the title of European hill-climb champion.

In 1932 a special, highly streamlined body was built for one of the SSKL models. Manfred von Brauchitsch drove this 300-horsepower, supercharged machine in the 1932 Avus race, winning with an average about 6 miles per hour faster than Caracciola had made the year before with the regular body style. Brauchitsch's average speed was 120.7 miles per hour — a new world's class record for distances greater than 200 kilometers.

Hans Stuck won the Alpine master championship that year, driving the regular SSKL model. In 1933 Ebb won the Finnish Grand Prix, and von Brauchitsch established new records in the Kesselberg hill climb and the Schauinsland hill climb near Freiburg.

The sports-car participation by the Daimler-Benz works during this period added to the tremendous prestige which their production automobiles always enjoyed. The by now classic sports cars have many enthusiasts all over the world, and specimens are highly valued by connoisseurs.

Mercedes-Benz 6.8-liter, 180-horsepower
"S" sports car, 1927

Mercedes-Benz 7.1-liter, 225-horsepower
"SSK" model, 1928

Short and light Mercedes-Benz 300-horsepower
"SSKL" model, 1931

Mercedes "S" model sports car, 1928

Mercedes "SS" model touring car, 1928

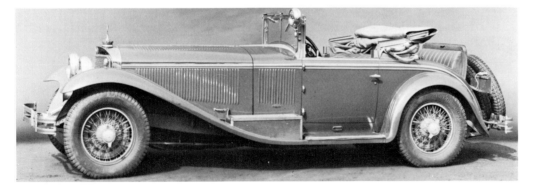

Mercedes "SS" convertible of 1928-1931

Chassis and engine of the "SSK" model, 1928

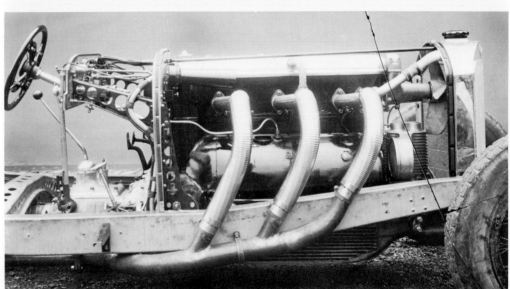

The exhaust side of the 7.1-liter engine

The 750-Kilogram Formula (1934-1937)

Of all the periods of automobile racing, the five years beginning with 1934 were unquestionably the most glorious ones in the star-studded history of Mercedes-Benz.

The fuel which kept the wheels of time turning had run out for the super sports cars. The evolution of the promising Mercedes-Benz S model had run its prescribed course, and had found its ultimate fulfillment in the excellent SSKL model. Manfred von Brauchitsch had driven the improved SSKL model at an average speed of 120.7 miles per hour on the fast Berlin Avus track in 1932. That average seemed to be beyond the limit of safety for any sports car. Still the public demanded, unmercifully, more speed.

The A.I.A.C.R. (Association Internationale des Automobile Clubs Reconnus), the governing body, hoped to hold down the ever-increasing speed by reducing the size of the power plants of the machines. It unanimously adopted a new racing formula that year, to become effective in 1934 and remain in force for three years, which stipulated that the weight of the car should not exceed 750 kilograms (1,650 pounds) and the minimum frontal width should be 34 inches. The weight excluded the driver, fuel, water, oil, and tires. It was about half that of the huge sports cars of that year. The new formula aimed to reduce engine sizes and thus to reduce the speed considerably and bring it within the limits of safety.

Despite the critical economic situation in Germany, the Daimler-Benz directors decided to build racing cars to the required specifications and enter international Grand Prix competition vigorously.

The same year four German automobile manufacturers had formed a combine to better their respective competitive positions. The Horch, Wanderer, Audi, and D.K.W. companies were now known as the Auto Union, and as a new company they had the problem of making their new name quickly known to the motoring public. The combine proposed to spend 1,200,000 marks (nearly $300,000) over a two-year period for this purpose. However, rather than enter a concentrated newspaper advertising program, the directors decided to sponsor a Grand Prix racing team. They acquired the offered P-Wagen project, a proposed rear-engined racing car designed by the famous Dr. Ferdinand Porsche, who had been responsible for the Mercedes-Benz S series. The cost was estimated to be 2,000,000 marks annually.

With their racing reputation at stake, Daimler-Benz decided to go all out in their racing participation. The abilities of Dr. Porsche were, of course, well known to the Stuttgart concern. Undisputed leadership over the years had brought tremendous prestige to Daimler-Benz, and the company rose now to its equally enormous task of maintaining pre-eminence.

Yearly, 2,500,000 marks (nearly $600,000) was expended on the racing department. The government agreed to contribute annually 500,000 marks while a Grand Prix racing car was under construction to bear the silver colors, representing Germany, at the international events.

There was no magic formula to insure the incredible successes which the Mercedes-Benz racers achieved between 1934 and 1939. Detailed investigation of the Stuttgart racing department set-up indicated that the findings were as disappointing as killing the goose which had laid the golden eggs. There were no trade secrets and no mysterious, superhuman formulas. The magic touch which seemed to turn most of the Daimler-Benz efforts to victories was an unbelievable Teutonic thoroughness. A thoroughness of organization was evident. The manner in which every minute detail was attended to was astonishing. Nothing was ever left to chance. Every eventuality, however remotely possible, seemed to have been anticipated.

An entirely separate racing department was established under Director Max Sailer, a racing driver of repute. His first-hand knowledge of racing was put to excellent use. The designers responsible for the construction of the new racers were Dr. Hans Nibel, who had designed the Blitzen Benz of 1909, and Max Wagner, who had designed the rear-engined Benz racer of 1922. They were outstanding in their field. There were some 300 employees in the entire unit, experts in every phase of automobile construction. Alfred Neubauer, a man with apparently inexhaustible energy and a record as an expert behind the wheel of a Mercedes racer, was put in charge of the actual racing team.

This complete racing organization within the larger Daimler-Benz organization produced the Mercedes-Benz M 25 model for the 1934 season, with a straight-eight engine originally of 3.36-liter displacement which developed 354 horsepower. The power plant, however, was soon replaced.

Start of the Eifel Race at Nürburgring, 1934

The 3.36-liter, eight-cylinder racing car engine, 1934

Faglioli in the Monaco Grand Prix, 1935

It was believed that the 750-kilogram formula would limit engine displacement to about 2.5 liters. This proved later not to be the case.

Before the season ended the improved model M 25 B was used. It remained within the weight limitation. This eight-cylinder engine had a bore of 82 millimeters and a stroke of 94.5 millimeters, giving it a displacement of 3.99 liters; it developed, with the Roots supercharger, 430 horsepower at 5,800 revolutions per minute. Each cylinder had four valves, set at a 60-degree angle. The two overhead camshafts were driven by gears from the rear end. The welded water jacket and ports were of sheet steel. The supercharger provided a 12-pound boost. A single Bosch magneto was used. Single-plate clutch transmission and four forward gears were used. A relatively hard front suspension was furnished by the independently swinging parallel arms, with horizontal coil springs. Swinging half-axles, controlled by semielliptic leaf springs and friction shock absorbers, were used in the rear. The 42-inch-high car had a frontal area of 13.8 square feet and a 107-inch wheelbase, and weighed 1,570 pounds.

The Ferrari Monoposto Alfa-Romeos appeared with rebuilt bodies for the 1934 Grand Prix season and were victorious in many early events. Although the new Mercedes-Benz cars made astonishing times at the practice for the French Grand Prix and seemed to be certain of victory, unexpected teething troubles developed during the actual race, and they did not do well. However, by the end of the season it was clear that the German racing machines were superior to all others.

The Mercedes-Benz M 25 models had won the Eifel race at the Nürberg Ring, the Klausenpass hill climb, the Coppa Acerbo, and the Italian and the Spanish Grands Prix.

Entered to compete in ten major events in 1934, the cars won four times, placed second three times, and took one third place.

The 1935 racing season was incredibly successful for the sleek silver arrows with the three-pointed star insignia. Mercedes-Benz racers took part in eleven major events that year. Eight large Diesel trucks were permanently attached to the racing department, transporting six racers, several spare engines, and tons of equipment to the racing circuits of Europe. The two crews of mechanics numbered twenty-five men each. One of the

trucks was a wonderful movable workshop, equipped with the most modern machinery. Another truck, with a supercharged engine, was held in readiness to give speedy help whenever necessary.

Several days before a race the Mercedes-Benz racing team would be hard at work becoming familiar with every inch of the course. Usually the drivers would begin by driving their own sedans over the circuit, noting every detail. Then the practice cars would be used until the branches of every tree along the course were a familiar sight, and the exact angle of every turn was deeply fixed in the driver's mind. The racing department at Stuttgart would already have mapped out the elevations of the course, the degree of each curve, and have taken pains to record other pertinent information. Thus, the proper gears were installed in the cars for the particular course on which they were to perform.

Each driver had a comfortable seat adjusted to his own body. The pedals too were made to his individual measure, transferred by the factory from the car he had previously driven to the car he was now to drive. Close attention was paid to the comfort of each driver in the team. After a few laps the final adjustments were made to the racing machine. Starting positions were given according to the best practice lap, and so the drivers would take one lap all out before quitting practice.

Practice was an important and very active function. The tire experts from the Continental Tire company, which furnished all the racing tires, busied themselves with accurate measurements of temperature and wear, and computed the distance which could be traveled with safety in the race. The men from the Bosch company examined the spark plugs to see if the proper fuel mixture was used to insure maximum efficiency in operation. And the Shell Oil representatives watched over their especially mixed fuel supplies. The chief mechanics, Zimmer and Lindenmaier, were ready to make minor changes that the ever-present Alfred Neubauer or the chief engineer of the racing department might suggest.

With such preparation there was small ground for wonder that the Mercedes-Benz racers won nearly all the events in which they participated in 1935. Seven Grands Prix races were won that year — the Monaco, the Tripoli, the Barcelona, the French, Spanish, Belgian, and Swiss —

Start of the Monaco Grand Prix, 1935

Mercedes record car of 1936 and 1937

Von Brauchitsch at the Avus race, 1937

along with the Avus track race, and the Eifel race at the Nürburg Ring. It was a well deserved grand year, positive proof that the machines built at Untertürkheim and the organization which was running them were superior to those of the potent Auto Union at Zwickau.

Despite the outstanding successes during the 1935 racing season Daimler-Benz engineers decided that the road-holding ability of the racer with the 4-liter engine was inadequate. Various types of running gear were tried, and finally it was resolved to design an entirely new car. After the death of Dr. Nibel the work was begun under the direction of Dr. Rohr resulting in the new model, the M 125.

The 1936 season saw Mercedes-Benz racers in the winner's lane only twice at Grand Prix events — Monaco and Tunis — with Caracciola driving. The 6-liter V-type sixteen-cylinder Auto Unions won three times that year.

The new Mercedes-Benz power plant developed 645 brake horsepower at 5,800 revolutions per minute. The eight-cylinder engine had, with a bore of 94 millimeters and stroke of 102 millimeters, a displacement of 5.66 liters. Other engine details were similar to the M 25 model. The suspension was considerably softer than that of the earlier model. The front suspension was independent with parallel wishbones and coil springs, while de Dion torsion bar springing and double action hydraulic piston type shock absorbers were used in the rear. The wheelbase was 110 inches. The one-inch-lower car had a frontal area displacement of only 12.5 square feet and weighed 1,640 pounds.

The 1937 season also proved to be an excellent one for the Mercedes-Benz racers. Most of the racing events had now become battles between the two German giants, other competitors being hopelessly outclassed. However, occasionally the Mercedes-Benz and Auto Union racers would push each other at such terrific pace that both crossed their respective points of ultimate speed, blew up their engines, and let the lesser makes romp victoriously across the finish line. The magnificent music to the multitude, the horrible howl of the Mercedes-Benz superchargers, had been eliminated, being replaced by a gentler, but still quite audible, whine.

After each racing event the cars were returned to the factory and completely overhauled before the next event. They were constructed to last 500 miles. (Most of the Grand Prix races were over distances of 300 to 400.) Then they were equipped with proper gears, chosen by detailed calculations of the racing circuit, and the carburetors were set for the expected atmosphere, which had been carefully duplicated in the laboratory as to dust, heat, and humidity.

In the 1937 Avus track race, three streamlined Mercedes-Benz cars were started. The completely closed bodies had less wind resistance than the open models, but nothing definite was known about the tire problem under racing conditions. In three heats Caracciola's car beat Rosemeyer's Auto Union by seconds in the first race; von Brauchitsch won the next. The third heat was also a tight battle between the streamlined Auto Union and Mercedes-Benz racers. The 400,000 spectators got many thrills as the cars rounded at top speeds the steeply banked north turn, the "wall of death," even though they could not identify with certainty the numbers on the different cars which screamed around the track too fast for positive identification. Lang won the last heat, crossing the finish line two seconds ahead of von Delius's Auto Union. His average speed was a fantastic 162.5 miles per hour.

Contrary to expectations, the streamlined cars were easier on tires than the open models. Offering less wind resistance, the closed models attained greater speeds with less acceleration. The greater heat under the covers was apparently not an important factor. However, changing of tires was more complicated. The wheel covers had to be loosened, turned up, then turned down again and fastened. A complete change took more than forty seconds. The open models, entered as safeguard in the event that the faster cars should blow up in the hotly contested race, could be serviced with fuel and tires in less than thirty seconds.

On the fast Spa circuit a model M 125 was timed at 193 miles per hour, a truly phenomenal speed for a road racing machine. This was more than 30 miles per hour faster than the official Avus record of the year.

Mercedes-Benz won in 1937 the Tripoli, German, Monaco, Swiss, Italian, and Masaryk Grands Prix. On the Avus track Lang won the race with an

The 750-kilogram formula W 25 racing car of 1936

On the Avus track, Caracciola (35) Mercedes and Rosemeyer (31) Auto Union, 1937

Mercedes-Benz W 125 racing car with Lang, 1937

average speed of 162.5 miles per hour — probably still the fastest winning average in any automobile race in the world.

While the 750-kilogram formula was in effect, from 1934 to 1937, Mercedes-Benz racers increased in power output from 430 brake horsepower to 645, without increase of more than 70 pounds in weight. The clocked top speed of the M 125 was 269.4 miles per hour. Average speeds increased tremendously, although it had been hoped that the restrictive weight formula would keep them down. A comparison of speeds on the same circuit would not be a true guide, because alterations are often made from one race to the next. If not rebuilding the circuit or rerouting the course, chicanes were set up which created an entirely different pattern and allowed greatly differing average speeds.

Von Brauchitsch at the "Coppa Acerbo" Pescara, 1937

Caracciola, ahead of Lang, at the Italian Grand Prix, 1937

Caracciola at the International Eifel race, 1937

Von Brauchitsch ahead of Caracciola at the Monaco Grand Prix, 1937

Loading of the racing cars for Tripoli, 1937

Lang wins the Tripoli Grand Prix in 1937

Von Brauchitsch and Kautz at the Belgian Grand Prix, 1937

The 3-Liter Formula (1938-1940)

For the season 1938 to 1940 the new international formula allowed a displacement of 3 liters supercharged, or 4.5 liters not supercharged and a minimum weight of 850 kilograms. Instead of limiting the overall weight of the machine, the formula prescribed the actual displacement. The Daimler-Benz engineers under Max Wagner and Rudolf Uhlenhaut developed a 3-liter supercharged engine, the M 163.

The twelve cylinders were of 67-millimeter bore and 70-millimeter stroke, and the engine had a displacement of 2.96 liters. The compression ratio was 6.5 to 1. The engine developed 485 brake horsepower at 8,000 revolutions per minute.

The cylinder-block construction was of chrome-steel barrels with integral heads in the shape of an inverted V. Water jackets and ports were of welded sheet steel and formed two blocks of six cylinders at an angle of 60 degrees. The four overhead camshafts operating the four valves, set at a 60-degree angle in each of the cylinders, were gear-driven from the rear end.

The supercharger was a two-stage Roots blower, mounted horizontally at the front end of the crankcase and driven at 1¼ times engine speed. Front suspension was of parallel wishbone links with open vertical coil springs. De Dion torsion bar progressive action springing was used in the rear. Double-acting hydraulic shock absorbers were employed in both front and rear.

The hydraulic brakes had two leading shoes with twin master cylinders. The frame consisted of two nickel-chrome-molybdenum steel, oval-sectioned side members tied together by five cross tubes. The wheelbase was 107 inches. The weight distribution was 40.8 percent for the front and 59.2 percent for the rear, including fuel and driver. The total weight was 2,410 pounds. The fuel capacity, 75 gallons, was increased to 88 gallons for the next season. The new models were even lower than the previous ones and had a pleasing oval grille.

The five gears used for the Nürburg Ring gave the car the maximum speeds in first of 58 miles per hour, second, 97; third, 121; fourth, 139; and fifth, 164. As mentioned earlier, Daimler-Benz engineers installed the gears which would allow peak engine power output for the greatest possible distances of the particular circuit. This was done by diligent studies of the courses, considering all gradients, curves, and even estimating prevailing winds. Well over seventy different gear combinations were available by changing the final spur wheels, the gear pinions, or the diameter of the rear wheels.

Certain design features of the Mercedes-Benz, and the Auto Union racers as well, became so firmly established in the minds of the public that neither company would ever incorporate the other's design, even if it proved to be superior.

The Continental Tire Company, which supplied all the racing tires, had four different types of tire for Mercedes-Benz racers, depending upon the physical characteristics of the circuit. The type required for continued high-speed driving on a relatively smooth course, of course, was entirely different from that required by frequent braking and rapid acceleration on a twisty course. Hill climbs naturally made altogether different demands.

Fuel was supplied by the Shell Oil Company; and in 1938 the mixture consisted of 86 percent methyl alcohol, 8.8 percent acetone for cooling valves and pistons, 4.4 percent nitrobenzene, and 0.8 percent sulphuric ether.

Early in 1938 several of the new M 163 models were shipped to Monza for road tests. The Mercedes-Benz home circuit, the Nürburg Ring, where most of the testing took place, was still in the throes of winter. Daimler-Benz officials were well pleased with the performance of the new machines, and they decided to enter two in the coming Pau Grand Prix. Two 4.5-liter Delahayes, two new eight-cylinder Alfa Romeos, and several older Bugattis and Maseratis were on the starting line. But many minor ills developed in the new Mercedes-Benz cars during the race. Lang retired, after crashing into the hay bales, tail first. The others had troubles too. Nuvolari burnt up his new Alfa in the woods off the road but escaped the flames. Then Villoresi's Alfa Romeo was taken out of the race as a precautionary measure. Caracciola led until half through the race. When he became ill Lang took over his car. But minor trouble plagued him. Eventually the car came in second. The unblown Delahaye had won, but the Mercedes-Benz racers had made the fastest lap times.

Front view of the 3-liter racing car of 1939

The Mercedes-Benz W 154 in the pits, with Caracciola, 1939

At the coming Tripoli Grand Prix the Mercedes-Benz of Lang made the fastest time of the day; and for the second time in succession, Lang won the fast African race. Von Brauchitsch was second, and Caracciola third. The new Mercedes-Benz models were doing well now.

In races on extremely fast courses, such as Tripoli, the Neubauer technique of saving tires by lower speeds paid off in victories. The Auto Unions traveled awfully fast and lost a great deal of their gained time in the pits with tire changes. For instance, Rosemeyer had to change his tires after only five fast laps around the eight-mile course; and Stuck's Auto Union used up seven sets of tires in the 325-mile race. The Mercedes-Benz team drove more slowly and made only two pit stops of less than thirty seconds each. They won the race. The winner's average speed was still a fair 127.5 miles per hour in 1938.

At the French Grand Prix the two Auto Unions crashed during the first lap. Two other contenders did the same in short order. The Mercedes-Benz racers ran well again, although Caracciola's machine did not sound healthy. Von Brauchitsch won the race, followed by Caracciola and Lang; It was another triple victory of the silvery Mercedes-Benz cars.

At the German Grand Prix on the Nürburg Ring, von Brauchitsch had a close call when his car caught fire in the pits and later crashed. The almost certain victory did not materialize for him. Dick Seaman drove an excellent race and won, with Lang and Caracciola sharing the second place. Later Lang won the Coppa Ciano near Leghorn, after von Brauchitsch was disqualified for being assisted by spectators out of the hay bales.

The Coppa Acerbo was all Caracciola's race. Jupiter Pluvius gave a superb performance, and the racing circuit resembled a canal. While visibility was near zero, Caracciola drove as if by miraculous illumination. Other drivers slowed down to stay on the course. Caracciola roared past them, drove a magnificent race, and consequently won the event.

The Swiss Grand Prix was a clean sweep for Mercedes-Benz. Caracciola navigated the Bremgarten course in fine style and won the race. Seaman placed second, and von Brauchitsch took third place.

The new 3-liter, 485-horsepower Mercedes-Benz racers had won six major races — the Tripoli, French, German, and Swiss Grands Prix, and the Coppas Ciano and Acerbo — in their first year of competition.

The 1939 version of the M 163 model was slightly improved over that of the previous year. The frame was lightened to but 99 pounds. Although the fuel tanks were enlarged to hold 88 gallons instead of 75, the car weighed about 200 pounds less. There were some ten machines and ten spare engines available now. However, only one spare engine was brought along for an event, and one practice machine — together with one car per driver, of course.

The Daimler-Benz racing organization was improved, if anything. It reached the acme of perfection. Engineer Rudolf Uhlenhaut, who was responsible for the design of the racers, accompanied the teams to the various events. Pit work was perfected so far that it took less than thirty seconds to refuel a car and change all the tires. Fuel consumption was considerable. The cars used nearly a gallon for every two miles traveled at speed. The two tanks were filled by a pressure method which supplied five gallons of fuel per second. The rear tank was filled through the front saddle tank.

The cars were likewise greedy in tire consumption. Lang had made but four fourteen-mile laps on the Nürburg Ring in the 1939 Eifel race with his new experimental machine, when he had to come into the pits to change tires. At the time he made record laps and also set a new record for the course. Otherwise, tires lasted a bit longer.

At the first race of the 1939 season, the Pau Grand Prix, Lang won, setting new distance and lap records. Unlucky von Brauchitsch took second place. He made mistakingly an unnecessary pit stop, which cost him the race. In the already mentioned Eifel race Lang won, Caracciola placed third. The Belgian Grand Prix was won by Lang, with von Brauchitsch in third place. Caracciola won the important German Grand Prix that year. The Swiss Grand Prix was again a triple Mercedes-Benz victory: Lang won; Caracciola took second place; and von Brauchitsch, third. Lang also

Mercedes racing car for the 1938-1940 season

Engine of the 1938-40 formula car

Mercedes record car of 1939

won the Vienna hill climb and the German Grand Prix hill climb. The Tripoli Grand Prix is another story.

Mercedes-Benz cars won four of the five Grands Prix that year: the Eifel race, the Vienna hill climb, and the German Grand Prix hill climb. It was another banner year.

The 3-liter racers had been improved over the two years until their official top speed was 250 miles per hour. This was only 20 miles per hour less than the top speed of the 6-liter machines of 1937. Daimler-Benz engineers had been able to get three-fourths of the earlier power out of engines of half the size. The 1939 M 163 3-liter engine developed 485 brake horsepower against the 1937 M 125 6-liter engine's 645 brake horsepower.

The team of Rudolf Uhlenhaut, Alfred Neubauer, Hermann Lang, Rudolf Caracciola, Manfred von Brauchitsch, and many others was an outstanding Grand Prix combination. They had brought the intricate racing activities to the highest level. They were men of extraordinary ability in their respective fields.

It is highly doubtful that Grand Prix racing will again produce such a successful group.

Start for the "Coppa Acerbo" at Pescara, 1938

Lang winning the Pau Grand Prix, 1939

Von Brauchitsch, leader in the triple victory of the
French Grand Prix of 1938

Engine of the 1938 Formula racing car, and chassis detail of the driver's compartment

Another view of the engine of the 1938 car, and still another view of it

The 1.5-Liter Racer (1939)

To the other automobile manufacturers with entries in Grand Prix racing the constant victories of the German cars were monotonous and highly disagreeable. Without consulting the German contestants, the Italians decided in September 1938 to make several of their coming Grand Prix events contests for 1.5-liter-displacement engines. Italian manufacturers had tested and raced such cars, and they hoped that the Germans would not have time enough to produce this type.

But the Daimler-Benz engineers developed a 1.5-liter racer within the incredibly short period of eight months. Under the direction of Rudolf Uhlenhaut the Stuttgart racing department built two complete racers, miniatures of the M 163 in outward appearance, and three spare engines. Caracciola and Lang tested one machine briefly on the banked, short motorcycle track at Hockenheim, near Heidelberg. The engine hummed sweetly as the experienced Grand Prix drivers pushed the accelerator down. Director Max Sailer, Engineer Uhlenhaut, and Race Chief Neubauer watched anxiously to see how the new, little cars would handle under expert guidance. The deadline for entries for the Tripoli Grand Prix race was three days away.

The car looked like a baby brother to the 3-liter machines. Its eight cylinders were banked at 90 degrees, and had a displacement of 64-millimeter bore and 58-millimeter stroke. Its 1.495-liter engine developed 278 brake horsepower at 8,250 revolutions per minute. Its compression ratio was 6.99 to 1. In other engine details it was similar to the larger, well proved twelve-cylinder M 163 model. The five gears for the fast Tripoli circuit gave the racer a top speed of 56 miles per hour in first gear, 97 in second, 115 in third, 146 in fourth, and 170 in fifth at 8,000 revolutions per minute. The wheelbase of the M 165 was 96½ inches. The fuel tanks held 55 gallons, and total weight, including fuel and driver, was 1,750 pounds.

After a few practice laps by both drivers around the fast oval, Max Sailer nodded his head. It meant that the new Mercedes-Benz racers were entered in the Tripoli Grand Prix to compete with the twenty-eight tested Italian 1.5-liter cars for the rich prize. The courageous move would show that the Daimler-Benz engineers could construct a racing car, from the blueprint stage to the finished product, in eight months. The machines would appear on the starting line, even if both cars blew up during the race. The racers were trucked to Naples, and shipped across the Mediterranean Sea.

The Tripoli Grand Prix was always a gala event in the Italian colony of Libya. An immense lottery was held in connection with it. The air was full of expectancy. Practically all the inhabitants took a deep interest in the proceedings. The international atmosphere of a Grand Prix event was provided by the crowd of Arabs and Berbers, of Negroes and Turks, and of Europeans. The oddly assorted spectators were as unusual and colorful as the history of Libya.

Caracciola and Lang were chosen to drive the new machines. Caracciola was the senior driver, and Lang had won the African race twice before. During practice a passing car kicked up a stone that hit Lang in the forehead; blood trickled down his face, over his goggles, and onto his white coveralls. He had had a similar mishap twice before in Tripoli. Bad luck, it seemed, came in threes; and perhaps good fortune would do the same.

Race day was extremely hot, and the sky was filled with yellow dust from the North African desert. In addition, the minute particles of sand had a mysterious way of getting into the delicate car machinery. The Tripoli Grand Prix was always a most difficult race. The heat, the sand, and the terrifically high speed gave it a fatality rate among racers considerably above that of other Grands Prix.

Luigi Villoresi, who had made the fastest practice time in his monstrous, super-streamlined Maserati — an average of 134 miles per hour on the fast 8.15-mile course — sat in it in the front row with the two Mercedes-Benz cars beside him. At the green light the cars were off: the flag-waving Marshal Balbo was a few seconds behind the official signal. The two small silver arrows shot ahead, their superchargers whining like sirens above the tumult. The Alfa team and Villoresi's huge machine followed. Lang soon raced away from the field. Caracciola and Farina's Alfa Romeo battled for second place.

The race strategy, designed by Race Chief Neubauer to produce a Mercedes-Benz victory, was for Lang, in a car equipped with overdrive, to go as fast as possible and cause the leading competitors to blow up

Mercedes 1.5-liter racing car, 1939

Lang, winner of the Tripoli Grand Prix, 1939

their engines. Caracciola was to stay behind and save his machine. Half through the race, Lang, if he was still participating, would come into the pits for a tire change. The special Tripoli tires on his car and Caracciola's had an exceedingly thin, and very smooth, tread, they were designed for the great continuous speeds possible on the fast course and were quite different from the tires used on all other Grand Prix circuits. It was a gamble that Lang's machine could stand the punishment of setting the terrific pace for the 244-mile race. If not, with the fast cars out of the race toward the end, Caracciola could win easily.

The multicolored flags and pennants over the long white grandstand fluttered gaily in the hot breeze. Lang was setting a really frightening pace. His car hurtled through the many palm-lined fast bends at all-out speeds and made a lap speed of 131.4 miles per hour. The officials and the thousands of spectators could hardly believe this tremendous speed possible. Two years before, Lang had flung the much more powerful 6-liter racer around the course at a speed not much greater. The fast Maserati lasted only through the first lap. The other Maseratis also quit soon after that. And the Alfa Romeo cars fell behind, or went out.

The white-clad, sun-baked, brown-faced spectators watched eagerly as the red and the silver racing cars flashed past them. Many wondered, perhaps, at the devilish high-pitched screaming of the supercharged engines.

When Lang stopped in the pits at the planned time he had a lead of a minute and a half over the second-place Caracciola. After the fast stop for fuel and tires he slowed his excellently performing car slightly but kept the lead. His position seemed to be secure without further risk-taking. The foot pedals of his car got extremely hot and burned his feet, but he kept on driving. If the little silver bomb would stand another hundred-odd miles, the race would be his. And the car, and driver, performed admirably.

This was Lang's third Tripoli Grand Prix in a row. Caracciola took second place, three minutes behind the leader. An Alfa Romeo crossed the finish line five minutes behind Caracciola.

It is interesting to compare Lang's speeds in the Tripoli over the years. In 1937 his winning 5.6-liter Mercedes-Benz car made an average for the 320-mile race of 134.3 miles per hour. In 1938 he drove the 3-liter car the same distance at an average of 127.4 miles per hour. This was but 6.9 miles per hour less with half the displacement. He won the 1939 race in the 1.5-liter Mercedes-Benz at an average of 122.9 miles per hour. Again, the speed was but 4.5 miles per hour less, and the displacement had been halved again. However, Lang's speed of 1939 was actually five hours faster than the winning time of Varzi's 3.2-liter Alfa Romeo of 1934.

The double victory of this rapidly developed Mercedes-Benz M 165 racer was indeed in keeping with the outstanding performances expected of the oldest automobile manufacturer in the world. It was a magnificent feat.

Driver's compartment

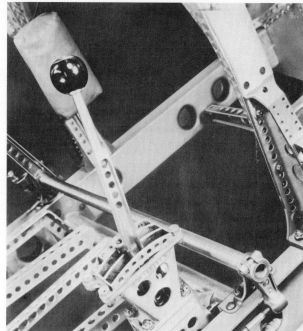

Gear shift detail

Brake detail

Rear axle of the racing car, 1938

Caracciola winning the German Grand Prix of 1926

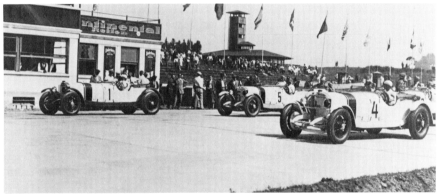

Start of the German Grand Prix of 1928

Caracciola sets new record at the Semmering race, 1928

Caracciola, driving an "SSK," wins the 1931 Mille Miglia

Zatuszek (SSK) wins the Argentine race in 1931

European Hill Climb Champion of 1931: Caracciola and his "SSK"

World Speed Record Cars (1901-1939)

The story of Daimler and Benz automobiles would not be complete without mention of the numerous world's records they set. Many such records have already been mentioned.

There was the early one-mile record of 49.4 miles per hour set by Barrow's 35-horsepower Mercedes at Nice in 1901. A year later Degrais bettered the mark in his 40-horsepower Mercedes at 51.6 miles per hour at the Week of Nice. And in 1904 Baron de Caters, with a flying start, drove his 90-horsepower Mercedes over the one-kilometer distance at 97.2 miles per hour.

The first automobile especially constructed for record runs was probably the twin-engined Mercedes of H. L. Bowden. With the two 60-horsepower engines, he established a new one-mile record of 109.6 miles per hour at the 1905 Daytona Beach speed carnival.

In 1908 Dario Resta drove his 120-horsepower Mercedes racer to a new half-mile world's record of 95.4 miles per hour, on the fast Brooklands track.

Then came the bountiful 1909 record year. Camille Jenatzy established a 500-meter record of 111.8 miles per hour at the Ostend speed week. From a standing start Barney Oldfield drove a 150-horsepower Benz at Indianapolis one mile at 83.8 miles per hour. At Brussels, Victor Hémery won the world championship race with a 200-horsepower Benz, driving one kilometer, from a standing start, at 71.5 miles per hour. Later that year he drove the Blitzen Benz on the Brooklands track, and established a one-kilometer record of 127.8 miles per hour and a half-mile record of 115.9 miles per hour, both from a flying start.

Barney Oldfield drove the 200-horsepower Blitzen Benz at Daytona Beach in 1910 to a new world's record for the mile of 131.4 miles per hour, from a flying start. And a year later Bob Burman drove the same car to the record of 141.7 miles per hour, which stood unbeaten until 1924.

In 1913 in Russia, Hörner drove his 200-horsepower Benz over the one-verst distance near St. Petersburg at a speed of 73.7 miles per hour. And Hornsted established a new half-mile world's record of 70.7 miles per hour and a new one-kilometer record of 73.8 miles per hour, from a standing start, on the Brooklands track before the First World War.

The record speed of the Mercedes-Benz SSKL streamlined model of 1932 has already been mentioned. Von Brauchitsch drove this 300-horsepower model on the Berlin Avus track 120.7 miles per hour for the distance greater than 200 kilometers.

All the above world records were established with regular road racing machines, none of which had been especially constructed for record runs. Such machines were also used in road and track races. Some, like the Blitzen Benz, performed considerably better on a long straight run than on a curved, banked race track.

After the Daimler-Benz company had constructed the 750-kilogram formula racers, and the regular 1934 racing season had ended, engineers modified one machine. A low, coupé-like cover was placed over the open cockpit. The racer was then taken to Budapest to try for new speed records for various distances. On the arrow-straight road at Györ, Rudolf Caracciola established several new world's records in the 3- to 5-liter category, Class C. He drove the one-kilometer distance at 197.2 miles per hour and the one-mile distance at 196.6, both from a flying start. He also drove the one-mile distance at 117.1 miles per hour, from a standing start. His highest speed was 199.2 miles per hour. Later Caracciola drove the same eight-cylinder racer at the Avus track over the 5-kilometer distance at 193.8 miles per hour, making a new class record.

A specially built twelve-cylinder, 5.66-liter racer was clothed in an aluminum envelope-style streamlined body in 1936. New world-speed-record trials were made that fall on a straight stretch of the absolutely level autobahn between Frankfurt and Darmstadt.

Caracciola established several new speed records during those trials. All world's records were for the 5- to 8-liter displacement, Class B. The top speed reached was 231 miles per hour. The record speeds were 226.3 miles per hour for one kilometer, 227.8 miles per hour for one mile, 211.5 miles per hour for 5 kilometers, 209.2 miles per hour for 5 miles, 206.2 miles per hour for 10 kilometers, and 207.1 miles per hour for 10 miles. All records were, of course, made from a flying start.

The speed record of 162.5 miles per hour set by Lang and the streamlined 1937 Mercedes-Benz in the Avus track race has been mentioned.

Mercedes SSK record car

The 5.57-liter record car of 1938

Mercedes 3-liter, twelve-cylinder record car, 1939

Several of these streamlined racers were built, but the cars were not used elsewhere. The drag coefficient of the streamlined machine was only 43 percent of that of a regular-bodied racing car. However, a marked instability at high speeds was among the aerodynamic effects. Still, Daimler-Benz engineers constructed a modified streamlined body, with all wheels enclosed, to be run in the 1940 Tripoli Grand Prix. The event never took place.

By late 1937 the twelve-cylinder, 5.66-liter record car of 1936 underwent some modifications. Again, after the close of a fine Grand Prix season, the speedster was taken to the Frankfurt-to-Darmstadt autobahn. Bernd Rosemeyer had reached a speed of more than 400 kilometers (248.6 miles) per hour with his streamlined Auto Union machine. It was up to Caracciola to better the mark with the Mercedes-Benz car.

The early morning mist still hung over the meadows and in the thick forests through which the autobahn knifed its unswerving concrete way. After some hot coffee Caracciola climbed into the cockpit of the already warmed-up record machine, pulled his goggles over his eyes as he received a friendly slap from Race Manager Neubauer on his white cloth helmet, and was pushed off by half a dozen mechanics for a short trial run. The record car was checked over again by the engineers. Then there was a short conference, and the car was pushed off for the real effort. The factory representatives watched anxiously as the brilliant aluminum-bodied car gathered speed. The high polish of the body reduced wind resistance to a minimum. Caracciola was successful in his task, driving 436.9 kilometers (271.3 miles) per hour. His one-kilometer record was 268.7 miles per hour, and his one-mile record was 268.5 miles per hour, from a flying start, for Class B. It was the highest speed reached on a public highway.

The 1938 Class B records were expected to stand for some time. The Daimler-Benz racing department modified two twelve-cylinder, 3-liter racers to establish new Class D (for 2- to 3-liter displacement) records the next year. Two streamlined bodies were constructed. The one used for record runs from a flying start had a thin, narrow opening in its flattened, gradually rising front end. A long, pointed tail helped the car to stay on the road. The brightly polished record car had a neat streamlined, bullet-shaped body as near aerodynamic perfection as was humanly

possible. But in the first speed-test run the front opening was pushed together slightly, the extremely thin metal skin having been bent by the force of the resisting wind. The other car was considerably shorter and had greatly improved acceleration, so important in standing-start trials.

The autobahn near Dessau was closed to regular traffic so that the 25-feet-wide half of the highway might be used for the speed trials. Caracciola established new world records in the 2- to 3-liter category, Class D, for the one-kilometer and the one-mile distances. From a flying start he traveled the kilometer at 247.3 miles per hour. He continued to gain speed after that distance and made the mile at 248.4 miles per hour. From a standing start he reached 108.7 miles per hour for the kilometer and 127.1 miles per hour for the mile.

These record runs were impressive performances. The Daimler-Benz engineers gathered valuable information during the test runs and incorporated their findings in what might have been the most powerful and fastest automobile ever built. The constructed record car was complete in every detail but was never tested. This is its story.

Conceived by the pioneering, resourceful engineering genius Ferdinand Porsche and the aerodynamics specialist von Fachsenfeld, the T 80 was built by the Daimler-Benz racing department in 1938. It was to bring the world's speed record to Germany.

A new world's speed record of 367.181 miles per hour had then been set by British John Cobb with his Railton Special on the Bonneville salt flats of Utah. So the Mercedes-Benz record car was designed and built to do more than 400 miles per hour. The Continental Tire people tested the tires to withstand speeds up to 440 miles per hour. The unorthodox, three-axle car was powered at first by a Daimler-Benz 600 aircraft engine and weighed 5,656 pounds. Later in the year the engine was replaced with the newer-type Daimler-Benz 601. This huge 44-liter (2,685 cubic inches), twelve-cylinder engine developed a whopping 3,000 horsepower.

When German officials heard of the plans to send the record car to the United States for a new speed record on the Utah salt beds, they refused permission to the Daimler-Benz company. Instead, a seven-mile-long strip of concrete road for the speed run was constructed near Dessau. The

T-80 World's record car

Chassis of the T-80 car

Rear view of the record car

land is flat there, and officials felt that the terrain offered an excellent substitute for the vast expanse of the American salt beds.

However, before the trial runs could be undertaken, World War II had begun. The power plant of the car had again been changed to an improved type, the Daimler-Benz 603 aircraft engine. The output of this twelve-cylinder engine was rated at 3,030 brake horsepower. The weight of the car remained under 6,000 pounds, and the theoretical top speed was near 500 miles per hour.

The speed-record car is of a remarkably advanced design by present standards, despite its age of twenty-eight years. The extremely light metal body, with its wing stubs and long tail overhang, gives the illusion of speeding along even while it stands motionless in the quiet museum at Untertürkheim.

The world's speed record stands now at 394.196 miles per hour, set by John Cobb in his twin Napier-engined Railton Special in Utah in 1949. The Mercedes-Benz speedster could probably exceed that speed in its present form. Further developments of the T 80 do not appear to be too difficult, however, should they become necessary. But the Daimler-Benz people are more interested in their production program than in this highly specialized, and exceedingly costly, phase of automobile racing.

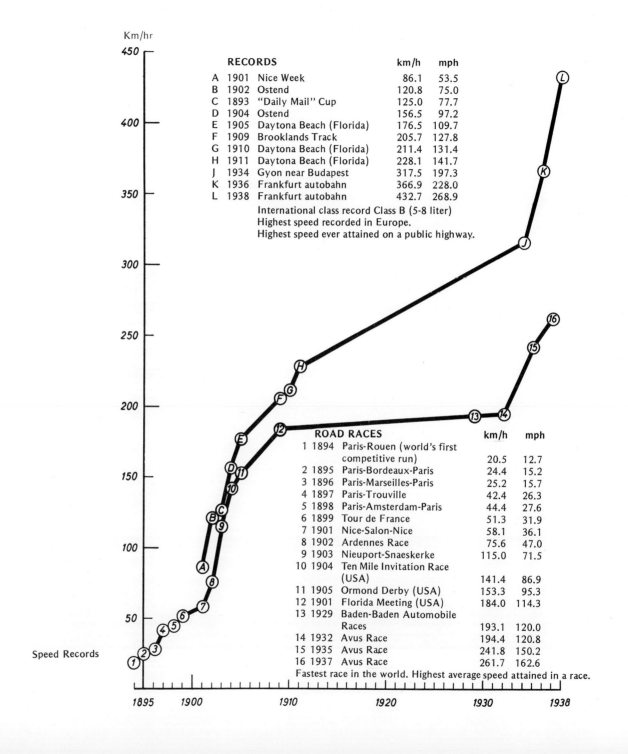

Km/hr

RECORDS

			km/h	mph
A	1901	Nice Week	86.1	53.5
B	1902	Ostend	120.8	75.0
C	1893	"Daily Mail" Cup	125.0	77.7
D	1904	Ostend	156.5	97.2
E	1905	Daytona Beach (Florida)	176.5	109.7
F	1909	Brooklands Track	205.7	127.8
G	1910	Daytona Beach (Florida)	211.4	131.4
H	1911	Daytona Beach (Florida)	228.1	141.7
J	1934	Gyon near Budapest	317.5	197.3
K	1936	Frankfurt autobahn	366.9	228.0
L	1938	Frankfurt autobahn	432.7	268.9

International class record Class B (5-8 liter)
Highest speed recorded in Europe.
Highest speed ever attained on a public highway.

ROAD RACES

			km/h	mph
1	1894	Paris-Rouen (world's first competitive run)	20.5	12.7
2	1895	Paris-Bordeaux-Paris	24.4	15.2
3	1896	Paris-Marseilles-Paris	25.2	15.7
4	1897	Paris-Trouville	42.4	26.3
5	1898	Paris-Amsterdam-Paris	44.4	27.6
6	1899	Tour de France	51.3	31.9
7	1901	Nice-Salon-Nice	58.1	36.1
8	1902	Ardennes Race	75.6	47.0
9	1903	Nieuport-Snaeskerke	115.0	71.5
10	1904	Ten Mile Invitation Race (USA)	141.4	86.9
11	1905	Ormond Derby (USA)	153.3	95.3
12	1901	Florida Meeting (USA)	184.0	114.3
13	1929	Baden-Baden Automobile Races	193.1	120.0
14	1932	Avus Race	194.4	120.8
15	1935	Avus Race	241.8	150.2
16	1937	Avus Race	261.7	162.6

Fastest race in the world. Highest average speed attained in a race.

Speed Records

1895   1900   1910   1920   1930   1938

The banked curve at the Avus, Berlin, 1937

Record trial, 1939

Rudolf Caracciola, in his best years

Enclosed-cockpit record car of 1936

Alfred Neubauer, in later life

Mercedes-Benz Drivers (1894-1955)

Of all the ace drivers *(Spitzenfahrer)* in Mercedes-Benz history, Rudolf Caracciola is unquestionably the most prominent. However, some 170 drivers have contributed since 1894 to the uncounted victories of this famous name. In the earliest stage of automobile racing the emphasis was on the reliability of the vehicles. Speed was of importance in winning a contest, but it was more often a matter of reaching the finish line.

Fritz Held was perhaps the first *Herrenfahrer* (sportsman-driver) of note. This man of fine features, full mustache, and well trimmed, pointed beard always appeared in an immaculate blue suit and yachting cap, the accepted fashion of the day. He was a familiar figure with his 1899 model, two-cylinder, 8-horsepower Benz at most distance runs. He won the early reliability runs from Frankfurt to Cologne and from Mannheim to Pforzheim and return.

Wilhelm Werner is the first outstandingly successful Daimler competitor on record. He was a big man, wore a mustache and always a smile. Werner really showed his driving ability when he won, later, the famous Nice La Turbie hill climb in 1901, driving a four-cylinder, 35-horsepower squatty Mercedes racer.

Wealthy Emil Jellinek should be included in the roster of early Daimler enthusiasts. This banker was so impressed by the reliable Daimler automobiles that he invested heavily and became a member of the board of directors of the company in 1900. He won the first Semmering hill climb with his 16-horsepower Daimler. This event was the first of a long series of important yearly race meets, eleven of which were subsequently won by Mercedes cars. Jellinek's pretty daughter Mercedes gave her name to the entire line of Daimler-built vehicles, beginning in 1901.

Now came, with the new century, the era of the gargantuan racing machines. They thundered down the often dusty, and almost torturous, roads and carried their badly needed supply of spare tires tied securely to their rear decks, continental style. Driving was tough and hard. Keeping the 2,000-pound behemoths on the road at roaring speeds of a hundred miles per hour or holding them in at the turns required brute strength as well as the utmost skill. When not busy with temperamental machinery, the riding mechanic worked almost constantly at pumping fuel to the guzzling engine. Drivers of that time looked as formidable as they actually were.

Camille Jenatzy was one of the best and fastest Mercedes drivers when the 60-horsepower monsters were in style. He also drove in the United States frequently, and won the fourth Gordon Bennett Cup in Ireland for Mercedes in 1903.

Christian Lautenschlager, with cap reversed and flowing mustache trailing behind, was a popular and successful Mercedes driver in Europe and abroad. He fitted well into the colorful age of powerful machines and brawn and stamina. He won the 478-mile French Grand Prix in his 140-horsepower Mercedes in 1908 and repeated the feat in 1914.

Ralph De Palma should, of course, be included in the roster of Mercedes drivers. Although he drove many other makes, his greatest international fame came undoubtedly from winning the Elgin road race and the Vanderbilt Cup in 1912 with his 140-horsepower, 1908 Grand Prix model Mercedes. That was the memorable year when he lost the 500-mile race at Indianapolis, pushing his car the last two heartbreaking miles to the finish line after having led the second-place car by ten miles, but won the hearts and the admiration of all automobile fans. But the great De Palma managed to win the 1915 Indianapolis speed classic with his Mercedes at an average of 89.84 miles per hour.

In 1914 De Palma won the Vanderbilt Cup race at Santa Monica, California, against the famous Barney Oldfield. By a ruse he indicated a pit stop for tires which Oldfield observed. Oldfield then stopped, thinking that he had plenty of time to do so. However, De Palma kept on, and won. And the 300-mile Elgin road race netted him the large sterling trophy and a fine wrist watch again. De Palma contributed greatly, as did the other winners, to the popularity of wrist watches.

Victor Hémery, the original Blitzen Benz driver, is one of racing's immortals. He established many sizzling world speed records with the 200-horsepower Benz racer, as the ace driver for Benz. In 1908 he won the tough 438-mile road race from St. Petersburg to Moscow. He might have captured the first place in the significant French Grand Prix as well that year; but a flying stone shattered his goggles, and he stopped to have the splinters removed from an eye before continuing with the race and placing second. Race driving in the early part of the century was arduous indeed.

Benz vehicle in Paris-Bordeaux race, 1895

First international track race, Frankfurt, 1900

The popular Eddie Hearne won many honors in his clean-looking low-slung 1907 Benz on circuits in the United States. In 1910 he won the Fox River Cup at the Elgin road races. That same year he also won the 100-mile race and a purse of a thousand dollars at Indianapolis in his 150-horsepower Benz, with an average of 89 miles per hour.

The American David Bruce-Brown set three new world records at Daytona in 1909, driving a 150-horsepower Benz. And the following year he won the 415-mile American Grand Prix at Savannah, Georgia. Battling all the way against Hémery, for 5 hours and 53 minutes, Bruce-Brown gave the spectators a thrill long to remember when he led his rival at the end by just one second. It was Grand Prix racing at its best.

Other successful Mercedes pilots of that time were Hieronimus, who was victorious in 1903 at the Week of Nice, and Braun, who repeatedly won the Semmering events, from 1903 in his 60-horsepower Mercedes until 1906 in a 100-horsepower model. And then there were Erle and Hörner, who drove various Benz machines to victory in Europe.

Other fine Mercedes drivers of the circuit races were Ladenburg, Hutton, Baron de Caters, Poege, von Stern, Salzer, Wishart, and Wagner.

The wealthy American sportsman William K. Vanderbilt, whose racing activities gave such a tremendous impetus to the infant American automobile industry, was a Mercedes driver of renown. In 1902 he tied Jenatzy's kilometer record of 65 miles per hour on the speed track at Achères, France. In 1904, at the annual "speed carnival," Vanderbilt drove his 2,000-pound, 90-horsepower Mercedes mammoth racer more than 92 miles per hour down the firm beach at the Daytona meet. In fact, he set seven new American records that time, when Mercedes racers were victorious in no fewer than twenty-three events. The dashing Croesus established the Vanderbilt Cup races the same year, and his many activities contributed greatly to the popularity of road racing in the United States.

International racing resumed three years after the First World War but most of the old drivers had driven their last race.

Some names of sports-car drivers, however, were still familiar. There were Lautenschlager, Hörner, Walb, and Kappler. Count Giulio Masetti, driving a 1914 Grand Prix model Mercedes, won the Targa Florio, the difficult Sicilian mountain race, in 1922 and the 269-mile Italian Grand Prix the previous year.

Christian Werner drove his 2-liter, supercharged Mercedes to a double victory at the Sicilian meet in 1924. With the same car he broke the fifteen-year-old record at the Austrian Semmering race. Otto Merz won the Klausenpass hill climb at the fast French Grand Prix in 1914 with the fastest Mercedes there, and won the Coppa Florio in 1921. Now a director of the Daimler-Benz company, he heads the racing and experimental departments. To keep abreast of developments, he still participates occasionally in competition.

Fritz Nallinger and Alfred Neubauer also appear on the roster of successful Mercedes drivers of that period. Dr. Nallinger is now chief engineer and one of the directors of the company. Alfred Neubauer was the capable director of the racing team during its finest years and still directs those factory activities. Mercedes-Benz race participation cannot be imagined without the portly leader in absolute command.

A few of the young men who had driven the wonderful sports cars of the early postwar period had developed into outstanding racing drivers when Mercedes-Benz cars dominated the Grand Prix scene some ten years later.

Luigi Fagioli had driven Grand Prix races since 1926 for Maserati and in 1933 for Alfa Romeo. All this before he began to drive the new 750-kilogram-formula Mercedes-Benz racers in 1934. He promptly won the Coppa Acerbo at Pescara and the Spanish Grand Prix at San Sebastian in this new-formu'a car; and with Caracciola he won the Italian Grand Prix. Fagioli won two Grand Prix races in 1934 and one more in 1935.

While the experienced Italian pilot drove the Mercedes-Benz machines in true championship style, he did not always blend well in personality with the other drivers. Especially was this the case with Alfred Neubauer, who directed Mercedes-Benz races from the pits. He, and not the drivers, planned the races; but the temperamental Italian ace often wanted to employ his own tactics.

Camille Jenatzy and the 60-horsepower Mercedes, winner of the 1903 Gordon Bennett race

Prince Heinrich of Prussia, driving a Benz in the Herkomer Trophy competition of 1906

Neubauer's little red and black flag when held below the position board meant, "Slow down." Held above the board, it meant, "Speed up." To Fagioli the signal always meant to speed if he thought it expedient.

However, the Italian undoubtedly contributed greatly of his vast Grand Prix experience to the new Mercedes-Benz team during his two active years with it — he won six Grand Prix events, took five seconds, and two third places for the silver arrows.

Manfred von Brauchitsch appeared on the international racing scene in a highly dramatic manner. Caracciola had already been driving Mercedes sports cars successfully when von Brauchitsch's streamlined, supercharged 7.7-liter SSKL model appeared on the fast Avus circuit at Berlin in 1932. Driving a sensational race, the young von Brauchitsch won from Caracciola who, admittedly, had a slightly slower car. He set a new class world's record of more than 120 miles per hour for distances in excess of 200 kilometers, and went on to win several hill climbs and other road races that year. It was inevitable that he should be chosen as a top driver for the new Mercedes-Benz racing cars when they first appeared two years later.

From the very start of the powerful, new 750-kilogram-formula, eight-cylinder, 3.99-liter, and 430 brake horsepower Mercedes-Benz racers at the twisty Nürburg Ring, von Brauchitsch beat a strong field of other works drivers and the new rear-engined Auto Unions. These were the sensational P-Wagen of famed Dr. Porsche's design. Von Brauchitsch won the 212-mile race and established a new record for the Eifel circuit. In the next seven years the red-cloth-helmeted von Brauchitsch was a familiar figure on the circuits of Europe whenever Mercedes-Benz cars raced. However, he was the unluckiest driver of all. His misfortunes were many.

Soon after the 1934 Eifel victory von Brauchitsch crashed at practice for the next German Grand Prix, ending his participation for the season. The following year he took second place in the French Grand Prix at Montlhéry and, together with Fagioli, finished second in the Belgian Grand Prix, run at the Spa-Francorchamps course. At the 1935 German Grand Prix on the Nürburg Ring, von Brauchitsch was in the lead, ahead of the masters Nuvolari, Caracciola, and Rosemeyer, when suddenly his tires tore into shreds. He held the car securely on the course, but the almost certain victory slipped through his fingers.

In 1938 von Brauchitsch won the Monaco Grand Prix. By having made the fastest lap in practice, he had the center spot in the starting line-up. Halfway through the race many of the contenders had dropped out. Caracciola, who had won this event the previous year, tried vainly to pass the leading driver on the twisty two-mile circuit through the narrow streets of the famed gaming resort; but, after establishing several new lap records, he had to pull into the pits for new plugs. Von Brauchitsch's lead was now secure. Mercedes-Benz cars had now won the Monaco Grand Prix three years in a row, and had taken the first three places each time. Also in 1938, the red-helmeted driver took second place in the German, Masaryk, and Donington Grands Prix and the Coppa Acerbo.

At the running of the 1938 German Grand Prix, von Brauchitsch was in great form. His fastest lap time of 9 minutes 49 seconds was just 3 seconds slower than the course record held by Rosemeyer, and he was well in the lead during the race, having bested Nuvolari, who piloted an Auto Union, and the other fine Mercedes drivers. As arranged, von Brauchitsch came into the pits for fuel and tires on the sixteenth lap. Some fuel spilled over in the filling of the tanks, and when the racer started again a flash from the exhaust ignited it. In an instant the rear of the car was enveloped in flame. Von Brauchitsch tore the steering wheel off and, with the help of the ever watchful Neubauer, got safely out of the car. The fire was extinguished quickly, and von Brauchitsch, covered with the sudsy foam of the fire-fighters, got into the car and roared away, trying desperately to regain his precious lead.

At the Flugplatz (airport), which is indeed correctly named, the racers leave the road momentarily and bounce, at some 125 miles per hour, into the air. Hitting the road after this "flight," von Brauchitsch had his steering wheel in his hands. It had come off the column. The car left the road, but the driver miraculously escaped serious injury. It was another link in the long chain of unfortunate incidents which plagued von Brauchitsch during his driving career.

Lautenschlager at the French Grand Prix, 1908

Salzer, winner of the French Grand Prix, 1908

In 1938 von Brauchitsch won second place in the French Grand Prix, and several thirds. The next racing season he placed second in the French and the Pau Grands Prix.

During the 1934 to 1939 Grand Prix racing seasons the eternally unlucky Manfred von Brauchitsch won two Grand Prix events, placed second eight times, and took third place six times. He was a valuable member of the Mercedes-Benz team.

Richard Seaman, the only English driver on the Mercedes-Benz works team, had a promising but short career. His style was similar to that of the great Caracciola. At the 1937 Vanderbilt Cup race on Long Island, he was billed as "the young Briton from Cambridge's cloistered halls," which indeed he was. With Caracciola he defended the Mercedes-Benz honors against the Auto Unions of Rosemeyer and von Delius. The Alfas and other contestants were hopelessly outclassed. When Caracciola retired with a broken supercharger drive after a terrific battle with Rosemeyer, Seaman was ahead of the pursuing Auto Unions, and the race was up to him. He drove a superb race, but had to stop for fuel at the last lap and was 51 seconds behind the winner.

The following year, the "daredevil Dick" won the greatest race of his life, the 312-mile German Grand Prix at the Nürburg Ring. Coming in ahead of Lang and Caracciola, the young Englishman had reached the pinnacle of success. The same year, he also finished second in the Swiss Grand Prix.

Richard Seaman, killed in an accident in 1939, had won one Grand Prix event, placed second twice, and taken third place once for Mercedes-Benz.

On the long list of championship drivers who have won victories for Mercedes-Benz, the name of Rudolf Caracciola appears first in 1932. The astonishing career of this remarkable automobile race driver began in a *Reichsfahrt* that year, sponsored by the German Automobile Clubs, in which he accumulated, with his 1.5-liter supercharged Mercedes, the largest possible number of points in the touring class. In time, the name Caracciola became synonymous with victory, and he became a national idol. Yet, in all his sixteen years of driving for Mercedes-Benz, there was never anything extraordinary, or highly spectacular, about this quiet and popular man. He always drove a capable race.

The only spectacular thing about Caracciola was that he won just about all the races in which his car performed perfectly. He calculated his chances before every race and seemed to drive coolly and collectedly. He seldom made mistakes. There was nothing theatrical about him. He never jumped up and down in his seat, as "campionissimo" Tazio Nuvolari did whenever he became excited. Like Hans Stuck, he never had a spectacular wreck on a circuit; and while the anxious crowd was wondering about him he would walk nonchalantly into the pits with his detached steering wheel, miraculously unhurt. In fact, on the days of practice and of racing for Grands Prix, Caracciola never left the road more than half a dozen times. He was a purist, and always drove a smooth race. Watching him, one had the feeling that the car and the driver were one and the same. He had the uncanny ability to sense what the car would do under any given circumstance, and so seemed to anticipate its every move.

Caracciola drove superbly and with perfect calm. His speeds were calculated to preserve the precious tires, and often when other drivers had to make an extra pit stop he could afford to stay the extra time on the track, and win the race handily.

Caracciola executing a masterful power slide, which hurtled his racing car across the road and into the turn at exactly the proper spot at every lap, was an amazing sight to behold. Others might touch the grassy edges of the track, but Caracciola always seemed to bring his car to a particular spot at precisely the same speed. After timing him on a circuit, you could set your watch by the lap speeds he made, unless the portly Neubauer manipulated his little flags in the pit to suggest a change of pace.

If a situation warranted it, Caracciola could hurtle his silvery racer competently through an opening which appeared much too narrow to emerge intact. His uncanny ability to seize upon a circumstance and make a split-second, and correct, decision, made him the "ausgezeichneter Meisterfahrer" (excellent master driver) which he was.

Caracciola always drove to win a race, never to show off. And, during his time of competition, this wizard won more than a hundred times for

Tire changing at the French Grand Prix, 1908

Racing car engine of 1908 and of 1914

Mercedes Grand Prix racing team of 1914

Mercedes-Benz, and more than three hundred trophies. Despite his name he was a German. He was born in the small town of Remagen on the Rhine River, which until the Second World War was known to few people as anything else than the home town of the famous race driver.

After the First World War, Caracciola first drove a Mercedes sports car in 1922 on the Avus track at Berlin. He placed fifth in the race, which was run in a steady downpour. Impressed by the performance of the twenty-one-year-old youth, Daimler officials invited him to drive for their company. And he continued to drive Mercedes cars, except during the extremely difficult economic situation after the next war when the Stuttgart factory did not participate in racing.

During that one season Caracciola drove Alfa Romeo machines and won, as was expected of him, the German, the Monaco, and the Lemberg (Poland) Grands Prix and the Eifel race at the Nürburg Ring.

In 1924 he made the fastest time for sports cars in the Klausenpass hill climb in Switzerland, driving the supercharged 1.5-liter Mercedes. The next year he drove the last-built Mercedes model sports car to several victories.

Caracciola was the overall winner in the sports-car category in 1926, driving a 2-liter, eight-cylinder Mercedes Benz in the German Grand Prix at the Avus track. In the Semmering race, he won in the racing-car category, driving a supercharged 4.5-liter 1914 Grand Prix model racer.

Caracciola lived up to expectations of him by driving his new Mercedes-Benz S model to victory when the complicated Nürburg Ring opened in 1927. The next year, he repeated in the German Grand Prix, on the same circuit, with the SS model. In 1929 he won the Prague hill climb and the Belfast Tourist trophy race.

In 1930 Caracciola won the Prague hill climb, the Irish Grand Prix, the Swiss Klausenpass hill climb, and the Austrian Semmering race. And at the Freiburg hill climb he established a new record with his Mercedes-Benz SSK model. He became European Champion that year.

With Sebastian as copilot, Caracciola won the 1931 Mille Miglia in a Mercedes-Benz SSKL model. The average speed of 63 miles per hour was a new record for the event. He also set a new record for the Prague hill climb and the Avus race. That year he won the 193-mile Eifel race and the 311-mile German Grand Prix on the Nürburg circuit in the highly successful SSKL model, and won again the European hill-climb championship.

While driving an Alfa Romeo racing car at the 1933 Monaco Grand Prix, Caracciola had a bad accident and was hospitalized for several months. As a result, his right leg is slightly shorter than his left; but this did not deter him in the least from pushing the accelerator as far down as anyone.

When the new 750-kilogram-formula racing cars first appeared, in 1934, Rudolf Caracciola was ready for the gleaming, silvery Mercedes-Benz machines. That year, he won the Klausenpass hill climb, and with Fagioli shared the Italian Grand Prix. He placed second at the Spanish Grand Prix.

But 1935 was a richer year for Caracciola. He won the Tripoli, the French, Belgian, Swiss, and Spanish Grands Prix. He placed second in the Penya-Rhin Grand Prix at Barcelona. That year, he also won the titles of German Champion and European Champion.

The duels between Caracciola and the Auto Union ace, Bernd Rosemeyer, were thrilling to watch. Often their shining, silvery sleek racers would stand idle side by side at the starting line, the low and long Mercedes-Benz of Caracciola and the stub-nosed and squatty, rear-engined Auto Union of Rosemeyer. Then the steady rhythmic hum of the engines warming up would fill the crisp air. As starting time neared, the loud, ear-shattering noise would become almost unbearable, shaking the ground. The deep throaty Mercedes-Benz and the higher-pitched Auto Union would reach a deafening crescendo, and then, with a terrifying scream and a horrible tire screech, the powerful racers would streak ahead like bullets. Usually Caracciola made the faster getaway. The Mercedes-Benz had better acceleration than the Auto Union, and he was a master of the rapid start.

Count Masetti at the Targa Florio, 1922

Rear-engined Benz at the Grand Prix of Europe, 1923

In 1936 Caracciola won again the hazardous Monaco Grand Prix and the Tunis Grand Prix. On the whole, however, it was an Auto Union year.

The following year, Caracciola won the German, Swiss, Italian, and Masaryk Grands Prix, and placed second in the Monaco Grand Prix. Again, he won the German Championship and that of Europe.

With the new 3-liter-formula twelve-cylinder car, Caracciola won the Swiss Grand Prix in 1938. He placed second in the French and German Grands Prix, sharing the latter honor with Lang. And for the third time he won the European Championship.

In 1939 Caracciola won the German Grand Prix on the Nürburg Ring, was second in the fast Tripoli and the Swiss Grand Prix. He had now won the German Grand Prix for the sixth time — an amazing achievement, considering the strong Auto Union competition in addition to the drivers of his own team. And, once more, he was German road racing champion.

The 1939 German Grand Prix was a colorful affair. It was the last big race for the 3-liter cars, and the last international event before the Second World War. The line-up of participating cars was impressive. The Daimler-Benz works had four cars; Auto Union started five. The new, promising 3-liter Maserati, and two Delahayes were there, and many others. Nineteen cars started.

It had rained during practice, and the difficult circuit had not dried up entirely. There were occasional patches of water, especially in the heavy wooded sections. By virtue of their best practice times, three Mercedes-Benz cars with Lang, Caracciola, and von Brauchitsch were in the front starting line. Nuvolari, Stuck, Mueller, Hasse, and Meyer, driving Auto Unions, and Brendel's Mercedes-Benz, and the others followed behind.

By the time the starting gun had reverberated, the cars were already disappearing around the Mercedes curve. Lang, driving the fastest car, equipped with a two-stage supercharged 3-liter engine which developed 483 horsepower, set the pace. On the third lap he came into the pits for new plugs. One more fast lap, and he retired for good. In the light drizzle, the pace was terrific. Caracciola stayed well behind the leaders. Then Brauchitsch pulled in with engine trouble. And the Mercedes-Benz driven by young

Brendel crashed just before he was to stop to relinquish his car to the more experienced Lang. That left Caracciola alone against the four Auto Unions, still running fine.

As the rain came down, pouring steadily, the old master was at his very best. With poor visibility, Caracciola made the fastest lap of the race, at 82 miles per hour. He had driven this Eifel circuit more often than any other driver. Every one of the 172 turns, every rise and every dip, of the fourteen-mile course was familiar to him. Eventually, the opposition got into trouble. Nuvolari, Stuck, and Hasse went out of the race. The pace was too fast for them. Their machines did not stand up to it.

Caracciola had driven in true championship style. When he crossed the finish line to receive the checkered flag he had won the German Grand Prix for the sixth time, a truly astonishing feat.

During the 1934 to 1939 Grand Prix racing seasons Rudolf Caracciola had won sixteen Grand Prix events, had placed second ten times, and had taken five third places for Mercedes-Benz.

In 1934 Caracciola drove the especially constructed Mercedes-Benz eight-cylinder record car at Györ, near Budapest, and at the Berlin Avus track to several new world records in Class C (3 to 5 liters). His top speed was more than 199 miles per hour.

Two years later he drove the twelve-cylinder record car on the Frankfurt-to-Darmstadt autobahn to several new world's records in Class B (5 to 8 liters). His fastest run was 231 miles per hour. He drove the improved 1938 Mercedes-Benz machine on the same stretch of public highway more than 271 miles per hour.

In 1939 Caracciola drove a smaller, streamlined record car on the autobahn near Dessau to new world records in the 2- to 3-liter category, Class D.

The never-tried, 3,030-horsepower, streamlined Mercedes-Benz racer, built to bring the world's speed record to Germany, would certainly have been driven by Caracciola had it ever been raced. And, had it not been for the impending war, the ace driver might also have been the man who traveled faster than any other on God's good earth.

Kling and Klenk at the Carrera Panamericana
Mexico, 1952

Drawing of the 300 SL

An early version of the 300 SL

Rudolf Caracciola was, unquestionably, on the *Spitze* of all the illustrious *Spitzenfahrer* of the celebrated Mercedes-Benz Grand Prix contingent.

When the Daimler-Benz company decided to enter its newly developed 300 SL sports cars in several 1952 events, Caracciola was, naturally, one of its drivers. In the Mille Miglia road race he placed fourth. Following this, came the Berne sports-car race. The old master seemed to be in championship form. He was the first away at the start. The Bremgarten circuit consists of difficult curves and corners and no straights of any consequence. Caracciola's car appeared unsteady, and then he suddenly went off the road at the slippery Forsthaus curve. He was hospitalized with a fractured thigh.

Now living near the celebrated Lake Lugano, in Switzerland, Caracciola has retired from all racing activities. His rooms are crowded with hundreds of trophies, mute mementos of an amazing career.

Hermann Lang, the youngest of the prewar Grand Prix Mercedes-Benz drivers, should have come by his interest in automobiles naturally. He was born in Cannstatt, the birthplace of the Daimler engine. After working as a mechanic he became interested in racing motorcycles, and in 1931 he became German hill-climb champion for motorcycles with sidecars.

After a year as racing mechanic for Daimler-Benz, he drove his first race in the Eifel race at the Nürburg Ring, and placed fifth. In 1937 he won the Grand Prix of Tripoli and the unusually fast Avus-track race, where he averaged an astonishing 162.5 miles per hour for the 180-mile race. And he finished second in the Swiss and Italian Grands Prix.

In 1938 Lang won the Tripoli Grand Prix and the Coppa Ciano near Leghorn. With Caracciola he shared second place in the French Grand Prix. The following year, Lang won the Tripoli, the French, Belgian, and Swiss Grands Prix, and the Eifel race at the Nürburg Ring. He won the hill climb at Vienna, and the Grand Prix hill climb of Germany. He became European champion and German hill-climb champion that year.

Hermann Lang won nine Grand Prix events for Mercedes-Benz during his three years of the 1934 to 1939 season, placed second four times, and took third place twice.

Thirteen years later, after the last war, Lang placed second in the 1952 Swiss sports-car race at Berne, where he made the fastest lap with his 300 SL model. He also established a new lap record for sports cars. In the following Le Mans twenty-four-hour classic he won, driving with Fritz Riess, in the highly competitive sports-car class. In the extremely grueling Mexican road race he finished second. His average speed for the 1,934-mile cross-country event was 99.5 miles per hour.

His short but excellent career was interrupted by the war. Postwar successes indicate that he probably still has many productive years behind the wheel of a Mercedes-Benz car.

On the roster of Mercedes-Benz drivers after the Second World War appear several new names. The young Fritz Riess, who won the 1952 Le Mans event with Lang, also placed third in the Berne race.

Karl Kling drove the Mercedes-Benz 300 SL model to second place in the Mille Miglia in 1952. Later that year, driving a superb race, he won the third Mexican road race in the sports-car category. Despite hitting, at some 130 miles per hour, a low-flying buzzard which broke the windshield coming in and left by the rear window, he managed to win the difficult race at an average of 102.6 miles per hour.

In 1954 Kling won the Berlin Grand Prix at 133 miles per hour and placed second in the French Grand Prix. He placed third in the 1955 British Grand Prix. Driving the 300 SLR, teamed with Simon, Kling was in third place at Le Mans when the car was withdrawn. Assisting Fangio at the Ulster Tourist Trophy and the Targa Florio, he placed second. But Kling was beset by bad luck during most of his activities for these two years. When not racing, Karl Kling works as an engineer in the Daimler-Benz organization.

And then there were Helfrich and Niedermayr, who placed second at the 1952 Le Mans event.

The 300 SLs at the Nürburgring, 1952

At a tire depot at the Mexican road race, 1952

Juan Manuel Fangio was, of course, the most outstanding driver of the 1954 Grand Prix racing season. The selection by Daimler-Benz racing officials of this exceptionally able driver was exceedingly fortunate.

After five years of participation, the Argentinian won the world's championship in 1951 by driving his 440-horsepower Alfa-Romeo to victory at the Swiss, Spanish, and European Grands Prix, and to second place at the British and German Grands Prix. He also had made the fastest lap times at five of those events.

The 1954 Grand Prix season was even more successful for the skillful Fangio than the 1951. He and the new Mercedes-Benz formula I racing car proved to be an outstanding combination on practically all Grand Prix circuits. He had the coveted pole position in almost all events, having made the best practice times.

The expert Juan Manuel Fangio won the French, European, Swiss, and Italian Grands Prix, and placed third in the Spanish Grand Prix, driving a Mercedes-Benz, and won the Belgian Grand Prix driving a Maserati, thus easily capturing the world's championship for 1954.

The following year Fangio practically repeated his superb performance. He won the Argentine, Belgian, Dutch and Italian Grands Prix, and placed second in the British Grand Prix. Driving the 300 SLR he won the Buenos Aires and the Swedish Grands Prix and the Eifel Race, and placed second in the Mille Miglia, the Ulster Tourist Trophy, and the Targa Florio. He was well in the lead, with Moss, when withdrawn from the Le Mans race. Juan Manuel Fangio won his third world's championship in 1955, far ahead of his closest competitor.

Hans Herrmann, the youngest of the Mercedes-Benz team of racing drivers of 1954, had considerable success driving smaller sports cars in European events and the Mexican road race. Driving the Mercedes-Benz racer, he made the fastest lap at the French Grand Prix at Rheims. He placed third at the Swiss Grand Prix. Herrmann had an accident practicing for the 1955 European Grand Prix at Monaco which put him out of competition for that season.

The young English driver Stirling Moss proved himself to be a valuable member of the 1955 Mercedes-Benz team. He won the British Grand Prix, having driven the fastest practice lap. He placed second in the Belgian and Dutch Grands Prix. In the Italian Grand Prix he drove the fastest lap, but did not finish.

Driving the 300 SLR, Moss won the Mille Miglia, with Jenkinson as observer. Paired with Fangio, Moss was well in the lead in the Le Mans race. He won, with John Fitch, the Ulster Tourist Trophy; and with Peter Collins he won the Targa Florio, thus securing the world's championship sports-car title for Mercedes-Benz. Moss finished second in the Eifel race, the Buenos Aires Grand Prix, and the Swedish Grand Prix, where he drove the fastest lap.

These are some of the drivers who wrote automobile racing history on the open roads, the high-speed tracks, and the tricky Grand Prix circuits of the world, and were rewarded by the most welcome sight, the glorious checkered flag.

Drawing of the 2.5-liter Formula racing car
 1. Radiator
 2. Water pressure compensator
 3. Injection pump
 4. Air cooling for driver and rear wheel brakes
 5. Gear shift
 6. Transmission
 7. Oil cooler
 8. Cooled brakes
 9. Fuel tank
10. Oil tank

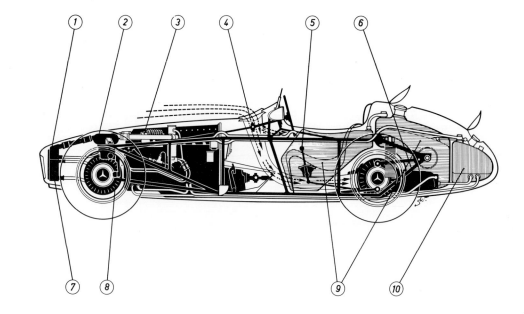

The 2.5-liter Grand Prix car with Nürburg type body

This Daimler won the Vienna-Salzburg race in 1900

A Benz before the start of a 1900 event

The Mercedes 18/22-horsepower car of 1903
(Wilhelm Maybach on left in car)

Baron de Caters in the 1904 Mercedes racer

Grand Prix Statistics (1934-1939 and 1954-1955)

In the following list of the winners of the Grand Prix events from 1934 to 1939, particular emphasis is given to Mercedes-Benz cars and drivers. Other winning cars are indicated by abbreviations — such as A-U for Auto Union, A-R for Alfa Romeo, Bug for Bugatti, Dar for Darracq, Del for Delahaye, Fer for Ferrari, and Mas for Maserati — and their drivers are not given.

The Grandes Epreuves (great trials) consist of the seven most important Grands Prix: the German, French, Spanish, Belgian, Swiss, Monaco, and Italian events. The great American classic, the 500-mile Memorial Day race at Indianapolis which is run according to its own special formula, and the Royal Automobile Club's Tourist Trophy, a sports-car race, are sometimes included. However, Mercedes-Benz cars did not compete in these events, and so they are not included in this listing. Minor Grands Prix in which Mercedes-Benz cars participated are included, except hill climbs.

In 1934 the competition in most races included Mercedes-Benz, Auto Union, Alfa Romeo, Maserati, and Bugatti machines. The German teams did not compete in the Monaco Grand Prix. In the French Grand Prix both German teams started, but their cars developed teething troubles and did not place. No German cars took part in the Belgian Grand Prix, which a Bugatti won. Seven Grandes Epreuves were held that year, and Mercedes-Benz cars won two.

By 1935 the Maserati and Bugatti cars ceased to appear in Grand Prix competition. Alfa Romeo stayed in the race and won the German Grand Prix: Tazio Nuvolari took the lead in the last lap and won the race in a most dramatic style against Mercedes-Benz and Auto Union, both of which were dogged by bad luck. However, the eight-cylinder 3.8-liter and the twelve-cylinder 4.6-liter Alfa Romeo were no real competition against either of the German Grand Prix machines. Seven Grandes Epreuves were held that year, and Mercedes-Benz cars won five. Only four big events took place in 1936, when Mercedes-Benz cars were victorious once. In 1937 five races were held, and the Mercedes-Benz racers took the checkered flag four times.

In 1938, when the new 3-liter supercharged or 4.5-liter unsupercharged formula became effective, Maserati built a 3-liter blown, and Delahaye and Darracq each built a 4.5-liter unblown, machine, But none of the three was a match for the Mercedes-Benz and Auto Union machines. In fact, after 1937 the Germans won all the events in which their cars were entered, except one. That was the 1938 Pau Grand Prix, in which Dreyfus drove his Delahaye to victory over the sick Mercedes-Benz of Caracciola and Lang. In 1938, and in 1939, only four Grandes Epreuves were held on the Grand Prix circuits of Europe. Mercedes-Benz cars won three of them in 1938, and three in 1939.

When in 1954 Mercedes-Benz cars again participated in Grand Prix racing, the new formula of 2.5-liter unsupercharged or 0.75-liter supercharged was in effect. Mercedes-Benz racing cars were, for the first time, unsupercharged machines. Competitors were the well established and proved Italian Ferrari, Maserati, and later, the new Lancia machines and French Gordini racers. Fangio won the Belgian Grand Prix, driving a Maserati; Mercedes-Benz cars did not compete in that event. Of the seven Grands Prix (including Berlin) entered in 1954, the new Mercedes-Benz cars won five; the Ferraris were twice victorious.

For the 1955 Grand Prix season the participating Mercedes-Benz racing cars were practically unchanged from the previous year. The French, Swiss, German, and Berlin Grands Prix were canceled. And the Ulster Tourist Trophy and the Swedish Grand Prix were sports-car events. The year was perhaps the most successful yet in the wondrous sixty-one-year racing history of the Daimler-Benz company. In the six Grands Prix events of 1955 the Mercedes-Benz racing cars won five first places, four second, and one third against Ferrari, Maserati, Lancia, Gordini, Vanwall, and Connaught competitors. It was a truly astonishing feat which proved indisputably the superiority of the Mercedes-Benz racing cars and their excellent drivers over all others.

The Mercedes Grand Prix racing team of 1938

The Mercedes Grand Prix racing team of 1955

Year	Event	Distance (miles)	Site	Winner's Speed (mph)	First Place	Second Place	Third Place
1934	German Grand Prix	354	Nürburg Ring	76.4	(A-U)	Fagioli (M-B)	(A-R)
	Italian Grand Prix	311	Monza	65.4	Caracciola-Fagioli (M-B)	(A-U)	(A-R)
	Spanish Grand Prix	323	San Sebastian	97.2	Fagioli (M-B)	Caracciola (M-B)	(Bug)
	Masaryk Grand Prix	308	Brno	79.2	(A-U)	Fagioli (M-B)	(Mas)
	Eifel Race	213	Nürburg Ring	76.1	von Brauchitsch (M-B)	(A-U)	(A-R)
	Coppa Acerbo	321	Pescara	80.5	Fagioli (M-B)	(Mas)	(Bug)
1935	German Grand Prix	312	Nürburg Ring	75.2	(A-R)	(A-U)	Caracciola (M-B)
	French Grand Prix	311	Montlhéry	77.4	Caracciola (M-B)	von Brauchitsch (M-B)	(Mas)
	Belgian Grand Prix	315	Francorchamps	97.9	Caracciola (M-B)	Fagioli-von Brauchitsch (M-B)	(A-R)
	Swiss Grand Prix	317	Bremgarten	90.0	Caracciola (M-B)	Fagioli (M-B)	(A-U)
	Monaco Grand Prix	198	Monaco	58.2	Fagioli (M-B)	(A-R)	(A-R)
	Spanish Grand Prix	323	San Sebastian	101.9	Caracciola (M-B)	Fagioli (M-B)	von Brauchitsch (M-B)
	Tripoli Grand Prix	326	Melaha	123.1	Caracciola (M-B)	(A-U)	Fangioli (M-B)
	Penya-Rhin Grand Prix	165	Barcelona	67.0	Fagioli (M-B)	Caracciola (M-B)	(A-R)
	Avus Race	122	Avusbahn	148.8	Fagioli (M-B)	(A-R)	(A-U)
	Eifel Race	156	Nürburg Ring	73.0	Caracciola (M-B)	(A-U)	(A-R)
1936	Monaco Grand Prix	198	Monaco	51.7	Caracciola (M-B)	(A-U)	(A-U)
	Tripoli Grand Prix	326	Melaha	129.0	(A-U)	(A-U)	Fagioli (M-B)
	Penya-Rhin Grand Prix	188	Barcelona	69.3	(A-R)	Caracciola (M-B)	(A-R)
	Tunis Grand Prix	237	Carthage	99.6	Caracciola (M-B)	(A-R)	(Bug)
1937	German Grand Prix	312	Nürburg Ring	82.8	Caracciola (M-B)	von Brauchitsch (M-B)	(A-U)
	Belgian Grand Prix	315	Francorchamps	104.1	(A-U)	(A-U)	Lang (M-B)
	Swiss Grand Prix	226	Bremgarten	97.4	Caracciola (M-B)	Lang (M-B)	von Brauchitsch (M-B)
	Monaco Grand Prix	198	Monaco	63.3	von Brauchitsch (M-B)	Caracciola (M-B)	Kautz (M-B)
	Italian Grand Prix	250	Leghorn	81.6	Caracciola (M-B)	Lang (M-B)	(A-U)
	Tripoli Grand Prix	320	Melaha	134.3	Lang (M-B)	(A-U)	(A-U)
	Masaryk Grand Prix	271	Brno	86.0	Caracciola (M-B)	von Brauchitsch (M-B)	(A-U)
	Donington Grand Prix	250	Donington	82.9	(A-U)	von Brauchitsch (M-B)	Caracciola (M-B)
	Avus Race	96	Avusbahn	162.5	Lang (M-B)	(A-U)	(A-U)
	Eifel Race	142	Nürburg Ring	83.0	(A-U)	Caracciola (M-B)	von Brauchitsch (M-B)
	Coppa Acerbo	257	Pescara	87.6	(A-U)	von Brauchitsch (M-B)	(A-U)
	Vanderbilt Cup	300	Roosevelt Field	82.6	(A-U)	Seaman (M-B)	(A-R)
1938	German Grand Prix	312	Nürburg Ring	80.8	Seaman (M-B)	Lang-Caracciola (M-B)	(A-U)
	French Grand Prix	312	Rheims	101.3	von Brauchitsch (M-B)	Caracciola (M-B)	Lang (M-B)
	Swiss Grand Prix	226	Bremgarten	89.4	Caracciola (M-B)	Seaman (M-B)	von Brauchitsch (M-B)
	Italian Grand Prix	260	Monza	96.7	(A-U)	(A-R)	Caracciola-von Brauchitsch (M-B)
	Tripoli Grand Prix	320	Melaha	127.5	Lang (M-B)	von Brauchitsch (M-B)	Caracciola (M-B)
	Donington Grand Prix	250	Donington	80.5	(A-U)	Lang (M-B)	Seaman (M-B)
	Pau Grand Prix	172	Pau	54.6	(Del)	Caracciola-Lang (M-B)	(Del)
	Coppa Acerbo	257	Pescara	83.7	Caracciola (M-B)	(A-R)	(A-R)
	Coppa Ciano	144	Leghorn	85.9	Lang (M-B)	(A-R)	(A-R)

Schematic drawing of the 2.5-liter car

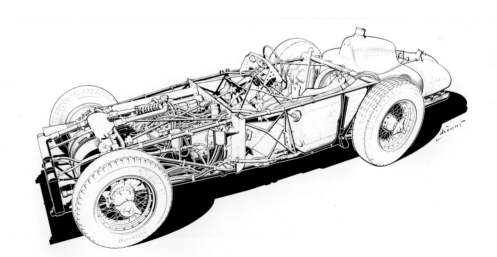

Another view of the Formula I car

Year	Event	Distance (miles)	Site	Winner's Speed (mph)	First Place	Second Place	Third Place
1939	German Grand Prix	312	Nürburg Ring	75.2	Caracciola (M-B)	(A-U)	(Mas)
	Belgian Grand Prix	315	Francorchamps	94.4	Lang (M-B)	(A-U)	von Brauchitsch (M-B)
	Swiss Grand Prix	150	Bremgarten	96.0	Lang (M-B)	Caracciola (M-B)	von Brauchitsch (M-B)
	Tripoli Grand Prix	244	Melaha	122.9	Lang (M-B)	Caracciola (M-B)	(A-R)
	Pau Grand Prix	160	Pau	56.1	Lang (M-B)	von Brauchitsch (M-B)	(Dar)
	Yugoslavian Grand Prix	86	Belgrade	81.2	(A-U)	von Brauchitsch (M-B)	(A-U)
	Eifel Race	142	Nürburg Ring	84.1	Lang (M-B)	(A-U)	Caracciola (M-B)
1954	French Grand Prix	307	Rheims	115.9	Fangio (M-B)	Kling (M-B)	(Fer)
	British Grand Prix	274	Silverstone	89.6	(Fer)	(Fer)	(Mas)
	European Grand Prix	312	Nürburg Ring	82.7	Fangio (M-B)	(Fer)	(Fer)
	Swiss Grand Prix	288	Bremgarten	99.2	Fangio (M-B)	(Fer)	Herrmann (M-B)
	Italian Grand Prix	313	Monza	111.9	Fangio (M-B)	(Fer)	(Fer)
	Berlin Grand Prix	312	Avusbahn	133.0	Kling (M-B)	Fangio (M-B)	Herrmann (M-B)
	Spanish Grand Prix	314	Barcelona	97.9	(Fer)	(Mas)	Fangio (M-B)
1955	Argentine Grand Prix	233	Buenos Aires	79.5	Fangio (M-B)	(Fer)	(Fer)
	European Grand Prix	195	Monaco	65.8	(Fer)	(Fer)	(Mas)
	Belgian Grand Prix	315	Francorchamps	118.8	Fangio (M-B)	Moss (M-B)	(Fer)
	Dutch Grand Prix	260	Zandvoort	89.6	Fangio (M-B)	Moss (M-B)	(Mas)
	British Grand Prix	270	Aintree	86.5	Moss (M-B)	Fangio (M-B)	Kling (M-B)
	Italian Grand Prix	315	Monza	128.4	Fangio (M-B)	Taruffi (M-B)	(Fer)

Moss at the British Grand Prix of 1955

Fangio taking a curve at the Nürburgring, 1955

Fangio leading Ascari in the Italian Grand Prix, 1954

Fangio, winner of the Argentine Grand Prix, 1955

Fangio and Moss, winning the Dutch Grand Prix, 1955

Tired, but victorious Fangio at the 1954 Italian
Grand Prix and

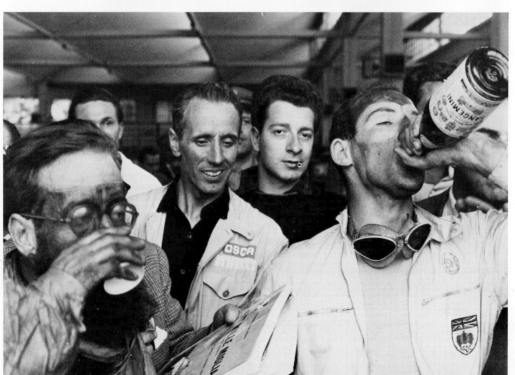

Joyful Moss after winning the Mille Miglia in 1955

Allied Automotive Products (1884-1977)

Ever since Gottlieb Daimler displayed a representative line of his manufactured goods at the great international exposition in Paris in 1889, the company has had various automotive products. Many of the early products were eliminated eventually in the concentration on superior engines and motor vehicles.

At the 1889 exposition a pavilion on the left bank of the Seine, near Pont d'léna and in the shadow of the Eiffel Tower, housed the V-type gasoline engine of Daimler. Near an open exhibition shed stood a Daimler streetcar on narrow rails. From observations at the time by Gustave Chauveau it appears that this vehicle attracted little attention from purchasing agents. The visiting crowds, however, enjoyed the comfort of the benches of the streetcar and used them constantly to rest from sight-seeing and consume lunches and other refreshments which they brought in picnic fashion to the fair.

A generating plant, powered by a 2-horsepower Daimler engine, supplied thirty brightly burning electric bulbs which were fastened to the walls in a huge hall. This exhibit, one of the marvels of the age, drew some interested spectators and many cursory glances. The Daimler steel-wheel carriage, along with the Benz vehicle, called attention to itself with its audible gasoline engine. The Daimler motorboats *Violette* and *Passe-Partout* cruised on the Seine, as floating advertisements.

When Gottlieb Daimler, his son Adolf, and Wilhelm Maybach visited the fair in the fall they livened up the stationary exhibits. Adolf Daimler and René Panhard drove the steel-wheel carriage along the river banks to the consternation of leisurely pedestrians. Papa Daimler and his party cruised on the lazy Seine in one of the motorboats. They made frequent excursions to near-by Saint-Cloud and Suresnes, and demonstrated the practicality of both modes of transportation.

These Daimler products were improved over the years, and even more varieties were constructed in time.

The State Agricultural Commission had enthusiastically endorsed two types of stationary gasoline engine which Gottlieb Daimler had submitted in 1892. In comparison with a steam engine the Daimler gasoline engine could be operated for almost one mark less per day, one experienced stoker being eliminated, besides. The smaller engines could also be used for many tasks on a farm in addition to harvesting.

Boat building was then an important activity of the Daimler company. In addition to the seven different types in production, light racing craft were built. Daimler suggested that these should glide atop the water rather than plow through it, to reach better speeds. His racing craft already reached the speed of 14 miles per hour. Huge marine engines for larger craft were most important in the production volume of the company for many years.

In 1892, three years after the first portable generating plant was built, one such unit was used to illuminate the Prag Tunnel of the Württemberg State Railroad. Its two 10-horsepower engines furnished the necessary current for eleven arc lights of 8.5 amperes each.

A Daimler fire pump got its first test in May 1892, when a featherbed factory in Cannstadt caught fire. The efficient pump was greatly praised by the local fire chief, who declared that it had kept the rapidly spreading fire under control. It worked uninterruptedly for five hours, throwing a sixty-foot-high stream of water on the roof of the factory, its performance being equal to that of thirty-two men. It pumped eighty gallons per minute, and a strong stream of water could reach the third story of a burning building with sufficient pressure to reduce a fierce blaze.

At the World's Columbian Exposition in Chicago in 1893 the Daimler Motoren-Gesellschaft with the New York Daimler Motor Company exhibited a complete portable gas-engined generating plant, three complete wagonettes, each with a 2-horsepower engine, a small streetcar with a 2.5-horsepower engine, a fire engine with a 6-horsepower pump, a 10-horsepower pleasure boat, a 2-horsepower gas motor, and a 3-horsepower gasoline engine. A working model of a fully equipped railroad switching yard, complete with turn table and miniature train, was also exhibited.

During the early part of that October, Gottlieb Daimler and his bride rode in his steel-wheel carriage through the grounds of the spectacular exposition.

WILLIAM STEINWAY,
PRESIDENT.

LOUIS VON BERNUTH,
TREASURER.

ADOLPH H. BURKARD,
SECRETARY.

ILLUSTRATED

CATALOGUE AND PRICE-LIST

OF THE

DAIMLER MOTOR COMPANY'S

Gas and Petroleum Motors

FOR

STREET RAILROAD CARS, PLEASURE BOATS, CARRIAGES,

QUADRICYCLES, FIRE ENGINES,

AS WELL AS ALL STATIONARY, MANUFACTURING OR OTHER PURPOSES.

Manufacturing Works and Principal Office:

Nos. 937, 939 and 941 STEINWAY AVENUE,

"STEINWAY," LONG ISLAND CITY, N. Y.

Branch Office: 111 East Fourteenth Street,

NEW YORK CITY.

1891.

First page of catalog by Steinway, New York, in 1891

In 1898 a lithographed poster illustrated twenty-four items currently manufactured by the Daimler Motoren-Gesellschaft. Two large stationary engines with upright cylinders and large vertical flywheels were shown — one model enclosed in a protective housing. As many as seven different types of boats were pictured against attractive backgrounds: a sailboat and a heavily loaded barge with Daimler engines, on choppy waters; a luxurious cabin cruiser with a 10-horsepower engine and a larger cruiser with a 20-horsepower marine engine, apparently traveling at some speed; two smaller excursion boats, one with a 2-horsepower and the other with a 4-horsepower engine, cruising on the charming Neckar River; a sleek cabin cruiser with a 6-horsepower Daimler engine on the Lake of Zurich. Boats were in demand from the Daimler company at that time.

A Daimler locomotive, a 12-horsepower self-propelled vehicle which was a movable four-wheeled power plant, and a two-wheeled 4-horsepower vehicle were also shown. A large streetcar and a wagonette, also with a double row of seats, were illustrated. The pictured draisine was an interesting vehicle named after its inventor, Baron Karl Drais of Mannheim. The 1813 original crude two-wheeled vehicle was also called a dandy horse, and was propelled by pushing with the feet on the ground. Eventually, it appeared in a greatly improved state as a velocipede.

Daimler's draisine was a four-wheeled affair, traveled on rails, and had seats facing front and back, with the gasoline engine in the center. It was much like the present small gasoline rail cars. The Daimler omnibus resembled a similar horse-drawn vehicle except that it had an engine under the driver's seat. The *Geschäftswagen* (business wagon) was a smaller edition of it. Another useful vehicle was a power saw and wood-splitting machine built on a heavy wagon bed. The fire engine with a power pump was already a well established product. The generating plant and the flat-bed truck had also proven themselves before.

A two-seated motor vehicle was pictured with extra seats for children and a large surrey top covering all. The Victoria model was also shown. And in the center of the large poster another Daimler motor vehicle rolled merrily along a busy thoroughfare. The dignified gentleman with a beard wore a top hat; his lady, a fluffly dress and an enormous picture hat decorated with flowers. A child wore a big bow over her dress and a large round hat and sat in the front seat. A dog ran along the cobbled street. Pedestrians stood on the sidewalk, obviously impressed by the horseless carriage.

The poster proudly listed twenty-nine honors which had been bestowed on Daimler products since 1893 by expositions where they had been displayed.

After the inauguration of the first motor-bus line on July 15, 1899, from Künzelsau to Mergentheim, omnibuses were an important item in the Daimler line of motor vehicles. Motor trucks, first built in 1896, also soon established a demand. After a Stuttgart draying firm and a Berlin brewery took delivery of trucks early in 1897 the Daimler company decided to build four different sizes of goods trucks, ranging in speed from two to eight miles per hour and in load capacity from 3,300 to 11,000 pounds. The five-ton trucks were guaranteed to take 8 percent grades at 2.5 miles per hour, fully loaded.

The automobile railroad cars began to operate in 1887 between Cannstatt and Esslingen. When these 5.5-horsepower vehicles found the trip difficult in time of snow or wet rails their engine was replaced with one of 10 horsepower. A car carried twenty-two passengers and eight standing. By 1898 the newest railroad car had a 15-horsepower engine and carried twenty-four seated passengers. In 1899 a railroad car with a 25-horsepower, four-cylinder engine, built to carry thirty-six seated passengers and eight standing at an average speed of twenty-two miles per hour, had been placed in service.

The locomotives, draisines, and railroad cars were built for Daimler by the Esslinger Maschinenfabrik.

As was only natural, the German army adopted motorized vehicles soon after their first appearance. The Emperor was fascinated by the Daimler automobile furnished to him during the 1898 maneuvers. He insisted that the chauffeur drive faster than the expressly ordered twenty miles per hour. During a stop the harassed chauffeur was severely admonished by

Narrow gauge locomotive with Daimler V-type engine, 1890

Daimler four-cylinder engine of 10 horsepower, 1890

Railcar for the Fried. Krupp company, 1890

his superior officer for exceeding the specifically commanded speed: "Remember that you are responsible for the life of his majesty!" The driver merely replied, "Mine, too," and promptly sped away with the Emperor at a lusty dust-raising tempo, as ordered by his majesty himself.

Late in 1899 the first army column was equipped with fifteen automobiles, after exhaustive tests on difficult terrain and practical instruction of the army personnel in the Cannstatt factory. The order of the military amounted to 150,000 marks (about $35,750). The following year the entire line of Daimler motor vehicles was driven in review before the interested Emperor.

Karl Wölfert, after the first trials of his airship in 1888, did not again demonstrate it publicly until 1896. Then he made several flights from the Tempelhof airdrome for the Berlin trade fair. The two four-cylinder Daimler engines which he used for steering had an aluminum engine housing. The first engines, built especially for the airship of Count Zeppelin, had the hot-tube ignition. This method proved to be unsatisfactory in tests, and electric Bosch ignition was used when installation was eventually made. The 92-feet-long and 36-feet-wide airship rose from Lake Constance in July 1900, equipped with two Daimler engines.

With these multiple activities of the Daimler Motoren-Gesellschaft it became necessary to enlarge the factory facilities. An area of 1,760 acres was acquired in Untertürkheim, near Stuttgart, and the building of new manufacturing facilities was begun.

However, from the advent of the Mercedes automobile all the emphasis was put on the construction of motor vehicles. Touring cars and sports models, trucks and buses of various types and sizes, and engines for many purposes were built under the guidance of Wilhelm Maybach and Paul Daimler.

By 1905 the Daimler company had built two 90-horsepower engines for Count Zeppelin's newest airship. Two years later the four-cylinder aero engines with pushrod-operated, overhead valves, developed 100 horsepower. By 1911 an eight-cylinder overhead camshaft engine was constructed which developed 240 horsepower. There was a marked similarity between these aviation engines and those used in the racing cars.

An earlier chapter has mentioned the superior 1914 Mercedes engine, which attracted such great interest at the French Grand Prix race. It was but the forerunner of the airplane engines built by the Daimler company in quantity during the First World War.

While the Daimler Motoren-Gesellschaft manufactured an extensive line of automotive products Benz & Cie. concentrated on motor vehicles. However, few related items other than the well established engines were produced in the early history of the company.

The exhibited Benz products received high praise at the 1885 World's Fair at Antwerp. One consequence was that Karl Benz delivered in 1886 a twin-cylinder engine which developed 20 horsepower for the city hall in Brussels. The power plant was used to operate the dynamos which furnished the electric current for the municipal building.

Karl Benz's first commercial vehicle ran into stubborn opposition in 1895 when he tried to demonstrate its worth. With Fritz Held he loaded oats from the railroad freight depot onto the truck, which they drove to the feed store. The surprised merchant refused to accept them, saying, "My customers will not buy any horse feed brought here by a motor vehicle."

The Benz company built the first motor omnibus in 1895: an eight-passenger Landauer with a 5-horsepower engine. In the Siegenerland, on the Siegen-Netphen-Deutz run, the Benz vehicle was the first omnibus used when the line was officially opened in 1896.

In 1896 the French Automobile Club sponsored a contest for trucks with a load capacity of at least 100 kilograms (220 pounds). Only eight of the fifteen entered vehicles were able to start, and they were steam-powered. That was the year when the Benz Mannheim factory had sold to the Bon Marché department store for 4,500 marks (about $1,075) a 5-horsepower delivery truck which created a sensation on the streets of Paris.

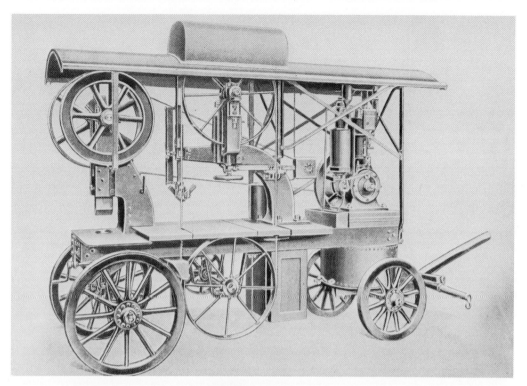

Mobile saw and wood splitting machine, 1888

Daimler fire pump of 1892

In 1898 the Hanover engineer Karl Jatho proposed that Benz furnish him with an engine for the flying apparatus he had designed. On August 18, 1903, Jatho managed to fly his primitive kitelike plane on a perfectly still day. Five years later, the four-cylinders-in-line Benz airplane engine was bench-tested, developing 45 horsepower at 1,600 revolutions per minute. Later the 120-horsepower racing-car engine was converted to airplane use.

The 1900 Benz factory catalog also listed a motor truck. Equipped with cogwheel differential and chain, and four gears, the 6-horsepower engine gave the 2,750-pound-capacity vehicle a speed of ten miles per hour and guaranteed the ability to climb 10 percent grades. With solid Kelly tires and with lights the price was 5,400 marks. The larger model, with capacity of 5,500 pounds and a 10-horsepower engine, sold for 6,000 marks. A huge 14-horsepower truck with a two-cylinder contramotor, for 11,000-pound loads, was also available with iron-shod wheels.

In 1901 the Benz works began construction of delivery trucks which could be converted into two-seat passenger vehicles by removing the delivery box from the rear. The combination vehicles had a 3.5-horsepower, one-cylinder engine and could carry 660 pounds.

In 1907 the Benz company acquired the Süddeutsche Automobilfabrik, G.m.b.H., in Gaggenau for 350 shares of Benz stock. This company had made the "Orientexpress" automobiles especially for sale in France and England, but its main products now were trucks and buses. From this time on the commercial vehicles were handled entirely by the Gaggenau factory, and the Mannheim works produced only passenger cars.

After a light Benz truck had been successfully driven through Spain in 1909 and French and Italian competitors had been eliminated in the grueling test run, the Spanish war department immediately ordered fifty vehicles for North African outposts.

The engine developed by Rudolf Diesel had found great favor in many fields, especially in large installations. The savings in fuel were considerable; but a complicated injection mechanism was required for spraying the heavy fuel oil under terrific pressure into the combustion chamber, and the compressor absorbed as much as 20 percent of the engine's power.

Benz engineers tried early in 1909 to simplify this system and thus increase the efficiency of the Diesel engine. A patent for a new process of front-chamber combustion was issued to the Benz Mannheim works in March 1909. Eventually engines were built which also incorporated the Swedish Hesselman principle. Two 260-horsepower marine engines were installed in the motor ship *Hermann Krabb*, which crossed the Atlantic Ocean to Argentina in 1913. A heavy Rumanian tugboat plying the Danube River was equipped with a similar power plant. Within a year the building of heavy Diesel engines increased sixfold in the Benz factory. It was halted temporarily by the war.

The earliest aeronautical application of the Daimler engine has been mentioned previously. But the unsuccessful airship experience of Wölfert culminated eventually to a highly successful airship period when Count von Zeppelin overcame his many disasters to prove that his own version of dirigibles was superior to all others.

The first zeppelins were powered by Daimler engines. From the 2-horsepower engine for Wölfert and the first zeppelin engine in 1899 of 16 horsepower and in 1909 of 115 horsepower, to the Schütte-Lanz airship in 1911 which developed 360 horsepower.

The first true aero engine in 1909, a four-cylinder unit of 110 millimeter bore and 140 millimeter stroke, developed 60 horsepower at 1,500 revolutions per minute. The overhead valves were operated by a camshaft with pushrods and rocker arm. In 1911 the 70-horsepower engine had a 120-millimeter bore and 140-millimeter stroke and 1,400 revolutions per minute. It had inverted cylinders and a geared-down propeller hub. The 85-horsepower six-cylinder engine with steel cylinders and welded-on jackets of sheet steel construction indicated an important advance. The thin steel cylinders had been first adapted in 1906 and were generally used for the aero engines.

In 1911 Mercedes auto engines were awarded first prize by the Society of Automobile and Aeronautical Engineering. Flying records were set in

Prospectus drawing for trucks by Daimler of 1896

Benz truck, engine forward-mounted, 1901

1914 with the Daimler 100-horsepower engine when Lange flew his *Pfeil* for 14 hours and 7 minutes, Ingold his *Aviatic* 16 hours and 20 minutes, Baser his *Rumpler* 18 hours and 30 minutes, and finally Böhm his *Albatros* 24 hours and 12 minutes. Limekogel reached an altitude of 21,260 feet, but soon Ölerich bettered it by climbing to 26,575 feet, and Hirth won first prize in a climbing competition in his *Albatros* with the 100-horsepower Mercedes engine.

In 1913 a Kaiserpreis had been awarded to the best aero engine. The conditions, set forth the previous year, specified that the engine should be between 50 and 115 horsepower with a maximum engine speed of 1,450 and 1,350 revolutions per minute respectively, and that the power-to-weight ratio not exceed 6 kilograms (13 pounds) per horsepower including sufficient fuel for seven hours of operation. Twenty-six competitors entered 44 models and 24 replacement engines — three were two-stroke types, thirty-two were water-cooled and twelve air-cooled; thirty had stationary cylinders and fourteen were rotary engines. The largest number of cylinders were fourteen in a 95-horsepower double engine. Tests were carried out at the Experimental Establishment for Aviation at Adlershof, near Berlin.

Benz received the first prize of 50,000 marks for a four-cylinder engine of 130-millimeter bore and 180-millimeter stroke, developing 100 horsepower at 1,300 revolutions per minute, and Daimler second prize of 30,000 marks for the six-cylinder engine of 85 horsepower. The Benz engine, built under the direction of Arthur Berger, had overhead inlet and exhaust valves with a side-mounted camshaft and push rods and rocker arms. The carburetor was placed inside the crankcase to protect it against variations in temperature. Ignition was by two high-tension Bosch magnetos. Cooling was achieved by a centrifugal water pump at the rear of the engine. Soon, however, Benz went to the six-cylinder construction for better balance and the Bz 3 engine of 150 horsepower was the best known model of the pre-war period.

Daimler produced about fifty aero engines per month in 1914, but this was soon increased and improved designs were created. The output of the six-cylinder unit was increased to 160 horsepower and in 1915 a supercharger was adapted to ensure full efficiency at altitudes of about 10,000 feet.

The F 1466 six-cylinder engine with a bore of 160 millimeters and stroke of 180 millimeters and developing 160 horsepower at 1,400 revolutions per minute was superseded and an improved version went into production in 1915. That engine developed 260 horsepower at 1,450 revolutions per minute, had separate vertical steel cylinders with welded steel water jackets. An eight-cylinder engine of 238 horsepower at 1,400 revolutions per minute was also produced with the same cylinder dimensions of 140-millimeter bore and 160-millimeter stroke.

In order to decrease the length of the engine but increasing its power, a new eight-cylinder V-type with a bore of 106 millimeters and stroke of 170 millimeters and developing 185 horsepower at 1,800 revolutions per minute was created. It was the prototype of a 500-horsepower eighteen-cylinder engine and a 600-horsepower six-cylinder engine which went into production by 1918. Despite the shortages of proper raw materials, the aero engines had a power-to-weight ratio of between 1.3 and 1.7 kilograms (2.9 and 3.8 pounds) per horsepower and certain experimental models actually achieved a ratio of 1.2 kilograms (2.7 pounds) per horsepower. Aluminum pistons were occasionally used.

Eventually Daimler built complete aircraft and for this manufacture acquired some 598,000 square yards of property at Sindelfingen. This site later became the main automobile body and assembly plant of the company. Several types of military aeroplanes were built. The R II in 1916 had four Daimler DF 160 (D III) engines, each developing 170 horsepower. The L 6 (D I) fighter plane of 1918 had an eight-cylinder V-type engine, D III b, of 200 horsepower and the L 9 (D II) was a further development. The aircraft designer Hanns Klemm created the L 11 and L 14 which were used as mail planes after the war. The L 20 was the last design. It gained recognition by round-the-world flights and several record performances.

The twelve-cylinder V-type aero engine built by Benz in 1914 was the prototype of their successful designs for some time. Developing 250 horsepower, the engine weighed only 425 kilograms (937 pounds) and

Daimler truck built at Marienfelde plant, 1903

First Daimler omnibus in England, 1899

had a power-to-weight ratio of 1.7 kilograms (3.8 pounds) per horse-power. It was the first German engine with a reduction gear for the slow-turning propeller. Perhaps because of its advanced design, the engine was rejected by the authorities. The majority of aero engines varied in output from 85 to 150 horsepower, as did the Benz six-cylinder units, the Bz 1, Bz 11, and Bz 111.

The first large aircraft with twin engines built in 1915 was equipped with two Benz 150-horsepower engines. The same year, the Bz IV model was built. It was a straight six-cylinder unit developing 230 horsepower and weighing 370 kilograms (815 pounds), giving a power-to-weight ratio of 1.6 kilograms (3.5 pounds) per horsepower. This engine and the Mercedes D III were the finest aero engines produced in Germany at that time and were built in large numbers.

The Bz IV engines were supercharged in 1916 for high altitude flying. The first design was a straight six-cylinder unit developing 225 horse-power at 5,900 feet. A following model, the Bz III, developed 195 horse-power and had a power-to-weight ratio of 1.45 kilograms (3.2 pounds) per horsepower.

When it became apparent that still better performance was required, the twelve-cylinder V-type engine was designed. Built in limited quantity, this Bz IV engine developed 575 horsepower and achieved the lowest power-to-weight ratio yet, 1.2 kilograms (2.7 pounds) per horsepower. The cylinders were set at an angle of 60 degrees and it had overhead inlet and exhaust valves. A rotary water pump was used. Four carburetors and a pre-heating device were utilized and two high tension magnetos supplied the current to two sets of spark plugs. Based on this design in 1917-1918 an eight-cylinder V-type engine with cylinders at 90 degrees and 200 and 210 horsepower was built.

After the war, a lightweight aero engine, the F 7502, developing 23 horse-power at 3,000 revolutions per minute, was built and widely used for sports planes. In 1926, when the restrictions were lifted, research and construction work was resumed and a liquid-cooled twelve-cylinder engine developing 880 to 1,000 horsepower was constructed. Known as F 2 and F 3, these engines were also adapted to marine and rail vehicle

use. Development work on a sixteen-cylinder engine had progressed to the point that from 1928 on these units — the DB 602 (LOF 6) or MB 502 (BOF 6) — were built for airships and motor boats. With a bore of 175 millimeters and stroke of 230 millimeters, displacing 88 liters, they had a maximum output of 1,320 horsepower at 1,620 revolutions per minute. The power-to-weight ratio was 1.8 kilograms per horsepower, including the reduction gear.

The airship *Hindenburg* flew over 3,000 hours and more than 200,000 miles equipped with four such engines, as was the new *Graf Zeppelin II*, which was never put into service. A further development of the engine was the twenty-cylinder MB 501 model, not supercharged but having 2,000 horsepower. The supercharged version, the MB 511, and later the MB 518, actually developed 2,500 horsepower.

Large-scale production of the DB 600 (F 4) aero engine started in 1935 after intense efforts had been made to improve the supercharger and carburetor the previous year. The engine was then built with direct fuel injection as DB 601 (M 74) and developed, as V model, 2,770 horse-power at 3,100 revolutions per minute. This power unit was used in the Heinkel He 100 V8 plane which attained the absolute speed record for Germany on March 30, 1939. Using the same type engine in a Messer-schmitt Me 209 VI, Captain Fritz Wendel reached 755.1 kilometers (469 miles) per hour, a record to stand for thirty years. Production of all aero engines was considerably expanded at the Marienfelde and Gen-shagen factories.

The DB 601 range of 33.9 liters was further developed. The DB 601 A had 1,100 horsepower take-off power at 2,400 revolutions per minute and the DB 601 E/F had 1,350 horsepower at 2,600 revolutions per minute, and a further model, the DB 605 with 35.7 liter displacement produced 1,500 horsepower at 2,600 revolutions per minute. Further power increases were achieved by using special fuels, additional fuel injection into the air charge, and by means of exhaust gas turbo chargers. However, the actual propulsion unit was also enlarged, as in the DB 603, to reach a range of from 1,750 horsepower to 2,300 horsepower. These were supplemented by the combined double engines DB 606, 610, and 613 with take-off power of 2,750 to 3,500 horsepower.

Benz Kaiserpreis aero engine of 1913 and
the 8-horsepower aero engine Bz 1 of 1913

Hellmuth Hirth completed his Berlin-Mannheim flight
on factory grounds, 1913

The technical solution to the problem of reducing the high fuel consumption of the jet power units being then developed and to increase the range of these aircraft, the engineers in 1940 turned to the two-circuit jet propulsion unit DB 109-007. An additional secondary air compressor made possible an increase of air flow rate through the unit while reducing the velocity at the tail pipe compared to that of a single-circuit jet unit. This also reduced losses at the exhaust side and increased forward thrust. However, after successful tests in 1943, all such work was halted.

Resumption of aero engine construction was begun in 1955 and several designs of turbo units were tested. In 1962 the new turbo unit with a shaft output of 1,050 horsepower originally — subsequently increased to over 1,400 horsepower — was publicly shown. A Bell UH-ID helicopter was used for test flights in 1969 and the craft achieved far better speeds than ever before with the DB 720 F power unit. Another new development was a gas turbine unit, producing shaft outputs of up to 2,200 revolutions per minute.

These engines could also be converted to twin-circuit units by adding a blower stage at the front or rear and because of their economy could be used for a wide range of tasks.

In 1912 the first small marine diesel engines of 60 and 100 horsepower were manufactured in the Daimler Marienfelde plant. A heavier version was available for dynamo work. By 1914 engines developing 175 and 260 horsepower were built and the following year a series of smaller six-cylinder engines developing 300 horsepower at 500 revolutions per minute were produced. This was followed by a series of 550 horsepower at 450 revolutions per minute units and ended with a six-cylinder unit developing 1,700 horsepower at 380 revolutions per minute in 1917.

Experimentation in 1913 with some thirty diesel engines of 5, 8, 10, and 14 horsepower led to the adoption of fuel injection by injection pump and one such engine was exhibited at the Agricultural Exposition at Hannover in 1914. After the First World War work was again taken up during 1920, but based on the air injection system. In 1921, three experimental four-cylinder engines of 150 millimeter stroke and 110 milli-meter bore and developing 40 horsepower at 1,000 revolutions per minute were built, and an engine of this type with supercharger for air injection was installed in a four-ton bus with propeller shaft drive. During the next years, many extensive tests were carried out. In August a trip from Berlin to Frankfurt an der Oder with a three-ton payload was made with the engine performing well. Consequently a truck, a three-way tipper, and a bus with a diesel engine were exhibited at the Berlin Show in October 1923.

In the meantime, Benz also carried out experiments and tests with a high speed diesel engine. After the preliminary merger of the two companies in 1924, the Benz pre-combustion chamber system was adapted for further development.

From its earliest successful operation, the diesel engine had been a suitable power unit for large, stationary applications. Its utilization in commercial vehicles did not come until 1924 and in passenger cars in 1936.

Large stationary diesel engines were built in the Marienfelde plant and installations including the sixteen-cylinder LOF 1, or DB 602, of 1,200 horsepower at 1,600 revolutions per minute in the airship LZ 129 *Hindenburg* in 1936. Railroad locomotives used the MB 820 power units of 1,000 horsepower or the MB 820 Bb of 1,200 horsepower at 1,500 revolutions per minute, built in the fifties.

Production of stationary diesel engines ranged from 10 to 4,500 horsepower by 1968. Many of these units had identical cylinder dimensions and a constant output of 20 horsepower per cylinder. Built in series of two, three, four, six, and eight cylinders, these engines came with either liquid or air cooling. The twenty-cylinder MB 518 diesel was a high performance unit, developing 5,500 horsepower at 1,900 revolutions per minute with supercharger and air cooling, developed especially for speed boats and other naval craft. The typical representative, however, was the large production of the four-cylinder OM 636, derived from the OM 138, the first diesel engine for passenger cars, and the M 136 gasoline engine of 1935-1936. This engine range extended from 19 horsepower at 1,500 revolutions per minute to 42 horsepower at 3,300 revolutions per minute.

Patent documents for pre-combustion chamber design of 1909 and for the funnel-shaped insertion of 1919

PATENTSCHRIFT

№ 230517

KLASSE 46 a. GRUPPE 2.

BENZ & CIE, RHEINISCHE GASMOTORENFABRIK AKT.-GES. IN MANNHEIM.

Verbrennungskraftmaschine für flüssige Brennstoffe.

Patentiert im Deutschen Reiche vom 14. März 1909 ab.

Bei den nach dem Gleichdruckverfahren arbeitenden Verbrennungskraftmaschinen ist zum Einblasen des Brennstoffes Preßluft erforderlich.

5 Statt der Preßluft können zum Zerstäuben auch gespannte Verbrennungsgase, welche, wie z. B. bei Haselwanders Methode, durch die Vorexplosion eines Hilfsgemisches erzeugt werden, verwendet werden.

sprechender Bemessung des Inhaltes der Kam- 30 mer, der Zwischenöffnung und der Einspritzmenge pro Zeiteinheit ein stetiges Überströmen von Gasen mit dem Brennstoff zugleich stattfinden.

Die sofortige Entzündung des durch die 35 Kammer in den Zylinder strömenden Brennstoffes wird hierbei durch entsprechend hohe Kompression, eventuell Beheizung der Kam-

---

DEUTSCHES REICH

REICHSPATENTAMT

PATENTSCHRIFT

— № 397142 —

KLASSE 46a GRUPPE 2

(B 88823 I/46a)

AUSGEGEBEN AM 17. JUNI 1924

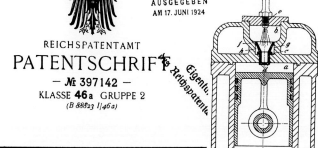

Eigentu. d. Reichspatents

Benz & Cie., Rheinische Automobil- u. Motoren-Fabrik Akt.-Ges. in Mannheim.

Verbrennungskraftmaschine mit Zündkammer.

Patentiert im Deutschen Reiche vom 18. März 1919 ab.

Gegenstand der Erfindung ist eine Verbrennungskraftmaschine mit hoher Verdichtung und Zündkammer, die mit dem Verdichtungsraum durch einen in den Zylinderkopf einge-
5 setzten, als Verdampfer und Zünder dienenden

kungen auf die Kolbenlaufbahn ausüben. Diese Übelstände sollen bei der Erfindung dadurch behoben werden, daß der Zündkörper in den 20 wassergekühlten Zylinderkopf so eingesetzt ist, daß nur seine Innenseite von den Verbrennungs-

These reliable industrial diesel engines have found a wide field of applications as power units for propulsion of numerous mechanical devices, in the railroad field, in the marine sector, and for generators.

In 1961 the Maybach Motorenbau, Friedrichshafen, was acquired and the larger units, the 800 line of diesels, were built there. The M.A.N. company worked together with Daimler-Benz on the development of aero-gas turbines since 1968.

When the basic patent of Rudolf Diesel for his engine expired in 1907, the Benz company decided to enter that promising and lucrative field and manufacture diesel engines in 1909. The design used was based on the orthodox Hesselman system, using fuel injection by means of compressed air and a cylinder output of 25 to 60 horsepower at about 200 revolutions per minute. Plans were made also for a light work unit at an engine speed of about 400 revolutions per minute.

Prosper l'Orange patented a unique pre-combustion chamber system and this became the basis of all produced diesel engines by Benz. The Swedish engineer Harry Leissner devised an effective injection system which overcame some of the difficulties encountered previously. This patent of 1919 was then applied and construction proceeded of engines up to 15 horsepower per cylinder at 400 revolutions per minute for all kinds of industrial purposes and high speed diesel engines for tractors and trucks.

In early January 1922 the first 30-horsepower engines were completed and mounted into tractors of the Benz-Sendling Motor Plow Trading Company. Tests proved so encouraging that a series of one hundred units was put into production and marketed by August 1923. In February 1924 a Benz truck of five tons capacity with propeller shaft drive fitted with a diesel engine of 50 horsepower and 1,000 revolutions per minute was exhibited at Amsterdam.

The first diesel engine, the BO 2 model, had a bore of 125 millimeters and a stroke of 180 millimeters, separate vertical cylinders, overhead inlet and exhaust valves, actuated by a camshaft housed on the left side of the engine and the usual push rods and rocker arms. The injection pump was arranged on the same side together with a centrifugal governor which the driver could regulate for any required speed.

Many regular-model Mercedes-Benz trucks were adapted for military use during World War II. Powerful engines for the Tiger and Panther tanks were also produced. The Daimler-Benz DB 601 aero engine was employed extensively in light bombers as well as fighters. Its unique fuel injection feature of eliminating icing in the highest altitudes, especially adapted superchargers, and many other special characteristics made it the best designed aero engine in the world at that time.

Concentrated daylight attacks during two consecutive weeks in September 1944 by Allied bombers brought devastation to the several Daimler-Benz factories. The long rows of machine shops and assembly lines were now rubble. Grotesquely twisted girders of the bombed-out plants reached into the gray sky. The destruction appeared to be complete and thorough. No more trucks to haul needed supplies nor powerful engines for the swift Messerschmitt fighter planes would come from these plants for the duration of the war.

A survey indicated that the Sindelfingen factory was 85 percent destroyed. The Gaggenau works suffered 80 percent damage. About 70 percent of the Stuttgart-Untertürkheim plant was damaged. The Mannheim factory was the least hurt. Only 20 percent of its buildings had been destroyed by the fire bombs. Therefore the Mannheim factory was the first to be restored after the war when production of heavy-duty trucks and buses was resumed. By 1949, 4,400 units were turned out. The production rose to 6,705 units the next year and to 9,600 by 1951. Production in 1952 reached 12,702 units of these heavy pieces.

The rebuilding of the Gaggenau plant, which had suffered much more during the bombing raids, presented a greater challenge to the Daimler-Benz officials. The task was immense, and production figures were consequently much smaller than those of the restored Mannheim factory. In 1950, 1,694 units rolled off the assembly lines. In the next year 2,621 units were built, and by 1952 production of heavy trucks and buses was 3,294 units. During 1953, 16,685 heavy units were produced in both factories; 12,759 were trucks of all sizes, 2,173 were buses and trolley buses, and 1,753 units were Unimogs.

The most useful and urgently needed vehicles were produced first. In 1949 a high-speed Diesel 3.5-ton truck, the L 3500 model, was intro-

Benz four-cylinder 50-horsepower diesel engine of
1923 and the twin-cylinder diesel engine of
30 horsepower, 1922

First diesel engine installed in five-ton truck, 1923

duced. The six-cylinder, 4.58-liter engine developed 90 horsepower at 2,800 revolutions per minute and had a top speed of more than 50 miles per hour. Combining passenger car comfort with rugged dependability, this model won such popularity that it was built with several panel sizes, as tank car, fire truck, and more than a dozen other different utility types. By the end of 1953 nearly 34,000 units had been sold.

The L 4500 model was a further development of this truck. Utilizing the same engine but built to carry 4.5 tons, it had an improved axle arrangement which made for better speeds and easier grade climbing. Its top speed was 45 miles per hour, and, like the 3500 model, it consumed less than 6 gallons of Diesel oil per 100 miles. For particularly difficult terrain the 4.5-ton truck with four-wheel drive was recommended.

The 5.5-ton truck had a six-cylinder, 7.3-liter Diesel engine which developed 120 horsepower and consumed 7 gallons of oil per 100 miles. It was equipped with a five-speed gear box and air brakes, and its top speed was 40 miles per hour. Fully loaded, it would climb grades of 37 percent.

The leviathan of the truck line produced at Gaggenau was the double-axle 6.6-tonner. Its 8.3-liter, six-cylinder Diesel engine developed 145 horsepower. The free-hanging engine rested on soft rubber blocks, and the patented fore-chamber ignition made for unusually silent and nearly complete burning of the fuel oil. The sixth gear operated similarly to that of an overdrive and allowed cruising speeds of 45 miles per hour. Consumption was slightly over 7 gallons of Diesel fuel per 100 miles. More than 7,500 units of this model were produced in the three years up to 1953.

One important factor in overland trucking in Europe is the practice of pulling at least one other fully loaded trailer, coupled close behind the truck. This custom naturally affects the actual hauling cost of the payload and accounts for the extreme heaviness and ruggedness of European trucks compared with their American counterparts.

In 1954 the model L 315 with a payload of eight tons was added to the line. (The former designation using the payload as model number was changed to the development number.) The hood was shortened and while the overall length remained the same, the loading space was increased.

The L 319/319 D was a commercial vehicle of 1¾ ton and was built in various models, as closed delivery truck or flat bed truck. Because of legally required changes in measurements and weights, lengths and axle loads in 1958, the LP 333, with three axles, was built. It had two steerable front axles, giving excellent cornering and straight line stability even on slippery roads. Powered by the OM 326 diesel engine of 200 horsepower, the truck had a payload of six tons.

When in 1960 a new regulation went into effect, the 334 model range with an overall weight of 19 tons and rear axle load of 13 tons was marketed. When the L 312 and L 328 models were discontinued after some 82,000 units had been sold, a new line of eight basic models in about eighty versions was introduced in 1962. The LP 608 to LP 1920 models covered the weight classes from 16 to 19 tons and 80 to 200 horsepower. The three-axle 2220 model was introduced in 1963, a vehicle of up to 26 tons overall weight and payload of 16 tons. The LP 1620, a long distance transporter, had a newly designed cab with the engine installed under the floor.

A more economical direct injection system for diesel engines was introduced in 1964 for the 126 to 210 horsepower range units.

Regulations were again changed in 1965 and the entire line ranged from the LP 608 of 5.9 tons to 19 tons total weight to the new 38-ton truck and trailer, the model 1623. The whole production consisted of twenty-eight basic models in twenty-four weights, including three-axle trucks of the LP 2223 models with two driven rear axles as a tractor unit for the 38-ton truck and trailer combination.

The new models were based on the previous 1620/1920 series. The medium class had a total weight of 8, 10.5, and 12 tons. Entirely new was the LP 810 of 9 tons, using the OM 352 engine of 110 horsepower. The LP 1013 was the larger version, and that engine developed 140 horsepower. The LP 1213 and LP 1418 were other models for that year.

In 1969 a new two-axle vehicle, the LP 1632, was introduced, incorporating the latest technical advantages. The cab tilted hydraulically for easier accessiblity to the engine, comfort for the driver was improved by better cab suspension and the compact OM 403 ten-cylinder V-type

Mercedes 40-horsepower diesel-engined truck, 1923

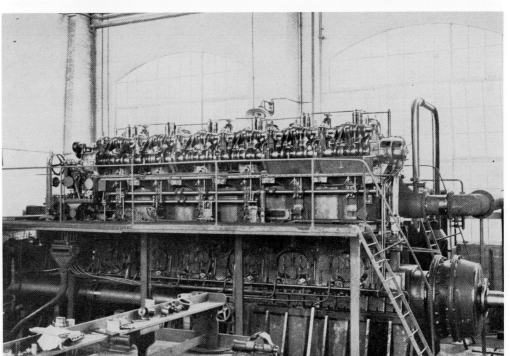

Diesel engine of 1,700 horsepower, built in 1917

engine of 320 horsepower had a lower power-to-ratio of less than three kilograms per horsepower.

A wider truck distribution system had been created through an arrangement with the Fried. Krupp organization in 1968 and contracts with the Rheinstahl company concerning the Hanomag-Henschel commercial vehicle line. In 1971 Daimler-Benz included the L 206 D and L 306 D transporter of 2.4 and 3.3 tons, based on the Hanomag models. All this gave the company its most extensive commercial vehicle program, consisting of 35 basic models in 800 standard versions of from 2 to 26 tons overall weight vehicles.

Commercial vehicle production decreased by 6.8 percent in 1971 because of poorer economic conditions and currency problems. In the over-3-ton category Daimler-Benz was in third place, behind General Motors and Ford. Production of commercial vehicles in 1965 had been 73,064 units and by 1970 it had increased to 196,149 and by 1974 to 205,344 units, down from the 1973 production of 215,935 units. (Production in foreign plants had increased to 43,944 units in 1974.)

A completely new line of medium weight trucks was added in 1975 to complete the entire range of New Generation trucks. The light transporters — 206 D, 207, 306 D, and 307 — had 60 and 70 horsepower engines. The four light truck models — 608, 808, 813, and 913 — had the 85 and 130 horsepower engines, while the new eighteen medium truck models 911 B and the 1013 to 1619 models had engines of from 130 to 240 horsepower. The new heavy trucks — 1621 to 2632 lines — were powered by engines of from 210 to 340 horsepower and came in nineteen various models. It was the most comprehensive line of commercial vehicles ever offered by Daimler-Benz.

Still, at the 1977 Auto Show, a brand new line of light vans and pickup trucks was shown to be built at the plant at Bremen. The 4- to 6-ton light trucks, manufactured at the Düsseldorf and the 6- to 10-ton vehicles from the Wörth factories were further improved to join the medium truck line from 10 tons to the heavy duty 38-ton GCW tractor and truck models. The driver's cabs had been awarded the Federal Styling Award for

1976-77 by the Ministry for Economic Affairs. Seven commercial vehicle manufacturers had competed for the prize.

The first bus with steel superstructure was built in 1929 and the following year the chassis from the Gaggenau and Mannheim factories were equipped with these new bodies. They found ready acceptance and production increased immensely.

When in 1948 bus production was resumed, the best known models were the O 3500 for 37 passengers, the O 5000 for up to 60 passengers, and the O 6600 for up to 66 passengers. All of them were powered by forward mounted diesel engines of 90, 120, and 145 horsepower, respectively. Later the H models, as in O 6600 H, from 1951 had rear-mounted OM 315 diesel engines of 145 horsepower. This engine location improved the driver's vision and allowed better utilization of the space. The same design was also used for the trolley bus H 6600 T with an electro engine supplied by an overhead line instead of the diesel engine.

In 1954 the H 321 H had the newly developed semi-integral construction, increasing the payload and providing a low vehicle weight, greater stability, and more luggage space. A torsion-resistant lattice type substructure replaced the former steel frame. The OM 321 H diesel engine of 110 horsepower was installed at the rear.

The line of buses in 1963 consisted of models carrying from 10 to 112 passengers. The Mannheim factory was the largest bus-producing plant on the continent, building the four basic models — the O 319, O 321, O 322, and O 317. The new O 317 K was a one-man city bus of 112-passenger capacity with a 200 horsepower engine; the overland bus O 321 had larger windows and many other refinements; the deluxe touring bus O 319 carried from 10 to 18 passengers, came with the four-cylinder M 121 gasoline engine of 68 horsepower or the diesel OM 621 engine, also used in the 190 D passenger sedan. Over 15,000 units of the medium sized O 321 line had been built thus far, the most successful series and widest variety of models.

The O 302 replaced the O 321 H after nearly ten years of production. It was available in five basic versions and numerous variations, equipped

Six-cylinder diesel engine OM 322 of 126 horsepower with pre-chamber

Six-cylinder diesel engine OM 352 of 126 horsepower with direct injection

Four-cylinder diesel engine OM 621 of 50 horsepower
for 190 D sedan, 1958

with the OM 352 engine of 126 horsepower, later 130 horsepower, or the OM 327 of 150 horsepower, later 160 horsepower. In 1968 the OM 360 engine of 170 horsepower, or 192 later, replaced the earlier OM 327 model. The OM 355 engine of 230 horsepower, later 240 horsepower, was added to the line.

The O 322 was a city bus, powered by a 138-horsepower engine, and carrying up to 94 passengers. The large sized O 317 — 12 meters (39.37 feet) long — had 34 seats and standing room for 111 passengers. Some 1,500 had been built.

In 1967 the O 319 was succeeded by the O 309 model of many versions and combinations, supplying practically any needs. There were two wheelbases and a choice of four engine sizes available: the 60-horsepower pre-chamber diesel engine, the 75-horsepower direct injection diesel, the gasoline engine of 75 horsepower using regular grade fuel, and one of 85 horsepower using premium grade fuel.

A new mini-bus from Bremen to seat 13 passengers — the 307 D with a 65-horsepower diesel engine, or a 308 with the 85-horsepower gasoline engine — was added to the line for 1978. The Düsseldorf bus range showed many improvements, as did the mainstay from the Mannheim factory, the O 303 model. New variations of the O 305 and O 307 models were also introduced.

In 1968 a special city bus (O 305) with air suspension and a 170 or 192 horsepower diesel engine was marketed. The O 302 line was increased by the addition of a city and touring bus with the newly developed three-speed transmission. The O 305 also had these features. The O 305 articulated bus had its premier showing at the Frankfurt Show in late 1977. Identical with the O 305 in its major components, it had a capacity of up to 189 passengers, but featured many important improvements over the earlier similar buses. Over 8,000 standard O 305 and O 307 buses were on the roads.

The O 309 D small bus had a seating capacity for eleven persons and could accommodate twenty-nine standing passengers. It was the ideal vehicle for use as a shuttle between suburban areas and shopping centers, or as a bus where traffic was light. Powered by the 85-horsepower diesel engine and with a four-speed automatic transmission, this economical vehicle found ready use in many communities in the United States.

Production of these models was not only at Mannheim and Düsseldorf, but also at the factories in Brazil, Argentina, Iran, and Turkey.

A truly unique vehicle, a Universales Motor Gerät or Unimog, was introduced in 1948. It combined the abilities of a farm tractor, power unit for machines, and transporter; could negotiate difficult cross country terrain, reaching a maximum speed of 43 miles per hour and could also be driven at a crawl of 1.8 miles per hour, with a fully synchronized transmission.

Constructed with rigid front and rear axles, the multi-purpose vehicle was of exceedingly sturdy construction. It featured all-wheel drive on equally sized wheels, had weight distribution of two-thirds at the front and one-third at the rear, a differential lock on both axles, hydraulically tilting auxiliary loading platform for a payload of two tons or mounting appliances, and a standard double cab with heating and ventilating systems. It had six forward and two reverse gears, enabling the Unimog twenty different grades.

In 1965 it came in three versions — the 411 model had the OM 636 diesel 35-horsepower engine, the 406 the OM 312 diesel of 72 horsepower, and the 404 with the gasoline engine. Other models were built in later years.

The OM 312 engine was throttled down to 72 horsepower for the Unimog, with a torque of 20 mkg (144.7 lbs/ft), allowing a speed range of from 2.73 miles per hour to 40 miles per hour. The intermediate gear enabled the low speed of 0.18 miles per hour. The four farm tractor models, produced since 1973, had engines of between 65 and 125 horsepower. The models U 1000, U 1300, and U 1500 with up to 150 horsepower engines were offered that year in addition to the basic seven models from 52 horsepower. The S model had a speed range of from 0.93 miles per hour to 59 miles per hour and was powered by a 2.2-liter six-cylinder gasoline engine of 87 SAE horsepower and 15.8 mkg (114.3 lbs/ft) torque at 3,200 revolutions per minute.

Mercedes bus O 321 H for Postal Service, 1954

Chassis of the O 6600 H bus, 1951

The O 303 long distance bus, 1975

Over 200,000 Unimogs had been built by 1977 at the Gaggenau plant and the originally agricultural vehicle was widely used in forestry, building, municipal service, and various branches of industry, including rail and road service. It had found good use also as a military vehicle and in 1965 had been used as the first vehicle to cross the wastes of the Sahara, from west to east. Although conceived more than two decades ago, the Unimog was still considered a most progressive concept — a real universal power unit.

Industrial engines produced by Daimler-Benz included thirteen different models from 40 to 550 horsepower output. Annual production of these diesel units was about half a million units and in 1967 amounted to 184 million marks. The V-type 400 range and supercharged twelve-cylinder 550 horsepower units were prominently displayed at the 1977 Frankfurt Show.

The largest diesel unit produced now by the Daimler-Benz company is the 1,000-horsepower diesel locomotive, used as a reliable switch engine in many railroad yards. It is a gigantic step from the narrow spur locomotive, powered by the Daimler V-type engine of 5.5 horsepower of sixty-five years ago.

First shown at the 1955 Frankfurt Automobile Show was the 0319 lightweight bus for seventeen passengers. A 1¾-ton delivery and pickup truck, built with cab over the engine and powered by similar diesel engines, was also introduced. The self-supporting construction, employed successfully in the 180 and 220 models of the passenger cars, was used. The improved four-cylinder diesel engine developed 46 horsepower and the vehicles had a maximum speed of 51 miles per hour. Fuel consumption was less than 4 gallons per 100 miles.

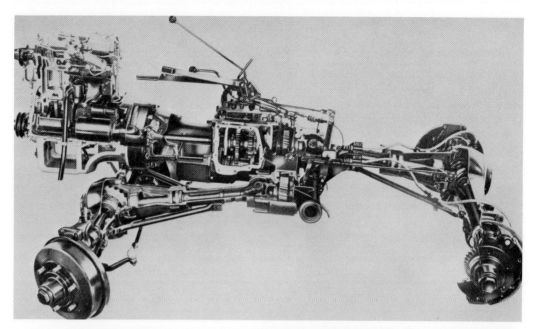

The Unimog engine, transmission and axle, 1951

The Unimog as rail switching unit, 1965

The Unimog with low-bed lifting truck, 1965

Mercedes-Benz trac 1300 aiding harvesting

The LPS 2020 semi-trailer unit

Mercedes-Benz transporter model 2070

The O 305 G articulated pusher bus

Daimler and Benz Production Models (1885-1939)

Many of the pioneering Daimler vehicles have been described in an earlier chapter. The major principles of the motorcycle of 1885 were later the valid basis of Gottlieb Daimler's first four-wheeled vehicles. Its one-half horsepower engine was started by igniting the pilot light under the glow tube and cranking the motor. A muffler softened the exhaust noise. A lever engaged the belt-drive gears, which could be regulated to the desired speed. Moving the shift lever into a neutral position disengaged the gears, and a brake could be pulled to stop the vehicle. But the motorcycle failed to win the hoped-for acceptance, and it was never put into production.

The elegant Daimler motor coach of 1886, like the horseless carriage which it was, had whip socket and harness attachment hooks in addition to a one-cylinder, 1.5-horsepower engine. The body was built by W. Wimpff and Sohn, the Stuttgart coach builders, on a frame purchased from Zuhr & Bobsin of Hamburg. The dark-blue-lacquered and red-trimmed "Americain" carriage of this first motor vehicle cost Daimler 795 marks (about $190). In the then preferred American style the door for the passengers was at the rear. The Stuttgart firm supplied the bodies for many models through the years.

By 1888 some newspapers were talking about the "steam-engined" Daimler vehicles, either through ignorance or, more likely, through a deliberate effort to avoid alarming readers by calling attention to the "dangerous petroleum product" which was carried as fuel.

The steel-wheel carriage, the tubular-frame vehicle, followed in 1889. It was light and was an entirely different motor vehicle from the carriage type of earlier and later years. Equipped with a V-type two-cylinder engine, it had independent, tangential front steering and a four-speed transmission.

After the Sultan of Morocco received his fanciful Daimler motor vehicle in 1892, many other rulers ordered special models from Daimler. Nicholas II, the Czar of all the Russias, had an unusually high automobile built for himself: he was tall and did not care to stoop when entering a conveyance.

A heavier vehicle of 1892 was but the forerunner of the improved Vis-à-Vis motorcar of 1894. This comfortable vehicle had facing seats. The 4-horsepower engine had the hot-tube ignition system, and was in a housing at the rear that kept the noise and odor from the passengers. Coil-spring suspension was used at the rear, while the front had leaf springs. Side curtains and a large surrey top, complete with fancy fringe, protected the four passengers from inclement weather.

The 3-horsepower, twin-engined Victoria of 1895 had the driver's seat at the front in the accepted style of the fancy coaches of the time. In other details it was similar to the Vis-à-Vis model of 1894.

A model designed in 1896 had the engine in front of the driver, a steering wheel which rose straight up, the shift and brake levers on the right side, and the gasoline tank under the driver's seat. A large top folded back, behind the passenger seat, but left the driver exposed to the elements.

A year after the sudden death of William Steinway in 1896, the Daimler Motor Company was organized in New York under the direction of Friedrich Kuebler, who had been active in the technical department of the Cannstatt factory for many years. However, the Sheldon patent affair made the selling of imported automobiles difficult, because the licensing company threatened every purchaser with a court suit. This threat was widely advertised in the press.

The Daimler Motor Company of Coventry was organized under the young engineer Frederick Richard Simms, who did so much to advance the cause of the motor vehicle in the British Isles. The company built several models. The most popular was a wagonette with a V-type hot-tube ignition engine which developed 5.5 horsepower at 800 revolutions per minute. The light automobile sported a smart "one-man" folding top, which seems still to be an important part of many British automobiles.

The Prince of Wales (later, King Edward VII) was an enthusiastic customer, and the Daimler became "by appointment" the official automobile of the royal house.

The business volume of the Daimler Motoren-Gesellschaft in 1897 amounted to 815,668 marks.

One of the first Daimler belt-driven carriages in England

Daimler two-cylinder, 1.8-horsepower car, the only motorized vehicle exhibited at the Chicago World's Fair in 1893

Daimler vehicles made an excellent showing in the torturous 1898 Austrian Alpine Rally. They accomplished what had been considered to be impossible — reaching 28 miles an hour on level ground. What was more spectacular, the participating vehicles climbed the difficult mountain passes across the Semmering. To go on like this for two days over almost impassable roads and arduous terrain was extraordinary.

Daimler's products were sold in Austria from 1890 on. Eventually, with the tremendous increase in demand after reliability exhibitions such as the Alpine Rally, the Oesterreichische Daimler Motoren-Gesellschaft was organized in 1899. All products were to be manufactured in the Wiener-Neustadt factory under the management of Paul Daimler.

The 1899 "Paul Daimler Wagen," the last model built in Germany to carry the Daimler name on its front radiator, was a great improvement over the earliest models. Built under the direction of the founder's oldest son, Paul, it featured many revolutionary advances. It had a low-tension break-and-make-type ignition utilizing the Bosch unit. A foot-pedal accelerator was provided for easier driving. The lever to manipulate the four gears was attached to the steering column instead of being on the floor, on the driver's side. The honeycomb-type radiator helped cool the engine, which was placed at the front. The 1,650-pound vehicle sped more than 30 miles per hour on pneumatic tires.

Volume by 1899 reached 1,584,011 marks, and 333 workers were steadily employed in the Daimler factory.

Although a four-cylinder engine had been built in 1890, it was not used in a motor vehicle until the Mercedes made its first appearance on the Côte d'Azur in the spring of 1901.

The building of this epoch-making automobile had begun a year before under the guidance of the capable Wilhelm Maybach. It is impossible to ascertain the influence of Gottlieb Daimler, who died on March 6, 1900. The negotiations with Consul Jellinek ended on April 2, when Cannstatt factory agreed to construct a totally new automobile. Sixteen days later, after seeing the designs, the financier formally ordered the entire first production of thirty-six cars at a cost of 550,000 marks (about $130,000). The first completed car made its successful test run on November 22,

1900. Several automobiles had been delivered to Jellinek the following spring when the first Mercedes was shown on the sunny Riviera playground at Nice.

At the Week of Nice, from March 25 to 29, 1901, the new 35-horsepower Mercedes cars were victorious in every event in which they were entered. They created the greatest excitement so far known in the short history of automobile construction. A square brass outline framed the honeycomb-type radiator, and a long low hood housed the four-cylinder T-head engine, whose crankcase was made of aluminum alloy. The inlet and exhaust valves were mechanically operated. The newly developed Bosch electric ignition system was provided. Twin carburetors were used. There were two sets of brakes to stop this sensational new car, which was capable of 55 miles per hour. The lower chassis, with a slightly longer wheelbase than the previous Daimler model, had semielliptic spring suspension. A rakishly twisted wide sheet of metal acted as a mud-guard over the wheels. The shiny steering column slanted gracefully. The gear lever was on the right side. Besides the large, highly polished, more than adequate acetylene headlamps, two bulb horns were provided. One was attached to the steering column, while a larger one snaked ornamentally along the side of the car and was fastened to the hood.

The first Mercedes was a beautiful automobile, years ahead of its time and of its competitors, and it had a great effect on the steadiness of the automobile market. A new age for Daimler automobiles began with the young century.

The brilliantly new styling and outstanding mechanical features of the glamorous new Mercedes were so advanced that Paul Meyan, editor of *La France Automobile*, warned French automobile manufacturers "to rise to the occasion and not let the Mercedes set the style for all cars in France, or the world." However, the excitingly impressive Mercedes did just that.

The glamorous Mercedes racing cars dominated the early years of the new century. The 1903 touring models, of which many more than the specially built racing models were sold, were available in several body styles. They came in four different chassis. They were offered with four-

Mercedes "Simplex" phaeton, 1905

Mercedes "Stuttgart" sedan of 1926

Mercedes "Mannheim" touring car of 1926

cylinder engines of 28, 40, 60, and 70 horsepower. The next year, timing gears were enclosed and oiled automatically. Ball bearings were used for crankshaft and connecting rods.

Built on the long chassis with a mammoth four-cylinder, 60-horsepower engine, the impressive chain-driven white touring car of 1903 was considerably larger than the first Mercedes model. The round radiator and the hood were larger and higher to accommodate the huge power plant. The large sprocket wheels supplied the power through immense driving chains to the rear wheels. Several cocks on the dash had to be adjusted to oil the machinery properly. The oil was pressure-fed into the lines from the drum which rested on the side of the car. Three sturdy pedals were set on the floor boards — for the brake, the clutch, and the accelerator. The huge rounded underpan went nearly the length of the automobile. The car had white leather upholstery. The front bucket seats and large rear seats were roomy and comfortable. A large white canvas cloth top with roll-up curtains was removable. Large narrow wicker baskets were attached to the sides. As on all Mercedes models, four large brass lamps added brilliance to the exquisite white automobile.

A six-passenger limousine for luxurious long-distance travel or short bus service was built on the 70-horsepower long chassis. The body resembled two elegant carriages which were closely attached to each other. The rear wheels were duals to adequately support the heavy body, the passengers, and a huge amount of luggage, which could be carried on the extremely sturdy roof.

In a deluxe town car the seats of the passengers were a step higher than those of the driver and the footman. The interior was splendidly fitted in the opulent fashion.

An American Mercedes was advertised about this time, built on a 45-horsepower chassis. It was assembled in the Long Island factory from parts made at Untertürkheim. The price for the heavy tonneau, with doors at the rear, was $7,500 f.o.b. New York. The car was equipped with four headlights, two horns, and comfortable leather upholstery, but no protective top.

After the resounding success of the 1908 French Grand Prix at Dieppe, Mercedes chassis for touring-car bodies, or specially designed custom bodies built by artisan coach builders, could be had in a great variety. Built on a 107-inch wheelbase chassis, the 12.8-liter, four-cylinder T-head engine of the Grand Prix model developed 120 horsepower. Similar four-cylinder engines were available with an output of 40, 45, 55, or 65 horsepower. Six-cylinder power plants of 70 and 80 horsepower were also built that year. The wide choice of models available, as indicated by the many chassis types produced, should have suited even the most fastidious prospective purchaser of a Mercedes automobile.

Faded pages of a factory catalog of the period reveal some interesting models. The small shaft-driven 20-horsepower sports car looks quite austere by Mercedes standards. The barrel-like cowl extended smoothly into the doors and ran up considerably higher than on previous models. It offered fine protection to the driver. The bucket seats look comfortable. Front and rear fenders were held together by the running board in one continuous line. The spare tires were carred flat on the rear deck. The open touring car, a four-passenger limousine, and a fancy landaulet all were built on the same chassis.

A plain-looking sports sedan without a top, for four passengers, was shown on a 30-horsepower chassis. Other body styles were available.

The deluxe limousine, built on a 40-horsepower chassis with a shaft drive, was an elegant-looking vehicle. The furnishings of this early town car were in fine style. A special deluxe open touring car was built for the Belgian monarch. The amply upholstered seats in the rear compartment appear to have been most comfortable. The brightly painted body was offset with bold gold stripes, and highly polished brass hardware added extra sparkle to the royal vehicle.

Two phaeton models are shown, built on the chain-drive 45-horsepower chassis. The standard model, with a high folding top, had fancy, decorated side panels to offset the otherwise one-color paint job. The deluxe version had slightly different body lines and featured fancier brassware. Another light phaeton was especially equipped for long-distance touring. The

Mercedes exhibit at the Paris Auto Salon in 1902
and the Benz exhibit there

folding top extended well over the driver's compartment; but, as in all phaetons of that time, there were no doors to protect him. In addition to the huge headlamps, two smaller lamps were fastened to the cowl, just over the hood. An especially fitted, large trunk filled the space behind the body snugly and completely.

A luxurious landaulet was built for the German Emperor on a 55-horse-power chassis. This sumptuous white and black automobile was fitted by the finest artisans. Expert craftsmen made special luggage to fit. Atop each of its brass lamps rested an exquisite hand-wrought miniature imperial crown, and the royal emblem decorated the doors. The Emperor was a Mercedes enthusiast, and used no other car.

A sport phaeton with a smooth, streamlined body was built on the six-cylinder, 70-horsepower chain-drive chassis. Another interesting model was the limousine for long-distance traveling. Especially fitted luggage in the rear and trunks for the top were available. In addition to the usual brass lamps, a large high-powered lamp between the two headlights gave extra illumination for night driving. A spotlight was attached to the steering column, well in front of the wheel.

One reason why so many body styles were available was the immense popularity of automobile tours on the Continent. The yearly Herkomer tours of the Bavarian Automobile Club began in 1905 and were replaced by the annual Prince Henry Tours in 1908. They were reliability runs of the first order and tested the dependability and endurance of vehicles and drivers. Although they were as long as 600 miles, they were tremendously popular. Prince Henry, the brother of the Emperor, always drove Benz automobiles, and was an enthusiastic participant in many Alpine rallies.

In order to satisfy almost every possible need, the Daimler company offered seven different chassis types by the end of 1910. The four-cylinder F-head engines developed either 20 or 30 horsepower. The four-cylinder T-head engines were offered in 40-, 50-, and 70-horsepower versions. And two six-cylinder T-head engines, developing 80 and 90 horsepower, could be had. The first three models had a shaft drive while the last four were chain-driven.

The new Mercedes cars of 1910 had many novel features. Three push-rod-operated overhead valves per cylinder made their appearance on the 90-horsepower engine, which had four main bearings. The chain drive was completely enclosed, to eliminate noise and to protect the assembly from dirt. The pointed Mercedes radiator made its debut.

This powerful Mercedes was a favorite of the sporting world, and, despite its New York price of $7,500 for the chassis alone, many cars were imported to the United States.

As an early attempt at streamlining, a 90-horsepower Mercedes had a smooth body with plain lines and disk wheels, and a simple, folding top.

One of the more interesting automobiles close before World War I was a specially constructed Mercedes, a Jagdwagen. The body, on the four-cylinder, 60-horsepower chassis, was styled like the open touring model. The upholstery was of leather as in the other open models, and a heavy canvas cloth top was provided; but the body panels were fashioned out of exquisite wooden sections. The hood section, although of metal, was painted to resemble wood. Station wagons even two decades later had a similar arrangement of wood paneling on their bodies.

After the First World War the six-cylinder, 95-horsepower engine was improved and found its first use in the Targa Florio sports car of 1921. Then it appeared in the large Mercedes touring cars and limousines. These models continued to be manufactured until the merger with Benz & Cie. in 1926.

With the change-over to the four-wheeled motor vehicle in 1891, Karl Benz left the idea of a three-wheeled carriage definitely behind. Within a few years many different models were produced. The Benz catalog of May 1896 showed an improved Victoria model. The two-seated vehicle, with a 3-horsepower engine, sold for 3,875 marks (slightly over $900). It could also be purchased with a 5-horsepower engine and additional seats for 4,000 marks. The catalog also showed the popular, light Velo, which had been produced in quantity since 1894, a year after this 2,000-mark (less than $500) vehicle first appeared. Velo production reached 1,200 units by the end of 1897. The Phaeton, to sell for 4,700 marks, the Landauer, the Vis-à-Vis, the Dos-à-Dos, and the Comfortable, all were built at this time.

Benz "Dos-à-Dos" of 1897

Opposed twin-cylinder engine

Benz "Comfortable" with pneumatic tires, 1898

Out of the Vis-à-Vis developed a hotel omnibus with 5-horsepower engine, to carry eight persons. After the contra-motor had proved itself, Benz built a larger vehicle to carry twelve persons. However, the early 10-horsepower engine was replaced by one developing 14 horsepower. Now speeds of 20 miles per hour and successful climbs of 15-degree grades were guaranteed.

At the turn of the century the Benz works built a special automobile for King Leopold II of Belgium. Called the "Duc," the 1,700-pound vehicle incorporated all the newest improvements, had a luxurious body, four-speed transmission, pneumatic tires, and especially large acetylene lights.

The elegant Mylord model with an 8-horsepower contra-motor, costing 6,500 marks, was built in 1889. As a coupé, equipped with mirrors and fancy beveled glass in the doors, it came to 7,000 marks. The Americain phaeton was a slightly lighter model and featured the so-called "American top."

By 1900 the front-engined Spider, the Ideal, the Tonneau, and the luxurious Elegant-Tonneau made their appearance.

The newly developed Parsifal four-cylinder engine of 1902, built to counteract the disastrous Mercedes influence on sales of Benz cars, was available in chassis types of 10, 12, and 14 horsepower. The low hood sloped gently upward, and the steering wheel was slanted slightly backward. Shift and brake levers were at the right of the driver. Two huge brass headlights were mounted in front of the radiator. The bodies were clean in design, with smooth, pleasing lines and a minimum of fancy trim.

Although earlier Benz models were shaft-driven, a four-cylinder, 20-horsepower chassis in 1904 had sprocket wheels and heavy chains. The tonneau of that year was heavy-looking, with the entrance to the rear seats in the back.

A contest for a small, popular passenger car in 1910 resulted in an 18-horsepower automobile designed by Karl Ketterer. Production of 1,000 units was ordered at once, because the machine could be sold for 7,000 marks (about $1,700), which seemed to be a reasonable price. Eventually the most desirable features of the basic design of this automobile were expanded into eight different models.

To emphasize outwardly a changing trend, the name of the company was changed in 1911 to Benz & Cie., Rheinische Automobil und Motorenfabrik, Aktiengesellschaft. The building of stationary engines definitely took second place to motor vehicle production.

A new factory was built on 35,000 square yards of land at Waldhof, near Mannheim, to provide improved production of passenger cars.

In 1909 the Benz Company issued 2,000,000 marks' worth of stock, and in 1910 it issued 4,000,000. By 1912 the 12,000,000 marks available were not sufficient, and another stock issue was floated, so that by 1914 the capital of Benz & Cie. was 22,000,000 marks.

By 1912 the Benz works employed 5,381 men. At the end of that business year a 12 percent dividend was declared on the 16,000,000 marks of outstanding stock. The shares sold at 226 percent of their face value.

Also in 1912 the directors decided that it would be more profitable to limit construction to three basic models with 18-, 20-, and 30-horsepower engines. A four-cylinder, 100-horsepower Benz runabout was available as well — a fast automobile that was popular in the many competitive touring events of the time.

Time-yellowed pages of the Benz catalog of that time list a surprising number of different body styles. The four-seater runabout had clean-cut body lines. The door for the front compartment was on the left. On the right side were the gear and brake levers. The steering column was slanted at a 45-degree angle. Electric headlights were provided. The floor boards were covered with aluminum for tightness. A velour rug covered the floor in the rear. Colors available were ivory, gray, black, Russian green, dark blue, mail yellow, and red. Pencil-line trims were in black or in contrasting colors.

The sport bodies were similar to the runabout, but lacked the rear seat. Their flat rear deck accommodated a considerable reserve supply of tires, so important at that time. The elegant landaulet and limousine had practically identical body lines; electric lights, fancy cut-glass windows, and

Benz 8/10-horsepower "Parsifal" phaeton, 1903

Benz 24-horsepower "Double Phaeton," 1904

Benz 40-horsepower touring car, 1905-1906

upholstery of the finest material in delicate gray or brown made them sumptuous. The closed cars could be had in white, blue, green, yellow, brown, red and black, trimmed in black, gold, or yellow. They were stately vehicles and should have suited the most discerning wealthy customers.

After World War I the Benz works began construction of four different passenger-car models. However, the period was an extremely difficult one. Eighty-six automobile manufacturers were producing 140 different model types in Germany. The small four-cylinder, 18-horsepower sports car of the period had a pointed radiator, and its sleek body had a pointed tail. Wire wheels and one large chrome exhaust pipe on the side of the hood gave the sports car a racy appearance. Fenders and running board were a smooth, continued line. A cloth top was folded neatly.

The Benz directors felt that consolidation with the Daimler Motoren-Gesellschaft would be of untold mutual benefit and would ensure survival of the severe economic crisis. However, not much was accomplished in the negotiations of 1919.

After the terrible nightmare of inflation had passed and the German economy had begun to settle upon a more solid foundation, the merger discussions were resumed, and in June 1926 a contract was mutually accepted which combined the two leaders of the automobile manufacturing industry. The basis of consolidation was for Daimler 600, and for Benz 346 units.

It is difficult to evaluate the intangible technical assets which were brought together in the merger of Benz & Cie., Rheinische Automobil und Motorenfabrik, A.G., founded in 1883, and the Daimler Motoren-Gesellschaft, A.G., since 1890.

Gottlieb Daimler, soon after constructing his first four-wheeled motor vehicle in 1886, concentrated his efforts on the constant improvement and perfection of his gasoline engine. It appeared soon in boats, fire-engine pumps, primitive airships, buses, and other conveyances. Karl Benz seemed to be more interested in the construction and further development of the vehicle itself, and built a prodigious number of models before the end of the nineteenth century.

The merger proved to be beneficial to both companies. The various phases of automotive vehicle construction were consolidated, and the existing factory facilities used to better advantage. An earlier chapter has mentioned the sports and racing cars produced by the firms, first separately and later in a combined effort.

The first joint product of the Daimler-Benz A.G. was the large Mercedes-Benz K model. The six-cylinder engine had originally been used in the 1924 Mercedes model. The cylinders had a bore of 94 millimeters and a stroke of 150 millimeters. With the same 6-liter (378 cubic inches) displacement as before, it was now improved to give 110 horsepower at 3,000 revolutions per minute. The Roots supercharger boosted this output to 160 horsepower.

For the first S (sports) model, brought out in 1927, the engine was enlarged to 98-millimeter bore and 150-millimeter stroke. The output was increased to 120 horsepower. The supercharger increased the power of this 6.8-liter, six-cylinder engine to 180 horsepower. The engine was equipped with a single overhead camshaft, shaft- and gear-driven. The huge crankcase and cylinder block were fashioned of light aluminum alloy with cast-iron cylinder liners and head. The four-bearing crankshaft was made of chrome nickel steel, as were the tubular connecting rods. The dual ignition and the high-tension magneto were of Bosch manufacture. Two updraft carburetors were employed in the S model. The two-vane, two-lobe vertical Roots supercharger blew through the carburetors. Three gear ratios of 2.5, 2.76, and 3.09 were optional.

This automobile was produced in a touring model first, and it proved to be so popular and was used in competition so extensively and successfully that the Daimler-Benz company brought out a sports model. An even faster, improved model followed in 1928. The huge luxurious Mercedes-Benz limousine of that period was — while perhaps the heaviest closed automobile ever produced — the fastest as well. A large, massive touring car was also produced, utilizing a similar power plant and giving equally outstanding performance.

The SS (super sports) model of 1928 had a slightly larger power plant than the S model of the year before. The six cylinders were of 100 millimeter bore and 150 millimeter stroke for a displacement of 7 liters (428

Benz 5-horsepower "Ideal" of 1899

Benz 12-horsepower "Tonneau" of 1899

cubic inches). At the relatively slow 3,200 revolutions per minute the engine developed 160 horsepower, which increased to 200 horsepower with the shrieking supercharger engaged. Built on a 134-inch wheelbase, the open car was heavy. Its overall length was just over 16 feet. The chassis alone weighed 3,630 pounds. A top speed of about 120 miles per hour was easily attainable.

When the Museum of Modern Art in New York held its historic exhibition in the autumn of 1951, which was concerned with the ethics of motorcar design, a Mercedes-Benz touring car SS model was chosen as one of eight outstanding automobiles in the world.

The Museum stated:

> The eight automobiles in this exhibition were chosen primarily for their excellence as works of art, although no automobile was considered for inclusion unless its mechanical performance met the highest technological standards. A second consideration was their relevance to contemporary problems of passenger car design. The older cars, dating back as much as twenty years, were chosen not to show historical progression but to show prototypes of design that are still valid today.

The curator of architecture, Arthur Drexler, had this to say about the Mercedes-Benz:

> The designer of the Mercedes regards an automobile as four enormous wheels carrying a box. No detail relaxes for a moment its authoritative carriage, no intransigeant decoration mollifies its stern purposefulness; but for all that the Mercedes combines an extravagance of metal with quantities of hardware, in an amusingly solemn piece of stagecraft.
>
> The Mercedes had a mighty engine, placed well behind the front wheels for technical reasons of weight distribution and steering performance. But physical bulk, justly attributed to mechanical requirements, hardly accounts for the coherence of its grandeur. This is the art: each detail, regardless of mechanical necessity, is developed on a scale appropriate to the total effect. The body of the car serves as a backdrop for a glittering ensemble of circles and bars, a necklace of lights, bumpers, straps, horns, and handles, undecorated but nevertheless expressively decorative, as were the caps and goggles which used to ornament the serious motorist.

The Mercedes looks as large as it is because the parts applied to it, whatever their size, incorporate an amount of detail sufficient to reveal their complexity. Hundreds of wire spokes, for example, visually expand the wheels by their intricate radiating lines. No two details are quite alike: each part appears to have its unique, mechanically appropriate form. But in every case this form is justified by the total effect. Thus the removable canvas top, a practical expedient for a sports car, also avoids disrupting the horizontality of the hood and passenger compartment with their flowing, grandiose curves.

Like most twentieth century artifacts which make one think of the machine because of their precise details, the Mercedes represents the triumph of craftsmanship in an older meaning of the word. What makes it a classically conceived object, and a classic among automobiles, is the successfully concluded search for a particular form, patiently tooled and polished to give it a resounding finality.

The first rear-engined car, the unorthodox and highly streamlined racing Tropfenwagen, was built by Benz in 1922 and a sports model, complete with simple front and rear fenders and horizontal side panels, was later produced, but it was not a commercial success at that ruinous inflationary and economically most difficult time. When the construction offices of the Benz and the Daimler companies were combined in 1925, prior to the merger of the following year, this type of construction was not further developed.

Again, in 1927 and 1928, experimental cars were built with the engines placed in the rear, and using a center tube instead of the regular frame with independent wheel suspension. Twelve such cars were produced for exhaustive testing in 1931. The body types built included sedans, convertible sedans, and open touring models. These 120 H models had a four-cylinder opposed piston engine of 70-millimeter bore and 78-millimeter stroke, developing 25 horsepower at 3,100 revolutions per minute.

The 130 H model, shown to the public at the Berlin Automobile Show in 1933 and produced from 1934 to 1936, had an engine of 70-millimeter bore and 85-millimeter stroke, displacing 1,308 cubic centimeters and developing 26 horsepower at 3,400 revolutions per minute. The chassis had independent wheel suspension and two leaf springs in front and swing axle and coil springs in the rear. Hydraulic four-wheel brakes and an over-

Mercedes-Benz 150 H, rear-engined sports car, 1934

Chassis of the 170 H sedan, 1935

The rear-engined 170 H sedan of 1935

drive were provided. The four-cylinder water-cooled engine was placed on rubber mounts. Instead of the usual frame, a large central tube was used onto which the front and rear assemblies were hung. The total weight of the sedan was 880 kilograms (1,936 pounds) and fuel consumption was given as 9 to 10 liters per 100 kilometers. Maximum speed was 92 kilometers (57 miles) per hour. The price of the sedan and the convertible was 3,575 Reichsmark. A total of 4,298 units were produced.

A roadster with a slightly enlarged engine but placed ahead of the rear axle was also built during that time. The 1,498 cubic centimeter engine developed 55 horsepower and gave at 4,500 revolutions per minute the car a top speed of 125 kilometers to 140 kilometers (78 to 87 miles) per hour. But only twenty units of this special 150 H model were produced to be used mainly by factory drivers in competitive events.

A still larger version, called the 160 H, powered by an engine displacing 1,598 cubic centimeters and developing 38 horsepower, was produced in 1935. The weight was 1,100 kilograms (2,420 pounds) and maximum speed was 110 kilometers (68.3 miles) per hour. Production totaled 3,102 units. A four-wheel drive version was created for the armed forces, but only eight such units were built and delivered to the services.

A final version of the rear-engined passenger automobile was the 170 H, built from 1935 until 1939. This model competed directly with the front-engined four-cylinder 170 V, constructed at the same time but on a regular chassis. Comparison of production figures provides the answer for the demise of this rear-engined passenger car type. In 1935, when both models were introduced, production was eight units for the rear-engined car and twelve for the front-engined type. The next year, when 1,101 H cars were built, the V model production was 12,683 units. In 1937 only 50 H cars were produced while 18,864 of the V model were built. In 1938 the ratio was 250 H against 17,575 V units, and the final year, 1939, the ratio was even greater — 189 H types against 16,305 Vs. The total production figures for the five years of 1,507 170 H models against 65,439 V models clearly indicated the preference of the buying public for the orthodox front-engined model. The time for a rear-engined passenger automobile had not yet come.

The first Mercedes-Benz diesel-engined passenger automobiles were built in 1936. The model 260 D had a 2.6-liter, four-cylinder pre-chamber diesel engine. The patented method of preheating the fuel in a separate chamber before it was injected into the combustion chamber made for smoother operation, which is so desirable in a passenger-car engine. The top speed was 65 miles per hour, and fuel consumption was 2.6 gallons for 100 miles. The 260 D model was a medium-sized car in roominess, riding comfort, and performance, yet the reasonable upkeep of the diesel engine was suggestive of that of a small car. If no diesel oil was available, the engine would also operate satisfactorily on kerosene, shale oil, purified vegetable oil, or animal oil.

The fantastic Mercedes-Benz sports roadster, the fabulous 540 K model, was produced in 1937 and 1938. Approximately 300 automobiles of this model were built, and many chassis were produced to be fitted with luxurious, individually styled exquisite bodies. The 5.4-liter, eight-cylinder engine developed 115 horsepower. The Roots supercharger boosted this to 180 horsepower. The cylinders had a bore of 88 millimeters and a stroke of 111 millimeters. The powerful engine turned only about 2,000 revolutions per minute at 60 miles per hour, which would indicate a greater top speed than the conservative 105 miles per hour advertised by the factory. The big car had a 130-inch wheelbase and weighed about 5,800 pounds.

The large scooping fender ran in a pleasant flowing line down to the rear wheels. The pointed radiator sat more than a foot back from the front-fender line; the long hood, extensively louvred on its sides, came past the center of the car, and the space under it was crowded by the huge engine. The massive vehicle, with its polished exhaust pipes protruding gracefully on the left side of the hood, was reminiscent of the magnificent SS models of ten years before.

The front suspension used was an independent type with parallel arms and coil springs. The rear suspension featured swing-axle and coil springs. The road-holding characteristics of this marvelous automobile were excellent, and the steering was very accurate. The sturdy Mercedes-Benz limousine had a similar power plant and an even greater top speed.

The 170 V or D model, 1936—1950

Mercedes-Benz 540 K roadster, 1936

The "Grosser Mercedes" limousine of 1938

The "ne plus ultra" in extravagant sports cars was the "Grosse Mercedes-Benz" of 1937. Built on a tubular chassis, this gigantic 7.7-liter, eight-cylinder supercharged engine developed 230 horsepower. Top speed was reported to be 140 miles per hour. This great automobile was the acme of Mercedes-Benz motorcars, the summit of perfection in every detail. The price was an even 50,000 marks (about $12,000) in Germany.

During 1938 the Daimler-Benz company produced 27,762 passenger automobiles. The small diesel model made up a great share of the total. The smaller six-cylinder Mercedes-Benz sedan, the 230 model, was the most popular automobile of the entire line and accounted for the largest proportion of the units produced. The bodies of all models were manufactured in the Sindelfingen plant and shipped to Stuttgart-Untertürkheim for final assembly.

Then came again a period when passenger-car production was all but halted and all the resources were employed to construct superior engines. Using the valuable knowledge acquired through inexhaustible tests on the racing circuits, the Daimler-Benz company produced some excellent aero engines. All the newest technical improvements were incorporated into these powerful engines, which were eventually used in the Second World War.

Again, what could have helped humanity to better itself and lighten its load was used in an inhuman, terribly destructive war.

Six-cyinder diesel engine of the 260 D, 1936

Engine and transmission of the 260 D

Mercedes-Benz "K" model of 1926

The "Nürburg 500" model of 1931

The 500 K convertible of 1934-1936

The 540 K coupe, 1939

The 540 K convertible of 1939

The 500 G4 (W 31) cross-country vehicle, 1933-1939

Postwar Production Models (1949-1965)

Mercedes-Benz passenger automobile production had ceased during the war. Concentrated and accurate bombing attacks destroyed nearly three-fourths of the Stuttgart-Untertürkheim factory; and the Sindelfingen plant, where all the automobile bodies were produced, was almost a complete loss. Eventually, passenger-car production was begun; but commercial vehicles took precedence.

In May 1949 the first postwar passenger Mercedes-Benz automobiles — the 170 S and 170 D models — were officially shown, together with the L 3500 truck model.

The four-door 170 models resembled the prewar cars in the slightly slanting, pointed radiator, which immediately identified them as Mercedes-Benz even before the pointed star at the top could be seen. The X-frame was of oval steel tubing. The suspension was the independent Mercedes-Benz type first used in 1931 in their racing cars; it was used on all subsequent models. The four-cylinder gasoline engine of the 170 S model had a bore of 75 millimeters and a stroke of 100 millimeters. Displacement was 1,767 cubic centimeters. The L-head engine developed 52 horsepower at 4,000 revolutions per minute. The compression ratio of 6.5 to 1 ensured satisfactory service with the relatively low-octane fuel available in Europe. A four-speed syncromesh transmission was provided, and the gear-shift lever was attached to the steering column. The weight of the 112-inch wheelbase vehicle was 2,684 pounds. The top speed, like the recommended continuous cruising speed, was 75 miles per hour. Fuel consumption was 4.2 gallons per 100 miles.

The same basic 170 model was also furnished with a most economical diesel engine. Developed from the prewar patented pre-chamber diesel power plant, the 170 D model employed, as far as practical, the same engine as the 170 S model. The output reached 40 hosepower at 3,330 revolutions per minute. The compression ratio was 19 to 1. Fuel-oil consumption was 2.6 gallons per 100 miles. The cost of diesel fuel in Germany was one-fourth that of gasoline. Aware of the difficult starting of diesel engines in cold weather, Daimler-Benz engineers perfected a glow plug which warmed up the chamber first, ensuring an immediate start in even the most severe temperature, so that diesel engines performed satisfactorily and won acceptance in cold areas. Top and cruising speed of the 170 D was 62 miles per hour. The vehicle weighed 100 pounds more than the gasoline-powered model.

In the fall of 1952 the 170 DS model was introduced. In chassis and body it was identical with the lighter S model; and it used the diesel power plant of the D model. And the new 170 V model had a top speed of 72 miles per hour. It also had some improvements over the old 170 model in chassis, body, and transmission.

By the end of June 1953 the Daimler-Benz company had produced 38,513 units of the 170 S, 11,811 of the 170 DS, 32,665 of the 170 D, and 49,139 of the 170 V model. A total of 132,128 units of the 170 models had been manufactured. In 1953 alone a total of 24,657 units of all 170 models was produced.

The new six-cylinder 220 and 300 models were introduced at the 1951 Frankfurt International Automobile Show. It was Daimler-Benz's first step into the luxury automobile field. The chassis of the smaller 220 model was similar to those of the proven 170 models. Its interior furnishings were more like those of the elegant 300 model. The engine had a bore of 80 millimeters and a stroke of 72.8 millimeters. Displacement was 2,195 cubic centimeters. The six-cylinder overhead-valve engine developed 80 horsepower at 3,470 revolutions per minute. Compression ratio was 6.5 to 1. The weight was 2,915 pounds. Top speed was 87 miles per hour. Several different body styles were available: the four-door sedan, the two-door convertible sedan, and the two-door convertible coupé.

By June 30, 1953, 16,694 units of the 220 model had been manufactured.

In the 300 model the Daimler-Benz engineers and designers created again a superb motor vehicle. Its design was conservative by postwar standards. The outfitting was excellent. Seats were adjustable for reclining. The dashboard, like the trim around the windows, was of polished dark wood. The four-speed gear-shift lever was attached to the steering column. In the center of the two-spoke steering wheel shone the familiar Mercedes star.

The 170 V sedan, and
the 170 V convertible, 1936

The 220a sedan of 1954

The 300 sedan, 1951-1953

The typical Mercedes-Benz independent suspension on all wheels ensured an exceptionally smooth ride. The rear coil springs enclosed a smaller spring which reduced road shock to a minimum. The torsion bars could be adjusted when the car was fully loaded by switching on a small electric motor. The overhead-valve six-cylinder engine had a bore of 85 millimeters and a stroke of 88 millimeters. Displacement was 2,996 cubic centimeters. Compression ratio was 6.4 to 1, and the engine developed 115 horsepower at 4,600 revolutions per minute. The 120-inch wheelbase sedan weighed 3,895 pounds. Top speed was 96 miles per hour.

The luxurious 300 model was available in a four-door sedan or a four-door convertible sedan. Many body colors, with matching interior styling, were produced.

For the discriminating sportsman the faster 300 S (super) model was created. Similar in appearance to the 300 model, the super was built to carry on the Mercedes-Benz tradition which had begun twenty-five years before with the 6-liter K model of 1927. The superb S and SS models, and finally the 540 K model, continued the tradition of luxurious motoring.

With but half the engine displacement, without supercharger, and weighing a ton less than its illustrious predecessor (the 5.4-liter, 180 horsepower 540 K model), the new 300 S was actually faster, more responsive, safer, and more comfortable. This magnificent, luxury sports model was the culmination of the technical developments of Mercedes-Benz automobiles over the years.

With a displacement of 2,996 cubic centimeters, the six-cylinder engine of the 300 S model had three carburetors and developed 150 horsepower. The compression ratio was 7.5 to 1. The single overhead camshaft was driven by a noiseless Duplex roller chain, which was held in constant tension by a spring at even the highest speeds. Oil and water were thermostatically controlled. The temperature of the block was regulated by a heat exchanger. The top speed was conservatively given as 110 miles per hour. The wheelbase was six inches shorter than that of the 300 model, and the car weighed 3,565 pounds. Two body styles were available: coupé and convertible coupé. A great choice of colors was offered.

Roadibility was extraordinary, and handling of the 300 S was like that of a true sports car.

Of the 153,254 passenger cars built by Daimler-Benz from 1949 until June 30, 1952, 4,432 were 300 and 300 S models.

For 1954 two new 170 models were introduced: the S-V and the S-D. As their designating letters indicated, they were developed from the former types. The four-cylinder gasoline engine of 1,767 cubic centimeters displacement developed 45 horsepower at 3,600 revolutions per minute; and the output of the diesel unit was 40 horsepower at 3,200 revolutions per minute. Springing was improved, and seating space was increased. Other features of the 170 models — of which over 200,000 units had been put into operation — were retained.

The Mercedes-Benz model 180 was a new vehicle for 1954. Its body shell was completely new, and its chassis had some unusual features. A frameless construction eliminated the accepted Mercedes-Benz tubular frame. The combined body and chassis unit was the basic structure. The entire front end, the *Fahrschemel*, consisting of the front suspension, springs, shock absorbers, steering gear with linkages, and the front support of the engine, was like a stool. This independent unit with the engine, clutch, and transmission could be removed very easily.

The rear end featured Mercedes-Benz swing axles with coil springs and double-acting hydraulic telescopic type shock absorbers. Hydraulic brakes were provided. The squared four-door sedan body retained many accepted Mercedes-Benz lines. Passenger space was increased by nearly one-fourth over that of the 170 models.

The reliable four-cylinder L-head engine, of 1,767 cubic centimeters displacement, developed 52 horsepower at 4,000 revolutions per minute. The 180 model sedan weighed 2,530 pounds, and its top speed was 78.5 miles per hour. Fuel consumption was a moderate 27 miles per gallon at cruising speed. Also available in this model was a four-cylinder diesel engine which developed 40 horsepower at 3,200 revolutions per minute. Top and cruising speed was 68 miles per hour. Fuel consumption was less than 2.5 gallons of diesel oil per 100 miles. Expertly combining Mercedes-

The 180 D sedan, 1953-1962

The sporty 190 SL roadster, 1955

The large 600 limousine, 1963

Benz quality with moderate cost (about $3,000) the 180 model definitely competed in the world automotive market.

The volume of the export business of the Daimler-Benz company increased steadily after production of passenger automobiles was resumed. In 1949, the first year of limited production, the volume was 6,000,000 marks. In 1950 it rose to 66,000,000. In 1951 exports amounted to 156,000,000 marks, and in 1952 they were 225,000,000. With production of 208,339 vehicles from the end of World War II to June 30, 1953, the Daimler-Benz A.G. again led the German automobile industry in production of quality vehicles and in exports.

Several changes in models were introduced late in 1955. The 300 S model was fitted with a 200-horsepower engine with direct fuel injection, similar to the unit in the 300 SL model, but installed vertically. A single-joint rear axle with low pivot point and Hydrovac booster brakes bettered the performance of this elegant automobile. The engine of the 300 models was improved to develop 136 horsepower, and single-joint rear axles were fitted to the models. An automatic transmission was also made available.

The new 220 convertible, accommodating four or five persons, had new lines and an improved engine which developed 92 horsepower at 4,800 revolutions per minute. Compression ratio was 7.6 to 1 and the maximum speed of the luxuriously outfitted vehicle was 96 miles per hour.

The diesel engine of the 180 D was also improved to develop 46 horsepower at 3,500 revolutions per minute. This bettered the performance of the popular and highly economical automobile of which over 30,000 units had been manufactured by the end of 1955.

In 1955 the Daimler-Benz A.G. produced 83,200 vehicles, an increase of 37.4 percent over the previous year. Production of passenger cars was 64,000 units, a 30.5 percent increase over 1954; and 29,200 commercial vehicles were built, representing an increase of 53 percent over the previous year. An almost equal percentage of both categories, 42.4 percent of all vehicles produced in 1955, was exported.

In May 1956, Daimler-Benz introduced three new models of passenger cars. The 190, an economical sedan, was powered by the four-cylinder engine of 84 horsepower. The engine-transmission unit was mounted on four points in the U-frame, resulting in greater quietness of operation. The 219 sedan had a six-cylinder engine of 92 horsepower at 4,800 revolutions per minute, with a two-barrel down draft carburetor. It was the less luxurious of the six-cylinder cars. And the 220 S replaced the 220 model of 1954. The improved six-cylinder engine now developed 112 horsepower at 5,000 revolutions per minute, giving the car a maximum speed of 100 miles per hour. Improved brakes and new interior trim made this medium priced sedan indeed a fine automobile. A convertible version was also available.

In 1958 a fuel injection system was developed for this 2.195-liter six-cylinder engine. The injection pump, with two plungers, fed fuel into the intake ducts of each of the cylinders, achieving outstanding flexibility and smooth operation. At a maximum revolution of 6,000 per minute, the engine developed 120 horsepower, allowing a top speed of 103 miles per hour for this 220 SE sedan.

Several new models of the 220 series were displayed at the Frankfurt Auto Show in 1959. Substantial improvements were made in wheel suspension and outstanding road holding and driving comfort was achieved. The new body style was governed chiefly by functional principles rather than passing fashion trends.

In February 1961, in connection with the Jubilee Year celebration, a new 220 SE coupe made its appearance. Powered by the 120-horsepower engine with fuel injection, it embodied various new design features including front disk brakes. The 300 SE, also a new creation, had the 160-horsepower engine, fully automatic gear transmission of a special design with hydraulic clutch, air suspension with automatic adjustment, disk brakes with all-wheel servo energizer, and servo-steering. And new body styles, similar to the 220 line, were given to the 190 line of cars.

In the fall of 1963 Daimler-Benz offered fourteen passenger car models. The economical 190 D, now with a smooth-running diesel engine of 60 horsepower and a cruising speed of 78 miles per hour, and available with automatic transmission, had as its companion the gasoline-powered 190 sedan. Both cars were equipped with front disk brakes. The three six-

The elegant 220 convertible, 1953

The larger 300 S convertible, 1951-1952

The elegant 300 Sc roadster of 1956

cylinder sedans — 220, 220 S, and 220 SE — were characteristically Mercedes vehicles, with modern lines, good performance, driving comfort, true road-holding properties, fine suspension, accelerating power and comfortable interior design. With the same wheelbase and body dimensions, they only differed in their performance. The 220 engine developed 105, the 220 S had 124, and the 220 SE had 134 horsepower at 5,000 revolutions per minute. The 220 SE convertible and the coupe were luxury editions of that line of production cars.

A new addition was the 230 SL. Replacing the 190 SL — and to some extent the 300 SL as well — the elegantly styled two-seater roadster, or coupe with pagoda-style roof, had a 2.3-liter fuel injection engine developing 170 horsepower at 5,600 revolutions per minute. Standard floor gear shift or automatic transmission was available. Disk brakes were provided for the front wheels. A safe, fast and dashing, also comfortable, reliable and luxurious sports car, the 230 SL proved its superb qualities when Eugen Böhringer won the tortuous Spa-Sofia-Liége Rally. It was a truly spectacular performance for driver and car on this initial test against strong international competition.

The "Grosse Mercedes," the 600 model, upheld the tradition of luxury and prestige of Mercedes-Benz. A new V-style eight-cylinder engine of 6.3 liters developing 300 horsepower powered this newest edition of the great Mercedes to a top speed of 127 miles per hour. Available in two sedan styles, with wheelbases of 126 or 153.5 inches, this fine automobile incorporated all modern design elements — fuel injection, overhead camshaft, air suspension and shock absorber adjustment, disk brakes on all wheels, automatic four-speed transmission and power steering, central vacuum locking system for the doors and luggage lid, adjustable steering wheel, and two separate heating and ventilation systems. It was a majestic car of the highest order and an honorable descendant of the distinct "Great Mercedes" cars of bygone eras.

Front axle and engine for 220 SE model

The fine 220 SE convertible, 1958

The 230 SL sports car in the coupe version

and as open roadster

Another view as coupe, 1963

These two body styles never got into production:
A 170 V study for the 220 model of 1949, and

A 320 (W 142) study for the 300 model of 1949

The Sports- and Racing-Car Program (1952-1965)

Designers of competition sports and racing cars usually begin from entirely new, untried fields when designing the prototypes. Approaching the problem from exactly the opposite, Daimler-Benz engineers had used the tested 1926 K model to develop the successful S, SS, and SSK sports models which proved themselves so sensationally superior on the racing circuits of Europe.

Once again in 1951 this time-tested procedure was followed by the designing engineers in Stuttgart. Under the guidance of Fritz Nallinger, the technical director, and Rudolf Uhlenhaut, the chief engineer, who had done so well with the Grand Prix models of the late thirties, the designers developed the silvery, swift 300 SL (super light) sports car from the regular 300 series production models.

Less than eight months after the conception of the idea, three new cars were entered in international competition, after preliminary tests on the Hockenheim track.

With a modified 300 model power plant, the six-cylinder 2,996-cubic-centimeter engine developed 173.25 horsepower at 5,200 revolutions per minute. Compression ratio was 8 to 1. Forged light metal pistons, valves in head, overhead rocker arm shaft, and self-adjusting automatic chain drive were other features. Three Solex downdraft carburetors with twin fuel pumps were used. The gear ratios were 3.16 to 1 in first gear; 1.89 to 1 in second, 1.325 to 1 in third; and 1 to 1 in fourth.

For a lower hood line, the engine was tilted 45 degrees to the left. A new sump was designed, and the inlet and exhaust manifold were modified to fit the altered position of the engine. The carburetors were mounted vertically, and the large air chamber fitted tightly against the hood cover.

The aerodynamic coupé was of the envelope body type and less than fifty inches high. The seamless body, of thin aluminum, was extremely light. The doors were of an unorthodox airplane type, consisting of the framed windows and a portion of the top, and swung upwards. This revolutionary door design made possible a lighter and also a stronger body construction. The oval grille with the large-circled three-pointed star was reminiscent of the Mercedes-Benz 1939 Grand Prix racing machines.

The light steel tube X-frame had individual front-wheel suspension with parallel arms and frictionless soft coil springs with additional rubber springs and wheel springs. The oscillating rear axle had coil springs. Hydraulic telescope type shock absorbers were used in front and rear. The large oil-pressure four-wheel brakes had two forward shoes in the front drums and one forward and one reverse shoe in the rear drums. Total brake area was 258 square inches. An additional mechanical hand brake acted on the rear wheels. Special 6.70 by 15 tires were mounted on 15-inch rims. The wheelbase of the 300 SL was 94.5 inches, and the overall length was 166 inches. The dry weight was 1,918 pounds.

Tachometer and speedometer were advantageously placed almost at the driver's eye level. The steering wheel was removable. Floor shift for the four synchronized gears was provided. The bucket-type seats were comfortable, and an air-conditioning system was installed to enhance the comfort of the driver.

For the nineteenth running of the Mille Miglia in May 1952, three 300 SL models were entered, with Caracciola, Lang and Kling driving. Caracciola had won the event in 1931, driving an SSKL model. More than a week before the race the factory team, under the direction of Neubauer, the energetic race manager, practiced diligently. The drivers went over the 973-mile route time and again, to familiarize themselves thoroughly with every characteristic of road surface and memorize turns and curves of the twisty Italian road circuit. Refueling and tire changing were indefatigably rehearsed.

The appearance of the Mercedes-Benz cars in Brescia overshadowed the activities of the other 605 entries. After some hesitation the embarrassed officials allowed the automobiles with airplane-type doors to start. But it seemed highly irregular, and their rule book made no provision for such advanced construction.

The participants started at one-minute intervals on their tortuous journey. Kling arrived in Ravenna, after driving through heavy rain, in second place. Along the Adriatic, on an extremely fast road, he took the lead and held it into Rome. However, true to the proverb, he was not first into Brescia. He had troubles and, conserving his gains wisely, placed

Early version of the 300 SL

Another view of the same version

With the doors cut into the body of the 300 SL, 1952

177

second in the race. Caracciola, driving a coupé which did not seem to be the fastest of the trio, came in fourth. Lang hit a milestone on the wet cobblestone road as he accelerated out of a sharp turn and damaged his front wheel. This mishap put him out of the race.

The Mercedes-Benz 300 SL models had done fairly well in their first participation in international competition. Plagued by minor difficulties, they had placed second and fourth against seasoned and long developed competitive machines.

At the Prize of Berne four sleek Mercedes-Benz 300 SL models started at the Bremgarten circuit with Caracciola, Lang, Kling, and Riess driving. Caracciola was the first away. On the second lap the four 300 SLs were closing ranks and were running snugly together in the lead. Then Lang passed Caracciola in the third lap, and Kling passed him during the fifth time around the curving circuit. The Ferrari, Jaguars, Lancias, and Aston Martins stayed behind. Kling took the lead in the eighth lap and kept it until the finish of the race. The four beautiful, shiny Mercedes-Benz cars rounded the circuit in record time, traveling in close formation. In the eleventh lap Lang established a new lap record of 93 miles per hour. During the thirteenth lap Caracciola's car seemed to be unsteady, and he slipped off the road at the nasty Forsthaus curve. He was hospitalized with a fractured thigh. The Mercedes-Benz cars won a triple victory in the Swiss race with Kling, Lang, and Riess finishing in that order.

The entire sporting world eyed the silvery Mercedes-Benz coupés at the important Le Mans twenty-four-hour endurance run in June 1952. One of the swift cars appeared with an air brake during the practice runs. A large flap ran the width of the roof, behind the doors. A lever brought it into action when wanted, but the air brake was not used in the race.

The four Mercedes-Benz sports cars were not among the first of the fifty-seven starters. Their drivers had to adjust their removable steering wheels when they climbed in, before starting out around the 8.6-mile circuit. Competition was keen, and the leaders set a furious pace. Records fell by the wayside as the race progressed, and many well-established makes and models found the tempo too fast to sustain. Kling's car developed light trouble when an incorrectly laid wire of his dynamo broke, and he

left the race when night closed in. After twelve hours of racing, the Mercedes-Benz cars ran in second and third places.

At the finish of the race, forty-one cars had dropped out with various troubles. The two Mercedes-Benz cars made an indelible impression upon the 400,000 enthusiastic spectators by the steady, almost monotonous regularity with which they rounded the fast circuit. The winners Lang and Riess set a new distance record, having covered 2,320.07 miles in twenty-four hours, at an average of 96.67 miles per hour.

In August, when the German Grand Prix races were held, four 300 SLs were entered in the "Grand Jubilee Prize of the Nürburg Ring." During practice some of the sports cars used superchargers, and a gear-driven, ribbed Roots blower, installed on the right side of the tilted engine; but in the race all the cars started as unblown machines. The car Kling drove had a shorter wheelbase. The four open models ran like clockwork in close order around the Eifel circuit. The eventual winner was Lang; Kling, Riess, and Helfrich followed in that order. Lang's new course record of 79.98 miles per hour was but a few miles less than the time made by the Grand Prix racing cars.

The fifth appearance of the Mercedes-Benz sports cars was at the Third Carrera Panamericana Mexico in November 1952. For three weeks prior to the 1,934-mile cross-country race, the team of Kling, Lang and the American, John Fitch, practiced diligently. The drivers and their copilots covered every mile of the route at least ten times. Nine tire-changing depots were installed along the way. This work was carefully rehearsed, because in the race no pit crews were allowed to work on the cars. It took just one minute for the two men to change three tires. Material and equipment were neatly placed for rapid, unobstructed use.

The steaming jungle atmosphere at Tuxla Gutiérrez near the Guatemalan border was a great contrast to the 10,482-foot elevation between Puebla and Mexico City, and the desertlike plains of Chihuahua and Ciudad Juárez on the United States border. The long, difficult road itself made this Mexican race one of the world's greatest road races and a greedy reaper of capable drivers and their highly tuned, expensive machines.

The 300 SL at the Swiss Grand Prix, 1952

At the "Jubilee-Prize Race" on the Nürburgring, 1952

Lang on the Nürburgring, 1952

The Mercedes-Benz team drove carefully the first day, but placed second, third and fourth at the end of the second and third days. Fitch, who drove a 300 SL roadster, was disqualified for returning to the starting line for wheel adjustments after having once left it. Kling and Lang placed first and second into Chihuahua the next day. The Ferraris, Lancias, Gordinis, and other strong contenders were left behind as the two winning Mercedes-Benz cars roared across the finish line into Juárez.

A buzzard had broken the windshield of Kling's car and slightly injured his co-driver Klenk. And the front of Lang's car was badly smashed by his encounter with a stray dog, which reduced the speed of the 300 SL considerably.

Again meticulous preparation and tireless practice, highly skillful, experienced drivers, and superior machines had paid off in a double victory over the other twenty-four entrants in the sports-car class. Genial race manager Neubauer was well satisfied with the results.

Kling's winning average speed was 102.6 miles per hour for the 1,934 miles of tortuous, grueling road. On the last 230-mile leg he averaged 135.7 miles per hour.

It was estimated that some eight million people watched while the cars sped through the greatly diversified Mexican country. Indian sheep herders in ageless, colorful dress on the hills, and peons in the fields behind their burro-pulled wooden plows, watched as the cars raced past them. Gay senoritas, men and women with proud weather-beaten, wrinkled faces, and joyful barefoot boys milled around the cars and drivers at all overnight stopping places. The ultramodern glass and steel buildings of Mexico City were a great contrast to the many ornate, historic churches and the plain adobe huts in the fields or villages. It seemed that all the two million inhabitants of the capital were on the festively decorated streets when the participating cars arrived in the metropolis. In other cities the congestion caused by the spectators taxed the abilities of the authorities to the extreme limit. Crowds gathered at many choice spots along the highway, and their interest in the race was amazing.

The new 300 SL sports cars were now well established. Their superiority was proven in their five starts against formidable opposition. The

Daimler-Benz directors, feeling that they should conserve their financial and technical resources, canceled participation in further international competition for 1953.

A new version of the Mercedes-Benz 300 SL sports car was shown to the American public in February 1954 at the Third Annual International Motor Sports Show in New York. The new car looked even more streamlined and lower than the previous model and was considerably more elegant in outward appearance and luxurious in interior styling and outfitting.

It was the first time since the days of the SS models that a Mercedes-Benz competition machine was available to the general public.

In this first production automobile featuring the revolutionary fuel injection instead of the usual-type carburetors, the Daimler-Benz engineers added another first to their long list of innovations in automobile building.

The 2,996-cubic-centimeter engine developed an amazing 240 horsepower. The crankshaft had seven unusually strong four-metal bearings and could easily withstand a continuous engine speed of 6,000 revolutions per minute.

Driven by a silent Duplex roller chain, the overhead camshaft and valve mechanism operated quietly at high speeds. The valves were extremely large, and an immense air induction system supplied sufficient air for the proper fuel and air mixture. The fuel injection system ensured a perfectly uniform mixture at the lowest as well as the highest operational speed. A thermostat and an altitude compensator at the injection pump corrected automatically the air temperature and atmospheric density, eliminating the usual frequent, troublesome carburetor adjustments. In fact, the engine power was increased by 40 horsepower over that of the former conventional multiple carburetor installation.

The four-speed transmission was of the controlled synchromesh type. An oil-pressure pump supplied lubrication. All wheels had independent suspension. The front axle had wishbone arms, and the rear axles featured friction-free coil springs and large shock absorbers. The large aluminum brake drums quickly conducted the heat to the outside of the drum. Required pressure was reduced by a special booster which lessened the

Start of the 24 hours at Le Mans, 1952

Through the Esses at Le Mans, 1952

Schock at the Sestriere Rallye, 1956

necessary physical braking effort. The brake shoes were automatically adjusted.

The comfortable bucket-type seats were fully adjustable. The airplane-type doors, consisting of portions of the roof, window, and body side panel, opened upward. The steering wheel was demountable. Both front fenders were visible from the driver's position. The narrow corner posts and one-piece curved windshield made for excellent visibility. To ensure passenger comfort and shut out engine heat from the passenger compartment, a double partition was provided. Fresh air entered this space through a grille in front of the windshield and left through larger grille openings on the sides. Fresh air was supplied to the passenger compartment by air ducts. The side windows had revolving-type panes for additional ventilation. An air scoop in the roof drew out the used air.

The improved 300 SL coupé, built on a 94.5-inch wheelbase and weighing but 2,244 pounds, had a top speed of 166 miles per hour. The price was $7,463 in New York.

The new 190 SL sports roadster was a smaller version of the luxurious 300 SL. The front appearance and side body lines were similar to those of the more powerful coupé. The car was basically like the 180 model, utilizing a combination chassis and body construction. For participation in competitive events, the black cloth folding top and one-piece curved windshield could easily be removed. The regular doors could also be replaced with lighter cut-out doors which gave a racier look and reduced the weight considerably below the 2,380 pounds of the fully equipped model.

A steering-column gear-shift lever operated the four-forward-speed synchronized gear box. The four available speed ratios made for excellent acceleration, desired especially in competition. The real leather bucket-type seats added greatly to the comfort and appearance of the silvery sports car.

The four-cylinder engine had a bore of 85 millimeters and a stroke of 83.6 millimeters and displaced 1,897 cubic centimeters. Compression ratio was 8.5 to 1. The overhead camshaft engine, equipped with two horizontal carburetors, developed 125 horsepower at 6,000 revolutions per minute. The 94-inch wheelbase sports car had a top speed of 120 miles per hour. Outfittings and workmanship were in the finest Mercedes-Benz tradition. The instruments were grouped on the uncluttered panel in front of the driver for easy vision. The two-spoke plastic steering wheel had a horn rim combined with automatic direction indicators.

In the 190 SL Daimler-Benz engineers and designers had found a satisfactory answer to the problem of combining comfortable touring-car characteristics with the superior road-holding qualities expected of a sports car. It seemed to be an ideal automobile for daily transportation as well as occasional competition. The 190 SL sold for $4,126 in New York.

For the 1954 Grand Prix season, Daimler-Benz directors announced participation in the twenty-four-hour Le Mans Endurance Trial, the Italian Mille Miglia, and the Carrera Panamericana Mexico with their new 300 SLR models. As the last letter indicates (R for racing), this model was especially designed for factory participation in international competition. The new 3-liter vehicle had a new-type swing axle. The gearbox and differential housing were in one unit. The wire-spoke wheels allowed better brake cooling than the former perforated disk type. The new brakes were on the inside — a design which had been used successfully in the drastically advanced aerodynamic rear-engined Benz racer of 1922. The extra fifth gear on this model indicated that the top speed of the 300 SLR was nearly 190 miles per hour.

But the announced sports-car participation was canceled, and the new Mercedes-Benz Grand Prix formula I racing cars made their sudden and unheralded appearance in 1954 on the international circuits instead. The race department of the Daimler-Benz company decided to consolidate its efforts and concentrate on the Grand Prix races, rather than partake in both types of events.

Three secretly developed 2.5-liter Mercedes-Benz racing cars started on July 4 at Rheims for the running of the forty-first French Grand Prix. During practice the Argentine master driver Juan Manuel Fangio, who had been world champion in 1951, lapped the 5.18-mile, extremely fast

The 300 SLR for the Mille Miglia

The 300 SLR for a single driver

With the air brake installed

circuit in an amazing performance at more than the magic 200 kilometers (more than 124 miles) per hour. Next to him, in the first starting row, was Karl Kling; and Hans Herrmann started in the third row.

As the starting tricolor fell, the two leading silvery Mercedes-Benz racers sped away with tremendous acceleration, ahead of the field of twenty-one fast Ferrari, Maserati, and Gordini racers. In the very first lap the fastest Maserati, driven by Ascari, was forced to retire. In the second, Gonzales pushed his Ferrari briefly into second place, but soon fell behind the Mercedes-Benz driven by Kling. Herrmann drove his car hard, set a new lap record for the course, and was in third place after the twelfth lap. The Ferrari contingent with such outstanding drivers as Gonzales, Hawthorn, Trintignant, and Manzon, and the Maserati works cars with Filloresi, Marimon, Bira, and Ascari, who eventually used up several cars, did their excellent best to fight off the Mercedes-Benz threat, but to no avail.

When the halfway mark was reached, two Mercedes-Benz racers were well ahead of the remaining eight cars. The others had been unable to stand up to the terrific speed set by the leaders. The Mercedes-Benz of Herrmann had retired in the seventeenth lap. The average speed was over 118 miles per hour, but now the leading cars, changing positions frequently, slowed the brutal pace somewhat.

Fangio crossed the finish line first, with Kling a few feet behind. Manzon, driving a Ferrari, placed third. The average speed of the winning Mercedes-Benz car was 115.98 miles per hour for the 307-mile distance. In 1938 von Brauchitsch had driven his winning 485-horsepower supercharged, 3-liter Mercedes-Benz an average of 101.3 miles per hour over a similar distance.

The first showing of the new, streamlined Mercedes-Benz formula I racing cars resulted in an astoundingly impressive victory over the well proven, successful Italian Grand Prix machines. It was reminiscent of the French Grand Prix of 1914 at Lyons, when the new Mercedes racers swept all opposition aside and won the first three places decisively. Or of the 1939 Tripoli when the 1.5-liter Mercedes-Benz racing cars bested the large field of strong opposition. The impossible had been done at

that time by Daimler-Benz just as it was achieved again now, fifteen years later.

The second appearance of the Mercedes-Benz racers was at the British Grand Prix, run on the slow 2.93-mile Silverstone airport course. But their monoposto bodies were not ready for the cars. Rather than cancel their anxiously awaited appearance in the British Isles, the Mercedes-Benz racers started in their fully streamlined version, most unsuitable for the short circuit, which was entirely devoid of fast straightaways. Fangio started in the pole position, having incredibly made the fastest practice lap at an average of 100.35 miles per hour, the fastest time ever recorded at Silverstone. Kling was in the second row. Among the other twenty-eight starters were Ferrari, Maserati, and Gordini racing cars.

Until the fifty-fifth lap, the Mercedes-Benz of Fangio was in second place, although both front fenders were badly crumpled by numerous encounters with haybales and pylons. Even an experienced Grand Prix driver has to see his front wheels when rounding the tricky turns of the course. With considerably impaired visibility, Fangio was unable to take full advantage of the course and skirt the corners by a razor's-edge width.

After ninety laps, the end of the 274-mile race, Gonzales and Hawthorn, driving Ferrari cars, were first and second; and Marimon was third, driving a Maserati. Fangio placed fourth, and Kling seventh. The winner's average speed was 89.69 miles per hour.

When the European Grand Prix was held on the mountainous Nürburg Ring in Germany, the new-type bodies for three of the four Mercedes-Benz racers entered were ready. Ferrari and Maserati cars were well represented among the nineteen starters. Fangio had again made the fastest practice time. He bettered the lap record made by Lang in a supercharged 3-liter Mercedes-Benz. This remarkable achievement suggested a tremendous usability of available engine power, immensely improved suspension, brakes, and other mechanical parts of the car, as well as excellent driving ability.

After five laps around the twisty 14.17-mile Eifel Mountain circuit, the three Mercedes-Benz cars of Fangio, Lang, and Kling were in the lead,

The 2.5-liter Formula I car in monoposto form

The eight-cylinder engine of the Grand Prix car

The enclosed body version of the Formula I car

breaking lap records repeatedly as they roared around the 174 curves and turns of the punishing course. Herrmann, who drove the streamlined Rheims-type Mercedes-Benz, went out of the race during the seventh lap.

It looked as if the Mercedes-Benz cars would make the most of their opportunities on their home course. The cars, well prepared by the Daimler-Benz race department in Stuttgart, directed advantageously by the able race manager Alfred Neubauer, and expertly driven by the masters Juan Manuel Fangio, Hermann Lang, and Karl Kling, appeared invincible.

At the halfway mark the average speed was 84.2 miles per hour. Then Kling made the fastest lap of the race at 85.75 miles per hour, and Lang spun his car at a tricky turn and was unable to start it again. When Kling was forced to make an unscheduled pit stop in the nineteenth lap, the Ferraris of Hawthorn and Trintignant passed him. What had looked like another certain one, two, three win for Mercedes-Benz now became but a single victory. Fangio won the European Grand Prix at the Nürburg Ring at an average speed of 82.77 miles per hour for the 312 miles. Kling placed fourth.

The Swiss Grand Prix was run on the Bremgarten circuit near Berne. Three of the open Nürburg-type Mercedes-Benz cars with Fangio, Kling, and Herrmann started. Fangio led the field of fifteen cars after the first lap. At the halfway mark the Mercedes-Benz racers were in first, fourth, and fifth places. Fangio drove the fastest lap of the race with an average of 101.9 miles per hour. Kling retired his car at the thirty-ninth lap.

Fangio won, driving his Mercedes-Benz at an average speed of 99.2 miles per hour for the 288 miles. Gonzales, driving a Ferrari, placed second; and Herrmann in his Mercedes-Benz placed third. With this victory, the thirty-eight-year-old Juan Manuel Fangio of Buenos Aires secured the 1954 World Champion automobile racing title.

In the Italian Grand Prix at the fast Autodrome track at Monza, three Mercedes-Benz racers participated against seventeen other Grand Prix cars. Two Rheims-type, enclosed racing cars were driven by Fangio and Kling, while Herrmann drove an open Nürburg-type model. By virtue of the fastest practice time, Fangio had the pole position. Kling started in the second row, and Herrmann in the third. Fangio was first away, with Kling close behind him.

The lead changed several times during the fast race. Kling retired his Mercedes-Benz during the thirty-seventh lap. Fangio won the race, driving his Mercedes-Benz at an average speed of 111.9 miles per hour for the eighty-lap, 313-mile event. Hawthorn and Maglioli, driving Ferraris, placed second and third, respectively. Herrmann in his unstreamlined Mercedes-Benz finished fourth.

The Berlin Grand Prix was run on the extremely fast Avus track with its steeply banked high-speed turns. The only other works team entered was that of the French Gordini, although Ferrari and Maserati cars were among the ten starters.

The fully streamlined Mercedes-Benz racers finished in the first three places, after traveling well in the lead, and with great regularity, around the course for sixty laps. Kling won with an average speed of 133 miles per hour for the 312-mile distance. Fangio placed half a second behind the winner, and Herrmann was third.

Three Nürburg-type Mercedes-Benz cars participated in the Spanish Grand Prix in the 3.93-mile Pedralbes circuit at Barcelona. Fangio again started in the first row; but Ascari, driving a new Lancia, had made the fastest practice time by one second. In the front row were also a Ferrari and a Maserati. The Mercedes-Benz of Herrmann was in the third row, that of Kling in the fourth. There were twenty-one cars.

As early as the second lap one of the new Lancia cars retired. In the next lap a Ferrari gave up. The fast Lancia of Ascari quit after nine laps. The fast pace took its early toll.

At the halfway mark, Hawthorn, driving a Squalo Ferrari, was in the lead with Fangio in second place. When a nasty whirlwind blew papers and debris onto the racing cars and clogged their cooling systems, several retired promptly because of overheating.

Herrmann went out on the fiftieth lap. Hawthorn won the eighty-lap race at an average speed of 97.99 miles per hour for the 314 miles. Musso, driving a Maserati, placed second, and Fangio third. Kling placed fifth.

Fangio at the Swiss Grand Prix, 1954

Moss at the Belgian Grand Prix, 1955

Fangio, winner of the Belgian Grand Prix, 1955

Because the newly adopted Grand Prix Formula I limited supercharged engines to 0.75-liter displacement, the Daimler-Benz engineers decided to abandon their tradition and construct an unsupercharged engine of 2.5-liter capacity for their racing cars.

The remarkably successful Mercedes-Benz racer was powered by a straight eight-cylinder engine, placed at an angle to achieve a lower frontal area. The bore was 76 millimeters, and the stroke 68.8 millimeters (2.99 by 2.71 inches), giving it a total displacement of 2,496 cubic centimeters. Compression ratio was believed to be around 13 to 1, and output to be around 280 brake horsepower.

The engine had a central crankshaft drive which provided a power take-off from the center of the eight-cylinder engine. This minimized torsional vibration greatly and placed the strain of only four cylinders upon the crankshaft. The direct Mercedes-Benz fuel injection, with pump and nozzles of Bosch manufacture, was designed especially for racing purposes and took more than a year to develop. It ensured a better mixture distribution between the cylinders at all speeds and improved low-speed performance considerably. The throttling effect of a normal carburetor venturi was eliminated by the direct fuel injection, thus increasing the peak engine performance. The improved distribution of the mixture made also for more economy in fuel, because the fuel quantity injected into each cylinder was exactly the amount used. A large fuel tank was placed behind and to the left side of the driver. Refueling stops for races of the regular Grand Prix distances of 500 kilometers (310.8 miles) were completely eliminated.

The clutch was a single dry plate and the five-speed transmission was mounted directly on the rear axle, behind the wheels. Independent wheel suspension was used with a genuine swing axle with lowered pivot point in the rear. In this type the joint center of motion of the swing arms lay in the middle of the vehicle below the rear axle housing. The swing arms were longer, and the center of motion was lower, giving greatly improved driving qualities over the former double-joint axle.

Torsion bars were provided. The huge four-wheel brakes, with light metal alloy brake drums, were turbo-cooled and were mounted inside. Fresh air, for the comfort of the driver and to cool the rear brakes, entered through the grilled opening in the cowl in front of the windshield. Sixteen-inch wire-spoke wheels were used with tires of various dimensions, best suited to the different racing circuits; and the tires were improved so that, under ordinary racing conditions, the entire Grand Prix distance could be traveled without a change.

Two body styles were available in the Mercedes-Benz 2.5-liter Formula I racing car. The fully enclosed and highly streamlined Rheims type for long and fast courses, and the open monoposto Nürburg style for short and twisty circuits where visibility of front wheels and maximum maneuverability of the powerful racing machines were of prime consideration.

The formidable Mercedes-Benz Grand Prix racing cars had won five of the seven events in which they were entered in 1954. The long dominant, red Italian racing cars were now decisively beaten on the Grand Prix circuits of Europe by the Mercedes-Benz silver arrows. The winning combination of extensive Daimler-Benz engineering experience and superb workmanship, indefatigable race preparation and excellent team management, and faultless championship driving was again nearly impossible to beat. It seemed as if another era, similar to that of twenty years before, might once again be repeated.

The 190 SL touring sports car became available as a coupe with a removable hard top, fitted at six points and easily detachable. Production of the fast 300 SL sports car at the Sindelfingen plant passed 1,000 units early in December 1955. Over 93 percent of those cars were exported, mainly to the United States.

It seemed impossible to exceed the excellent results of their first Grand Prix season after World War II, but the Daimler-Benz company did just that. In January 1955, the Argentine Grand Prix was run on the 2.4-mile Buenos Aires autodrome. In the first starting row were four makes of cars — Ferrari, Mercedes-Benz (with Fangio), Lancia and Maserati. Kling, Moss and Herrmann, the other Mercedes-Benz drivers, were behind. Starting positions for the twenty-one participants were based on times made in a five-lap practice on the previous day.

Moss wins the British Grand Prix at Aintree, 1954

The Rheims-type Formula I car in action

The midsummer heat rose to 104 degrees Fahrenheit in the shade, of which there was none on the scorching track. Cars dropped out and drivers came into the pits for relief. Another car skidded and collided with Kling's Mercedes-Benz, putting it out of the race. Moss ran out of fuel on the track, and an eager first-aid crew, thinking that he had suffered a heat stroke as several drivers had, rushed the protesting Moss to a hospital where his protestations were finally properly understood. He was then speedily returned to the race course with equal rapidity. Herrmann was a victim of the heat, and Kling took over his car. Then Moss relieved him. The car placed fourth. Fangio proved his championship stamina by driving the entire three hours with but brief pit stops and winning two minutes ahead of the Farina-Gonzales-driven Ferrari.

The European Grand Prix was driven through the streets of gay and colorful Monaco and proved a most unpredictable race. Fangio made the best time during practice. Herrmann crashed and André Simon replaced him for the race. Two cars with a shorter wheelbase had been built for this race; the brakes were mounted outboard. The Mercedes-Benz cars of Fangio and Moss, with the Lancia of Ascari between them, started in the first row. By the fifth lap Fangio was closely followed by Moss, and this team seemed again in excellent form. Simon dropped out. Fangio made the fastest lap time, breaking the record set in 1937 by Caracciola. Then, at the fiftieth lap, Fangio dropped out with differential trouble. Ascari, trying to catch the now leading Moss, plunged with his Lancia into the bay and was quickly rescued from fifteen feet of water. Moss' car suffered engine trouble in the eightieth lap, causing Trintignant to win the race. It was a black day for Mercedes-Benz cars at Monte Carlo.

The Belgian Grand Prix was a very different race from the previous event. Fangio took the lead at once, followed closely by Moss. Kling drove in fourth place, but was forced out by a leaking oil line. The performance of the two leaders Fangio and Moss, and their well running Mercedes-Benz cars, set a pattern which was repeated with almost monotonous regularity in subsequent Grand Prix events. Soon it became evident that, barring trouble, the order at the end of the race would be the same. Fangio won the thirty-six-lap event and drove the fastest lap, setting a new record; Moss placed second, making it a double victory for the silver cars.

Three Mercedes-Benz cars, with Fangio, Moss and Kling, stood in the front row at the start of the Dutch Grand Prix. Fangio took the lead and never relinquished it. Moss soon passed the Maserati of Musso and followed, shadow-like, the excellent Fangio for most of the hundred laps. While driving in fifth place, Kling spun out at the Waldecke on the twenty-second lap and was unable to get his car out of the sand onto the track. Fangio won, with Moss close behind.

The British Grand Prix was run on a three-mile Aintree circuit instead of the Silverstone airport course. The competitors included the factory teams with four Mercedes-Benz cars, four Maserati, three Ferrari, three Gordini, two Vanwall, three Connaught, and one Cooper; three Maserati were privately owned. The Mercedes-Benz of Moss and Fangio and Behra's Maserati were in the first starting row. The Mercedes-Benz of Kling and Taruffi were behind. Fangio took the lead with Moss close behind, but Behra placed his car between them as they roared past the starting line after the initial lap. Moss passed Fangio in the third lap and kept the lead for fourteen laps, when the world champion took it again. Soon the terrific pace took its expected toll. Among others, Behra was also forced to quit. In the twenty-sixth lap Moss regained the lead and kept it to the finish. He drove the fastest lap at 89.8 miles per hour and won the race, becoming the first Englishman to win the British Grand Prix. Fangio placed second, Kling third, and Taruffi fourth. It was an overwhelming Mercedes-Benz victory and eradicated the decisive defeat of the previous year. Of the twenty-four starting cars, nine finished the race.

The Monza track had been rebuilt with a loop within a loop to allow even faster speeds and afford maximum visibility for the spectators. The extremely rough new speedway section caused great concern to the practicing participants and the Lancia cars were not allowed to start because of unsolvable difficulties with their tires; they came off during high speeds. Fangio and Moss, driving the fully streamlined Mercedes-Benz cars, and Kling in an open, shorter wheelbase car, stood in the first row of the starting lineup. Taruffi, also driving an open car, was in the rear. The average speed of the first lap, made by Fangio, was 124 miles per hour, from a standing start. For the three-mile speedway section he averaged 134 miles per hour; and after twenty laps his average was 129 miles per hour.

Moss and Jenkinson, winners of the Mille Miglia, 1955

Fangio congratulates Moss on the British Grand Prix victory, 1954

Böhringer, winner of the Liege-Sofia-Liege Rallye, 1963

Rosquist at the Monte Carlo Rallye, 1963

After but two complete laps, all four Mercedes-Benz cars were well in the lead, only a second separating each car. The windshield of Moss' car was shattered by a flying stone, and he stopped at the pits to have it replaced in the nineteenth lap. Having thus lost over one and a half minutes, he tried to catch the leaders, and made the fastest lap of the race, but seven laps later his car failed him. Kling was forced to retire at the thirty-third lap. The new speedway and road circuit was probably the fastest in the world, but the cars took a terrific punishment. Of the twenty-two starters, only nine finished the race. Fangio won the Grand Prix at an average of 128.42 miles per hour and the world's championship with forty-one points. Taruffi was less than a second behind the new 1955 champion.

The Buenos Aires Grand Prix, run in two heats of 175 miles each, was held two weeks after the Argentine event. The four Mercedes-Benz cars competing in this *formula libre* race were fitted with the 3-liter engines which were to be used later in the 300 SLR sports racing cars. Farina, driving a Ferrari, won the first heat with the Mercedes-Benz cars of Fangio, Moss and Kling following in that order. In the second heat Moss finished first, ahead of Fangio, Trintignant (Ferrari), and Kling. The final results placed the Mercedes-Benz cars of Fangio first at 75.06 miles per hour average, Moss second, and Kling in third place.

The 3-liter engines of the Mercedes-Benz 300 SLR (super-light-racing) cars were based on those of the Grand Prix model W196 which the cars closely resembled in outward appearance. The tilted straight eight-cylinder engine of 78-millimeter (3-1/16 inch) bore and stroke had direct fuel injection and developed 300 brake horsepower at 7,500 revolutions per minute on regular 80 octane gasoline. The tubular steel frame weighed only 132 pounds, and the dry weight of the sports racing car was about 1,785 pounds. Rear-mounted five-speed transmission and independent four-wheel suspension were provided.

The Mille Miglia was the first test for the complete Mercedes-Benz 300 SLR cars, which carried two spare tires and had special fuel tanks to hold 260 liters, necessitating but two stops for fuel and tires. After painstaking preparation and tenaciously determined training, which began in February for the May race, to become familiar with the 922-mile road,

four Mercedes-Benz cars started at Brescia. Unfortunately, they drew the first starting positions in their class, allowing their following competitors to know their elapsed times at every check point.

The larger Ferrari cars took the lead, and Taruffi was first at Pescara. At Firenge, however, the three Mercedes-Benz cars were in the lead. Moss and his observer Jenkinson arrived first in Rome and, contrary to the popular proverb, reached their goal before all others. Moss became the first Britisher to win this Italian race, and bettered the record by almost ten miles per hour. His speed of 97.93 miles per hour was also an indication of the tremendous progress in Daimler-Benz machines over the twenty-four years when Caracciola won the event at 62.72 miles per hour. Fangio, who drove alone, placed second, although his car did not always operate at top efficiency. Kling crashed outside Rome, breaking some ribs and damaging his car, and Herrmann punctured his fuel tank while climbing the Futa Pass.

In the production-sports-car category, Mercedes-Benz 300 SL cars took the first three places, driven by Fitch, Gendebien, and Casella. Fitch, incidentally, was fifth over all, a spectacular performance of the tall American driver. In the special diesel class, three Mercedes-Benz 180 D models won the first three places, the winner at over 60 miles per hour.

At the Eifel Race on the Nürburg Ring, the Mercedes-Benz sports racing cars beat all existing records. Moss bettered the lap record established by Lang in 1952, and drove the fastest lap of the race. Fangio won the 142-mile event at 80.98 miles per hour, and Moss was close behind in second place. Kling's car developed trouble in the last lap, placing fourth.

At the Le Mans endurance event, three teams of Mercedes-Benz drivers started. The cars were equipped with a flap-type air brake and had fifty-gallon fuel tanks. After about two and a half hours of racing, a series of situations which would probably never occur again in a similar sequence set off a spectacularly disastrous accident involving the car of Pierre Levegh, killing him and some eighty spectators. As an expression of sympathy for the victims of the catastrophe, the Daimler-Benz company decided to withdraw their cars from the race. After nine hours and forty minutes of racing, the Fangio-Moss car led the race by two laps, and the Kling-Simon car was in third place.

On the starting ramp at the Mille Miglia, 1955

Kling at the Swedish Grand Prix for sports cars, 1955

The 230 SL of Böhringer at the Liege-Sofia-Liege Rallye, 1963

The Swedish Grand Prix was run on the 4.06-mile Kristianstad circuit with Ferrari, Maserati, Jaguar, Aston Martin and Mercedes-Benz cars participating. The two Mercedes-Benz cars of Fangio and Moss took the lead and maintained it to the end of the 129.9-mile race. Both made the fastest time during the event. Famgio won at 100.43 miles per hour. Kling won the production-sports-car race of sixteen laps at 89.48 miles per hour, driving a 300 SL model. Lundgreen placed second, and Persson third, both driving 300 SL cars.

Fifty-five contestants were lined up at the 7.43-mile Dundrod circuit for the Ulster Tourist Trophy. The Ferrari, Maserati and Jaguar factories were also represented at this important 625-mile event. Stirling Moss was first away, and held the lead until the twenty-eighth lap, when a burst tire, which damaged the body of his 300 SLR, robbed him of this position. He drove the car about three miles on the rim to the pits at an only slightly reduced speed. After two minutes of feverish repair work by the mechanics, John Fitch took over. Hawthorn, driving a Jaguar-D model, was now in the lead. Seven laps later Moss took over again. When rain began to fall, it became increasingly evident that the Mercedes-Benz cars were greatly superior in road-handling ability than their competitors; all other cars slowed down while the 300 SLRs kept their pace. By the sixtieth lap Moss had regained the lead through his spectacular driving in the downpour, and twenty laps later he was actually three minutes ahead of Hawthorn's car when the Jaguar developed trouble and his only challenging adversary was forced out of the race. Moss-Fitch won the event at a speed of 88.32 miles per hour. Fangio-Kling placed second and Count Berghe von Trips-Simon third, making it another amazing triple victory for the Mercedes-Benz 300 SLR cars.

The Targa Florio was to be the decisive event for the world's championship for racing sports cars. Ferrari led with nineteen points, while Mercedes-Benz and Jaguar each had sixteen points. Eight points were awarded to the winner, six for second, four for third, three for fourth, two for fifth, and one point for sixth place. Thus, Mercedes-Benz cars had to win the first and second place of the Targa Florio to beat Ferrari. The winner of this difficult Sicilian mountain race then would capture the championship. Mercedes-Benz drivers practiced diligently for three weeks, trying

to familiarize themselves with the tortuous 45-mile road circuit. No driver was allowed to drive more than five continuous laps. Three teams were entered to drive the 300 SLRs — Moss and his countryman Peter Collins, Fangio and Kling, and Desmond Titterington with Fitch. Ferrari was well represented, but Jaguar did not compete.

Moss was off on a rapid pace, lapping at over 62 miles per hour, safely ahead of the pursuing Castellotti and his 3.5-liter Ferrari, when his Mercedes-Benz spun off the road. With the willing assistance of eager spectators he got his car back on the road and roared off with the damaged speedster in fourth place. Collins took over and drove excellently, trying to regain the lead, but he also went off the road, then gained third place. Meanwhile, Fangio had passed the Ferrari and, leading the race, turned his car over to Kling. Titterington-Fitch were in fourth place. Kling was able to brake properly when a car, standing across the road, suddenly blocked his passage. Collins, who had gained the lead by his spectacular driving, turned the car over to Moss. Kling came into the pits for fuel and a tire change, but the filler cap stuck and two valuable minutes were lost. Castellotti went past, in second place. Fangio took over in the realization that the second place was necessary to win the championship. In the eleventh lap he passed the Ferrari, and Castellotti then had to change tires. Moss-Collins won at 59.8 miles per hour; Fangio-Kling placed second, and Titterington-Fitch placed fourth. Mercedes-Benz won the championship with twenty-four points, one more than Ferrari.

When the German long-distance champion Werner Engel of Hamburg won the European touring-car championship for Mercedes-Benz by his victories and positions in various rallies, he added the third important title to the other two for the Untertürkheim company. It was the first time that any manufacturer had ever won three such outstanding honors in one year, attesting to the high standards of men and machines. Engel had participated successfully as over-all winner, driving a 220 model, in the Tulip Rally and the ADAC Rally at the Nürburg Ring and, driving the 300 SL, he placed third at the Wiesbaden Rally, was over-all winner of the Adria Rally and placed fourth in the Liége-Rome-Liége Rally. Some other important victories with the 300 SLs, not previously mentioned,

Böhringer at the Monte Carlo Rallye, driving a 220 SE, 1963

Rosquist at the six-hour race at the Nürburgring, 1963

Böhringer at the Deutschland Rallye, 1963

were achieved in Europe by private entries during 1955. Tak-Niemöller won the Tulip Rally; Gendebien was first in the Gold Cup of the Dolomites; Gendebien-Stasse won the Liége-Rome-Liége Rally; and Gendebien, with Thirion, won the Stella Alpina.

With the three 1955 achievements, the world's championship for Grand Prix racing cars, the international sports-car championship, and the European touring-car championship — perhaps suggesting a symbolism in the three-pointed Mercedes star — the Daimler-Benz company decided to retire from the active racing scene. The two-year postwar racing activities were a glorious chapter in the history of the work pioneered so many years ago by Gottlieb Daimler and Karl Benz.

The sports department competed in several rallies, using factory prepared production cars. In 1959 Karl Kling drove a 190 D to victory in the great 8,727-mile African Rally from Algiers to Cape Town, averaging 50.5 miles per hour across the vast Dark Continent's deserts, steppes and mountains. And the following year a 219 won the Coronation Safari, a speedy 3,200-mile journey across the wild territory of Uganda, Kenya and Tanganyika.

Participation in rallies was expanded and the selected drivers had excellent success in some of the most hotly contested and exceedingly difficult events. In 1960, Walter Schock won the Monte Carlo Rally, driving a 220 SE with two similar entries following. This triple triumph inaugurated a series of rally victories which resulted in winning the European Rally championship.

The 1961 African Rally, shortened to 7,200 miles, brought a double victory to 220 SE sedans, led by Kling. A third potential winner remained stuck in quicksand on the last lap. And for the third time, the East Africa Rally was won by a 220 SE. The Argentine Grand Prix, a tough 2,800-mile cross country race, resulted in a double Mercedes victory for Schock and Hans Herrmann.

In 1962, Eugen Böhringer, driving a 300 SE, won the Monte Carlo Rally, the Acropolis Rally, the Poland Rally, the Liége-Sofia-Liége Rally, and the German Rally, to become European champion. The team of Ewy Rosqvist and Ursula Wirth (220 SE) won the Argentine Rally. During the year Daimler-Benz drivers won 54 first prizes, 38 second prizes, and 34 third prizes in their class in international events.

Böhringer won the 1963 Acropolis Rally, the German Rally, and driving the new 230 SL at the Liége-Sofia-Liége Rally was again victorious. The Argentine race brought triple honors to Mercedes drivers Böhringher, Glemser and Rosqvist, and Glemser won the Poland Rally. Again, Böhringer became European Rally champion.

During the 1964 season the Mercedes-Benz rally team won five overall victories and thirteen first prizes in their class in the fourteen events entered. The Acropolis Rally was won by three-time winner Böhringer. The Grand Prix for touring cars at the Nürburg Ring was won by Böhringer-Glemser, but the Francorchamps 24-hour race was a great disappointment to that fine team. They were forced to quit because of brake trouble after leading, three laps ahead, for 23½ hours. For one lap Böhringer actually averaged 110.81 miles per hour. The Belgians Crevits-Gosselin (300 SE) won the fast event at an average of 103.68 miles per hour to startle enthusiasts and confound experts. The tough six-stage Argentine race found four 300 SEs entered to repeat the earlier victories, an ambitious assignment indeed. For the fourth consecutive time Mercedes won the race, this time with Böhringer-Kaiser, Glemser-Braungart, Rosqvist-Falk. The Herrmann-Schiek team held third place throughout the distance, but engine trouble slowed them so that they arrived at the finish line 27 seconds too late to be counted. Before going home to Stuttgart, Böhringer stopped at Hong Kong to win the Grand Prix of Macao, establishing a new record. It had again been a good season for Mercedes-Benz.

Döhringer at the start of the Acropolis Rallye, 1963

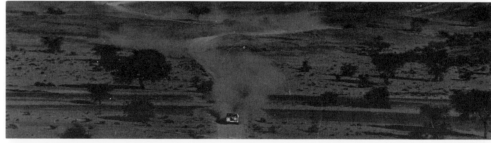

Kling (220 SE) in the Tamanrasset-El Golea desert at the Africa Rallye, 1961

At the Argentine Rallye start at 2 a.m., 1964

Fangio, Kling, and Herrmann at the Avus race, 1954

Fangio leading Moss at the Dutch Grand Prix, 1955

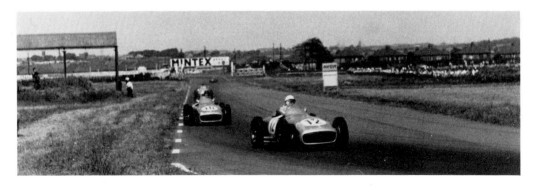

Moss leading Fangio at the British Grand Prix, 1955

The winning engineering combination: Uhlenhaut, Nallinger, and Scherenberg

Victory celebration after a successful season, 1955

Production Models (1966-1973)

Four entirely new models of passenger cars were introduced at the Frankfurt Automobile Show in 1965. This gave the company a total of seventeen models, ranging from the 200 D sedan to the 600 limousine. And all of the new models had modified body lines. Several inches of inside width were gained, and the small rear fins were gone. The new four-cylinder engines had five-bearing crankshafts and the new six-cylinder engines had seven main bearings.

The previous models were altered. The 190 became the 200 sedan, the former engine having been increased to 1,988 cubic centimeters displacement, and the power output from 90 to 105 horsepower at 5,400 revolutions per minute. The diesel had already been that size, but was now called properly the 200 D instead, and its speed boosted to 81 miles per hour from the former 78. Automatic transmission was also available. The 230 sedan, which replaced the 220 S, had a single carburetor six-cylinder engine of 2,306 cubic centimeters and 118 horsepower at 5,400 revolutions per minute while the two-carburetor engine of the 230 S developed 135 horsepower at 5,600 revolutions per minute.

The engine for the entirely new 250 series was a redesigned 2.3-liter using the same bore but an increased stroke, for a displacement of 2,496 cubic centimeters. The 250 S engine with two twin-choke carburetors had 146 horsepower at 5,600 revolutions per minute, and the 250 SE, with individual port fuel injection, developed 170 horsepower at 5,600 revolutions per minute. The 250 sedan line had disc brakes installed on all wheels.

The 300 SE and 300 SEL sedans had the former 3-liter engines developing 195 horsepower at 5,500 revolutions per minute, but with improved and restyled bodies. The more luxurious coupe and convertible were now available with three engine sizes as 220 SE, 250 SE, and 300 SE. The 230 SL and the 600 models remained unchanged. But early in 1967 the 230 SL was offered as 250 SL and equipped with the new 250 engine. Rather than increase the maximum power, the torque was increased by about 10 percent throughout the entire speed range. It was 174 pounds-feet at 4,500 revolutions per minute, as to 159 at 4,500 formerly, and made an appreciable difference in the performance of the car, although

the weight was 2,998 pounds now. The price of the 250 SL was $6,568 for the roadster against $6,343 for the 230 SL before.

For 1968 the "New Generation" models, first shown at the Brussels Auto Show, again underwent a change. The 200 D, 220 D, 200, 220, 230, and 250 received new bodies, quite similar to those of the 250 line of 1965. The new four-cylinder diesel engines now developed 60 horsepower for the 200 D and 65 for the 220 D. The gasoline four-cylinder 2-liter engine for the 200 sedan developed 105 horsepower, and the 2.2-liter for the 220, 116 horsepower. The improved six-cylinder 2.3-liter engine for the 230 gave 135 horsepower at 5,600 revolutions per minute, and the new six-cylinder engine for the 250 had 146 horsepower at 5,500 revolutions per minute.

All of the new models had fourteen-inch wheels with disc brakes fitted, and a new suspension geometry. The new 280 line consisted of the 280 S (two carburetors, 157 horsepower at 5,400 revolutions per minute), 280 SE and 280 SEL (fuel injection, 180 horsepower at 5,700 revolutions per minute), 300 SE and 300 SEL (fuel injection, 2.8-liter engine, 195 horsepower at 5,900 revolutions per minute). The 280 SL — still in the same body style as before — also had the fuel-injected six-cylinder engine of 180 horsepower. The 600 sedans remained unchanged. Prices were $4,360 for the 220 sedan and $5,060 for the 250 sedan.

The 280 SL showed, of course, considerable improvement in performance over the former 250 SL. With the 180-horsepower engine and weight of 3,120 pounds, this sports car reached 0 to 60 miles per hour in 9.9 seconds (10.3 with automatic transmission). Its maximum speed was 124 miles per hour. The list price was $6,731.

When in June 1968 the 300 SEL 6.3 sedan was introduced — appropriately at the Laguna Seca race course — the car immediately received high praise. Rudolf Uhlenhaut, Director of Passenger Car Development, pointed out that the car had better road-holding ability, braking potential, suspension stability, and maneuverability than any comparable automobile in the world. (The entire production for the balance of the year had already been sold.) With the 6,332 cubic-centimeter fuel-injected 300-horsepower V-8 engine installed in the slightly modified but outwardly regular 300

The 250 S or SE sedan, 1965

The sporty 280 SL of 1967

The 200 or 200 D sedan, 1965

sedan body the car weighed 3,835 pounds. Torque was 434 pounds-feet at 3,000 revolutions per minute. The wheelbase was 112.8 inches and overall length 196.9 inches. Tires were Dunlop SP FR 70-VR14. The actual performance of this "greatest sedan in the world," as the experts called it, was truly fantastic, and especially so when Uhlenhaut demonstrated its capabilities. The power to weight ratio was 12.8 pounds per horsepower. Acceleration, with the automatic four-speed transmission, from 0 to 60 miles per hour took 6.5 seconds and maximum speed was 137 miles per hour. The price was $13,997.

The 250 C coupe, announced for the 1969 model year, seemed a compromise between the regular passenger sedan and the sports car. The body style, with metal roof strips, suggested a sporty automobile. Powered, in the United States, by the 280 engine of 157 horsepower — elsewhere the 250 (146 horsepower) or 250 SE (170 horsepower) engines were used — the 3,538-pound vehicle had a maximum speed of 115 miles per hour and reached 0 to 60 miles per hour in 13.6 seconds. The performance of this coupe was decidedly more lively than that of the 250 or 280 sedans. Disc brakes were fitted on all wheels, ensuring excellent stopping and radial tires provided superb road-holding. The four-speed automatic transmission and independent rear suspension made for pleasant and effortless driving. The price of $6,260 did not include the many available extras expected in a luxury car, and such items as air conditioning, radio, power steering, and conveniences and comfort accessories brought the delivered price in Tucson, Arizona, to $8,998.

The unorthodox C 111 sports car, conceived as an engineering exercise with no future production in mind, was first publicly introduced at the Frankfurt Automobile Show in 1969. This advanced type of vehicle created a sensation at the exhibition and the speculation that such a sports car would eventually be produced and sold to the public, despite the statement by Daimler-Benz that it was strictly a research and development vehicle. Many remembered that the unique 300 SL sports car was also originally built as a purely experimental car and was produced only after victories in several international events.

The small coupe of steel monocoque frame with fibre glass panels and gull wing doors had a wheelbase of 103.2 inches, an overall length of 166.5 inches, was 70.9 inches wide and 44.3 inches high. Front suspension was by unequal length A-arms, coil springs, and telescopic shock absorbers with anti-roll bar. The 3-chamber water-cooled Wankel rotary engine, positioned ahead of the rear wheels, had a displacement of 1,800 cubic centimeters — the equivalent of a 3.6-liter reciprocating (Otto) engine — and developed 330 horsepower at 7,000 revolutions per minute. Compression ratio was 10 to 1. Torque was 220 pounds-feet at 5,000 to 6,500 revolutions per minute. A five-speed manual transmission was provided and all wheels had outboard vented disc brakes, similar to those of the 6.3 sedan. Tires were 195 x 14 radials. The curb weight of the vehicle was 2,524 pounds, and the power to weight ratio was 7.2 pounds per horsepower. Performance was truly incredible. Acceleration from 0 to 60 miles per hour took 4.9 seconds, and maximum speed was 162 miles per hour.

The compact 330-horsepower rotary engine weighed merely 275 pounds (the V-8 developing 230 horsepower weighed 495 pounds), but fuel consumption was about one-third more. The two fuel tanks of the C 111, one on each side, held 31.6 gallons. Service needed was estimated at 60,000 to 70,000 miles of hard driving, against the 90,000 for a conventional six-cylinder piston engine. But the Wankel engine had only 950 parts, while 1,750 parts were needed for the other type. The higher exhaust temperature of the rotary engine was definitely an advantage for an afterburner emission control for this much more pollutive offensive Wankel type engine and thus a bright future for it was predicted.

The following year an advanced model of the C 111, the Mark II, was shown to the public at the Geneva Auto Show. An additional rotary chamber had been added, raising the horsepower output accordingly, but also adding considerably to the engine weight. That was now 395 pounds. The new, refined body, longer by 8.3 inches, allowed improved vision because of an even lower hood and cut-outs in the rear buttresses. The drag coefficient was also lowered by 8 percent. But the curb weight was 2,735 pounds, due mainly to the greater engine weight. The performance of this four-chamber rotary-engined vehicle was appreciably increased, with acceleration from 0 to 60 miles per hour at 4.7 seconds and maximum speed of 186 miles per hour. But no further production of the vehicle was promised.

The 200 or 200 D and 220 or 220 D sedan, 1968

The 280 S or 280 SE sedan, 1968

The 250 C or 250 CE coupe, 1968

In fact, the vehicle was used extensively for experimental work. It had been driven over 20,000 miles by 1976. Suspension systems and brake circuits and designs were exhaustively tested on this high-speed car. But one of the more significant experiments was the endurance and speed test conducted with a turbo-charged diesel engine in early 1976.

The C 111 was slightly modified with aerodynamic headlight fairings and solid wheel covers so that the air resistant coefficients were below 0.3. Tires fitted were 215/70 x 15. For the trial the 12.6-kilometer (7.82-mile) test track near Nardo in Southern Italy was selected, where other tests had also been made by Daimler-Benz engineers of their prototypes and experimental creations.

The turbo-charged diesel sedan was driven by the engineers involved in the project: Joachim Kaden, Hans Liebold, Guido Moch, and Erich Waxenberger. Each man drove for 2½ miles when the 37-gallon (140-liter) fuel tanks had to be refilled. In about 64 hours, sixteen international class records and three world records for land vehicles were established, all considerably higher than the previous ones. The world records were for distances of 5,000 miles, at 156.928 miles (252.540 kilometers) per hour, for 10,000 kilometers, at 156.748 miles (252.249 kilometers) per hour, and for 10,000 miles, at 156.467 miles (251.798 kilometers) per hour. The other records were for nine distance and four time periods for vehicles with diesel engines of 2- to 3-liter displacement. These were for Category A, group III, class 8, at from 10 kilometers to 5,000 kilometers and speeds of 139.797 miles (224.971 kilometers) per hour to 157.155 miles (252.905 kilometers) per hour for the longer distance. The time periods covered 1, 6, 12 and 24 hours at speeds of from 158.368 miles (254.856 kilometers) per hour to 157.233 miles (253.030 kilometers) per hour.

Actually the regular OM 617 engine was reduced slightly to a capacity of less than 3,000 cubic centimeters by minor alteration of the cylinder bore diameter. The compression was lowered, changes in camshaft timing were made, and a special Bosch injection pump was installed. Especially made pistons were fitted with larger piston pins than those used in the regular production engines. Connecting rods were altered. The pistons were pin-point cooled by an oil spray system. Several parts were made of a different material or were especially treated because of the expected increased stress. However, remarkably, the crankshaft and main bearings were left identical with those of the production engines.

The exhaust gas turbo-charger T-04 B, made by Garrett Airesearch, reached a maximum of 135,000 revolutions per minute and compressed the intake air to a boost pressure of about 2 kilograms per square centimeter. The air temperature of about 220 degrees Celsius was reduced to about 100 degrees Celsius (212 degrees Fahrenheit). The unit was tuned to ensure that the highest boost pressure was reached at an engine speed of between 4,200 and 4,700 revolutions per minute to generate an output of 190 horsepower DIN (over 200 SAE). Torque was 275 pounds/feet (38 mkp) at 3,600 revolutions per minute. In emission and fuel consumption this special engine with a 2.17 fifth gear ratio did not differ significantly from the standard production unit. Average fuel consumption on the record run was 19.8 liters per 100 kilometers or 11.9 miles per gallon, and oil consumption was 0.7 liters per 1,000 kilometers.

In 1970 a newly designed 3.5-liter V-8 engine with fuel injection was installed in the more luxurious models, the 280 SE coupe and convertible and the 300 SEL sedan. This V-8 shared no parts with the 6.3 engine. With a stroke of 92 millimeters and a bore of 65.8 millimeters, this engine displaced 3,499 cubic centimeters. Compression ratio was 9.5 to 1, and power output was 230 horsepower at 6,050 revolutions per minute. The engine weighed 505 pounds, merely 55 pounds more than the 2.8-liter six-cylinder unit. The body lines of the coupe and convertible models, first introduced in 1961 as the 220 SE, were slightly altered. While other refinements had taken place over the intervening years, basically these cars really looked the same. But now the performance was greatly enhanced over that of the previous six-cylinder model. Acceleration from 0 to 60 miles per hour took 9.3 seconds, and the maximum speed was 125 miles per hour. The price of the 280 SE coupe was $13,430, which included most of the accessories, such as air conditioning, stereo radio, automatic transmission, electric windows, and such.

The new 350 SL sports car replaced the successful eight-year production run of the nearly alike 230 SL, 250 SL, and 280 SL. At 3,670 pounds, considerably heavier than the former sports car models, the 350 SL had

The 280 SE 3.5 coupe, 1968

The 350 SL roadster, 1971

The 350 SE sedan, 1972

a completely new and different body style. The wheelbase was 96.7 inches long, and the overall length was 172 inches. Tires were considerably larger as well, at 205/70 x 14. The improved suspension system utilized unequal A-arms in front and semi-trailing arms at the rear. An anti-roll bar in front was standard. The front disc brakes had ventilated rotors, while the rear ones were solid.

The 3.5-liter V-8 engine developed 230 horsepower at 5,000 revolutions per minute. A four-speed transmission or automatic was available. But in the United States the engine of 4.5-liter displacement was used with a three-speed automatic transmission. Because of the required emission controls this larger displacement engine was necessary to achieve the same power output as the 3.5-liter engine elsewhere. The list price of the 350 SL was $10,500.

When in 1971 *Road & Track* magazine selected the "Ten Best Cars in the World," the editors named the Mercedes-Benz 350 SL and the 300 SEL 6.3 (the sedan was also chosen as best in the over $10,000 sedan class). The editors stated, "The 350 SL is for the driver who is more interested in going fast really than looking as if he is going fast, and will keep him as comfortable, and as safe, as one can be in an automobile." And, the 6.3 "holds the top honors of sedans. . . . If we had to choose one car regardless of cost, to serve all our automotive desires, it would have to be the 300 SEL 6.3." And in the $6,000 to $10,000 sedan class, the 280 SE was selected. The magazine wrote, "It's meant to cover ground in a hurry, and the excellent seats and carefully controlled ride make it almost ideal as a luxurious transportation car."

It was not too long before the 4.5-liter engine also replaced the 3.5 unit in the luxurious coupe and convertible, as well as in the 300 SEL sedan. This enlarged version had the 65.5 millimeter stroke changed to 85 millimeters, and had a lowered compression ratio (from 9.5) of 8 to 1 to better cope with the stringent emission controls and to allow the use of regular low octane gasoline. It produced slightly less power, but actually smoother performance in the cars. Price of the sedan was $10,447.

In 1971 a total of 35,156 Mercedes-Benz passenger cars were sold in the United States. Total production of passenger cars was 284,230 and that of commercial vehicles about 160,000 units, with sales of 9.6 billion DM, according to the factory reports for that year.

Then, after nine years of production, the body style of the luxurious coupe and convertible line was discontinued and replaced. The new luxury coupe 350 SLC was a full four-seating coupe similar to the 350 SL sports car in style, but with a 14.2-inch longer wheelbase (111 inches) and mechanically the same. The weight was 3,820 pounds. It was the first Mercedes-Benz passenger car to adopt the low radiator styling of the sports car instead of the traditional radiator grille design. (In Europe, the 3.5-liter engine of 200 horsepower was used, but because of emission control problems in the United States the 350 SLC was delivered with the larger 4.5-liter engine developing 195 horsepower at 4,500 revolutions per minute and a compression ratio of 8 to 1 instead.) This elegant coupe — there was no longer any convertible — was available with the three-speed automatic transmission.

A double-overhead camshaft six-cylinder engine was introduced early in 1972 to better deal with the demands of stricter emission controls. The valves were operated by finger rockers, similar to those of the V-8 engines. A Solex four-barrel carburetor replaced the former two carburetors. Compression ratio was 9 to 1. This new six-cylinder engine, with carburetor, developed 130 horsepower at 5,000 revolutions per minute, and the fuel-injected version 160 horsepower at 5,500 revolutions per minute, compared with 134 and 155 horsepower, respectively, for the former single overhead camshaft units. But the new engines produced about 15 percent less hydrocarbon and 10 percent less carbon monoxide than the earlier design.

Late in 1972, at the Paris Salon de l'Automobile the entire new "S" line of passenger cars was first shown. Lower and wider than the previous models, all of them had the improved suspension of the SL and the SLC types. The double-overhead camshaft six-cylinder engines, with carburetors, now developed 160 horsepower for the 280 S, and the fuel-injection version 185 horsepower for the 280 SE sedan. The 350 SE model was powered by the 3.5-liter V-8 engine, developing 200 horsepower, with fuel injection. However, for the United States market, the 195-horsepower

The four-cylinder engine of the 200 model, 1965

Six-cylinder twin overhead camshaft engine M 110

4.5-liter unit was to be provided instead. These models were available with manual or automatic transmissions. (A total of 41,556 Mercedes-Benz passenger cars was sold in the United States in 1972.)

In fact, by the time these new models were offered to the public, several changes had been made. In Germany, a total of 21 passenger car models was available, but only nine models were offered in the United States: the 220 D sedan with a diesel engine of 57 horsepower, and the 220 sedan with the four-cylinder 85-horsepower gasoline engine. The 280 sedan had the new double-overhead camshaft six-cylinder engine of 130 horsepower, and the sporty 280 C was similarly powered. Now weighing 3,425 pounds against the 3,395 pounds for the sedan, the coupe would probably not be much livelier in performance.

The 280 SE 4.5 sedan with a wheelbase of 108.3 inches, the 280 SEL 4.5, and 300 SEL 4.5 with identical wheelbases of 112.2 inches, as well as the now designated 450 SL and the 405 SLC, all had the same 4.5-liter V-8 engine which developed 190 horsepower at 4,750 revolutions per minute. All of the gasoline engines had an 8 to 1 compression ratio to permit the use of low-lead or no-lead fuel. The 300 SEL 4.5 had air suspension and was a somewhat more luxuriously equipped automobile than the 105-pounds lighter 280 SEL 4.5 sedan.

Then the 450 SE and 450 SEL (with a 100-millimeter longer wheelbase) sedans were introduced, especially to be sold in the United States to simplify the distribution and sales. They actually replaced the 280 line of cars for that market. Powered by the 190-horsepower engine only, the three-speed automatic transmission was available, as in the 450 SL and 450 SLC. (In other countries, the 225-horsepower engine and both styles of transmission were used.) The new 450 models had yet longer, lower, and wider bodies, but were still similar in appearance to the previous sedans and unmistakenly Mercedes-Benz. The wheelbase of the 450 SE was 112.8 inches and the weight 3,995 pounds, 305 pounds more than the 280 SE. Overall length was 195.3 inches. Mechanically these 450 sedans were identical to the SL and SLC models. They were all solid and substantial cars and although quite heavy, fun to drive and extremely comfortable. Still, the figures given were indicative of superb performance of this new line of automobiles. The 450 SE reached 0 to 60 miles per hour in 9.3 seconds and had a maximum speed of 134 miles

per hour. The 450 SL and 450 SLC accelerated from 0 to 60 miles per hour in 8.8 seconds and had a maximum speed of 131 miles per hour. The price of the 450 SE was $13,491, fully equipped, and that of the SEL was $14,698.

Passenger safety had always been a major consideration in the construction of Mercedes-Benz automobiles, but the first of a line of special safety vehicles, the ESF (Experimentier-Sicherheits-Fahrzeug), was constructed in 1971. A vast number of outside and interior safety designs and devices underwent extensive tests. Actually, more than a hundred safety elements had been developed and tested since 1946, and have been incorporated into the cars built. The cone-type door lock was patented in 1949, and in 1952 a patented body design, standard in all models since 1959, was the safety body which upon impact would crush in front and rear but withstand exceptional forces in the extremely strong passenger compartment. Several ESF vehicles were built and exhaustively tested, and the ESF 24 looked startlingly similar to the 450 SE sedan.

Actually, the construction of safety vehicles was not new. In 1940 the experimental vehicle number 11 included the improved suspension system and such safety features as solid side protection and an extremely rigid floor and a three-part steering column. Design features over the years, adding to the safety of the cars built, were the complete independent wheel suspension in 1931 and the frame-floor construction and stressed chassis used since 1953. Engine features were the overhead camshaft design since 1952, the low pivot single-joint swing axle since 1954, air suspension system and automatic transmission since 1961, a dual circuit power braking with disc brakes for the entire passenger car line since 1963, a leveling adjustment device with coil springs available for all cars since 1965, the new diagonal-pivot swing axle from 1968 on, and electronic fuel injection since 1969. All of these advanced engineering designs made the cars safer to drive.

Conscious of ever-increasing concern of all environmental problems and in an effort to reduce pollution and noise, engineers have carried out tests and development work in the area of modifying available drive units and by developing new drive systems.

Experimental C 111 car with rotary engine of 350 horsepower

Experimental safety vehicle of 1971

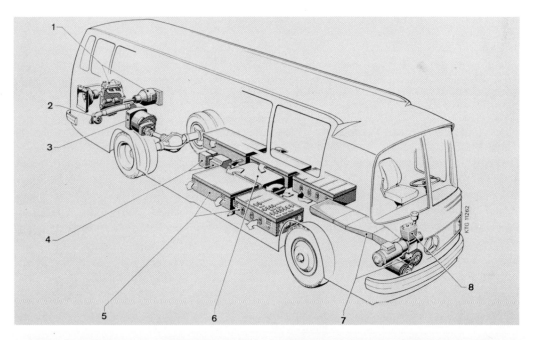

Drawing of OE 302 bus with hybrid power unit
1. Diesel engine with generator
2. Cooling fan for traction motor
3. Electric traction motor with reduction gear
4. High voltage section
5. Lead batteries
6. Electronic control unit
7. Fan for cooling batteries
8. Air compressor and auxiliary pump for power steering

A low-pollution commercial diesel engine in 1972 was the OM 402 unit. This water-cooled eight-cylinder V-type engine produced 256 horsepower at 2,500 revolutions per minute. Maximum torque was 83 mkp and weight 780 kilograms. The fuel was injected through a four-hole nozzle into a cylindrical piston recess where the air is set into turbulent motion by means of a twisted intake duct. This combustion process takes place according to the familiar direct injection system guaranteeing quiet engine running, favorable fuel consumption, and low toxic emission.

Carbon monoxide (CO) emission of the OM 402 engine was 3.8 grams per brake horsepower hour (gm/BHP-hr), actually less than a tenth of the 40 permitted by the 13-stage California test after 1973. The total emission of unburnt hydrocarbons (HC) and nitric oxides (NOx) was 7.2, less than half of the 16 permitted as of 1972. The 21-stage test for the other states produced practically the same results. By reducing the effective mean pressure there was no problem in meeting the exhaust gas regulations from 1975 of 5 for hydrocarbons and nitric oxides, although they were considerably stricter.

To reduce the noise level, an engine for the O 305 bus was especially well insulated by using a special casing. By closing the lower, open part of the engine compartment with a new type cover, it was possible to completely enclose the engine, apart from the necessary openings for cooling air circulation, air induction and exhaust gas emission. The fan was driven very quietly by a viscosity slip clutch and with just enough rotation speed to ensure sufficient cooling air for the particular operating conditions. These measures enabled the operating noise to be reduced by an average of twelve decibles. The sound level was actually so low that the human ear heard only a third of the noise produced by a vehicle with a conventional engine.

Another example in the search for new power sources was a regular model O 305 city bus which was converted to use natural gas as fuel, developed by the Linde Company. Four insulated tanks with a capacity of 286 liters (108.3 gallons) contained the liquified gas at a temperature of −162 degrees. This natural gas was drawn off in a gaseous or liquid state and switching over was automatically accomplished by solenoid valves, according to the container pressure.

Another vehicle, a refuse truck LPKO 1113, had the engine driven by liquid propane-butane gas. Transformed into a liquid state, not by cooling as with the natural gas but by means of pressure, this fuel was stored in a special pressure tank holding 120 liters (45.5 gallons) at 12 to 16 pounds per square inch pressure. A gas mixer ensured the correct gas-to-air ratio and this mixture was ignited in the individual cylinders by the spark plugs. The maximum engine speed was limited by a centrifugally controlled throttle.

Still another development was the OE 302 electro bus with hybrid drive. As the term suggests, actually two forms of energy were used in driving this vehicle. A diesel direct current unit transformed the heat energy of the fuel into electrical energy which is then stored in lead batteries for the supply of a direct current motor. This arrangement permitted extremely quiet charging with no exhaust gas emission when the diesel unit was not working, a great advantage in highly populated areas of the city. Less populated areas, as suburbs, could be used for recharging. The diesel engine of the sound-proofed generator functioned at the best thermal efficiency in accordance with the load and rotation speed, and exhaust gas emission was minimal. This compound motor could be switched directly from engine operation to braking operation and acted as a charging generator for the batteries. The engine could also be started under load, thus eliminating the need for a gearbox.

Using another form of electro drive, the smaller transporter, LE 306, was developed in conjunction with Hanomag-Henschel and the firms Kiepe and Varta. This new type of electro vehicle had none of the slow speeds of the former electromobiles, but was a fast and quickly accelerating transporter as the diesel-engined version. While the heavy lead batteries allowed only a relatively small operating radius, this disadvantage was compensated by a new battery-changing method. At a charging station, the huge battery was removed from one side and a new one was inserted from the other. The operation took not any longer than a normal fueling process and meant that the electro transporter could be used in an around-the-clock operation if desired. When the vehicle was not in service the battery could also be charged from the electric lines by means of a charging device.

The experimental hydrogen-powered bus and
280 E sedan

The transporter with metal hydrides hydrogen
storage unit

The use of hydrogen as another alternative source of energy had been examined carefully by Daimler-Benz engineers. A suitable hydride storage unit, replacing the massive and dangerous systems used previously, had been developed of special alloys which take up hydrogen under heat. These units can also serve as air conditioners to cool the interior of the vehicle, as independent vehicle heaters, or as reservoirs for engine waste heat with subsequent recovery for heating purposes.

Small buses have been tested over several years and it was found that hydrogen drive combined with carburetor engines and hydride storage units was possible without any particular problems. For instance, a 200-kilogram (440-pound) tank weight with a 60-horsepower engine allowed for a maximum cruising radius of 200 kilometers (125 miles). Efforts were made to extend this to 400 kilometers. With the cooperation of the University at Kaiserslautern, a further development with a mixed gasoline and hydrogen drive was built into a 280 E sedan. A significant improvement in the quality of exhaust gas encouraged the engineers to believe that such a system would provide a continuous transition from oil to hydrogen technology.

Riding in such an experimental sedan in 1977, the author watched the expert engineer-driver manipulate several buttons and switches when starting the car and during the drive, but found the performance only slightly inferior to that of the regular gasoline-engined sedan.

Generally thought of as manufacturers of fine passenger cars, Daimler-Benz also produced a complete line of commercial vehicles, ranging from the light transporter to heavy-duty truck, from the special purpose vehicle to the Unimog and all-wheel tractor, and from the touring bus to the intercity and city bus. In fact, about 12 percent of all trucks produced in Western Europe in 1977 carried the three-pointed star emblem. Passenger car production that year amounted to over 10 percent of all

such vehicles built in Germany. More than 130,000 people were employed by the company there.

In 1976, 45.9 percent of all passenger cars built and 64.7 percent of the commercial trucks built in Germany were shipped to over 150 countries. Besides the 1,272 servicing facilities in Germany which employed 57,000 people, some 3,800 sales and service stations in 169 countries employed about 54,000 people.

Passenger cars were manufactured at factories in Stuttgart-Untertürkheim, Sindelfingen and Bad Homberg; commercial vehicles in Mannheim, Gaggenau, Wörth, Kassel, Düsseldorf, Berlin-Marienfelde, Bremen, and Harburg. Through a part ownership of Motoren und Turbinen Union (MTU), Daimler-Benz is leading in the production and development of gas turbines, high-performance diesel engines for railroads, shops and special heavy-duty commercial vehicles, as well as diesel drive units for boats and numerous industrial purposes. The MTU companies employed about 11,000 people in their Friedrichshafen and Munich factories.

Commercial vehicles and diesel engines were also manufactured in seven factories abroad, either by wholly owned subsidiaries as in Brazil, Argentina, or by associated partner firms as in Spain, Iran, Turkey, South Africa, and Indonesia. Cooperation for the production of commercial vehicles existed with the Yugoslavian manufacturers Fap/Famos.

Total sales of the Daimler-Benz group in 1976 amounted to 23,503 million Deutsche Marks and of the home group 19,358 million DM, increases of 11.9 percent and 12.9 percent over the previous year. (Sales in 1966 were 5,822 million DM, about one-fourth of those of ten years later.) A total of 370,348 passenger cars and 247,756 commercial vehicles was produced in 1976, increases of 5.8 percent and 8 percent, respectively, over the previous year. (In 1966 production of passenger cars was 191,625 units and commercial vehicles 82,629.)

Chassis of the 170 S of 1949

Chassis of the 230 model of 1938

Engine and front axle, drive shaft, and rear axle
assembly of the 220a

The six-cylinder engine for the 300 model, 1955

The four-cylinder engine for the 190 model, 1956

The six-cylinder carburetor engine for the 220 S, 1956

The six-cylinder fuel injection engine for the 220 SE, 1958

The six-cylinder carburetor engine for the 250 S, 1965

The six-cylinder fuel injection engine for the 250 SE, 1965

Production Models (1973-1978)

In 1973 the 230/4 replaced the 220 sedan, produced from 1967 on. The four-cylinder engine had a bore of 93.75 millimeters and stroke of 83.6 millimeters, displacing 2,277 cubic centimeters, and developing 110 horsepower. The 2,970-pound sedan had a maximum speed of 106 miles per hour. The United States version developed 95 horsepower and the California engine 85 SAE horsepower because of more stringent emission controls. To offer the public another economical model, the 230/6 was developed. The six-cylinder engine displaced 2,292 cubic centimeters and developed 120 horsepower. Maximum speed was 109 miles per hour and fuel consumption was rated at 21.5 miles per gallon.

The following year, two new longer wheelbase sedans, the 280 SEL and 350 SEL, were introduced at the Geneva Auto Show. Both cars were essentially the same as the shorter versions, but offered greater comfort to passengers and were more economical to operate than the larger-engined long 450 sedan.

With the introduction of the new five-cylinder diesel-engined sedan, Daimler-Benz again startled the automotive world. The 240 D sedan, with a four-cylinder diesel engine of larger displacement than the earlier models, had been introduced in 1973. That engine had cylinders of 91 millimeter bore and 92.4 millimeter stroke, displacing 2,376 cubic centimeters and it developed 65 horsepower at 4,200 revolutions per minute. Engineers believed that the 600 cubic centimeter displacement was the ideal size for a passenger car diesel engine. In fact, the 240 D sedan proved to be an excellently selling car, production reaching 60,928 units in 1974, from 16,512 in 1973, when this model was first sold. (Production of the 220 D in 1974 was 27,510 units.) With a maximum speed of 138 kilometers (85.7 miles) per hour and fuel consumption of 9.5 liters per 100 kilometers (24.75 miles) per gallon, the 240 D was truly a most economical vehicle.

Thus it was no surprise that the unorthodox five-cylinder diesel automobile found overwhelming acceptance, especially by diesel enthusiasts everywhere. The car was first produced in May 1974 and designated in Europe as 240 D 3.0. The United States owners got the 300 D identifying badge on the rear trunk lid. The five cylinders had a bore of 91 millimeters and stroke of 92.4 millimeters, displacing 2,971 cubic centimeters.

Horsepower rating was 80 DIN and 77 SAE, with torque of 16 mkg or 115.7 lbs/feet at 2,400 revolutions per minute. Engine speed at 100 kilometers (62 miles) per hour was 2,980 revolutions per minute, 200 less than that of the four-cylinder model. With the 3.46 rear axle ratio (the 240 D had 3.69), the 3,146-pound sedan had a maximum speed of 148 kilometers (92 miles) per hour and fuel consumption of 21.5 miles per gallon. (The Environmental Protection Agency rated the 300 D mileage as 21 miles per gallon for city driving and 28 miles per gallon for highway travel.) The enlarged fuel tank for the 1976 model year, holding 20.6 gallons, would allow a driving range of 576 miles. Production in 1975 was 34,420 units of the 300 D, but many more could have been sold if engine production capacity could have been increased. Nearly half of the Mercedes-Benz passenger cars sold in the United States were diesel-powered and the proportion was expected to increase every year. The 300 D sold in 1974 for $11,782.

To give buyers of the sporty SL and SLC models a wider choice, the more economical version with the double overhead camshaft six-cylinder engine of 185 horsepower was introduced in 1974. The cars shared the body and appointments with the 350 SL and SLC and 450 SL and SLC line of cars. Performance of these lighter models was quite respectable. Maximum speed was 205 kilometers (127 miles) per hour and acceleration for the 0 to 100 kilometer per hour speed was 9.5 seconds, against the 8.5 for the 450 SL which had a maximum speed of 215 miles per hour.

The 450 SEL 6.9 sedan was first publicly shown in 1974. It was a fast, powerful luxury sedan and chassis of the larger S-class, but had a hydro-pneumatic suspension system with four spring units carrying the weight of the vehicle. A constant self-leveling device kept the car at an even level under all road conditions, giving it superb roadability. All of the technological improvements of the time were incorported in the construction, making it an excellent automobile in every respect.

The 6.9-liter V-8 engine was basically an enlarged version of the tested powerplant used so successfully in the former 6.3 sedan and the current large 600 models. Many refinements were, of course, included. The overhead camshaft engine had a bore of 107 millimeters and stroke of 95 millimeters, displacing 6,834 cubic centimeters and it developed 286

The sporty coupes 280 SLC, 350 SLC, and 450 SLC, 1974

The 200 D to 280 E range sedans, 1976

The S-class top model, 450 SEL 6.9, 1975

horsepower at 4,250 revolutions per minute. (The U.S. version had 250 SAE horsepower at 4,000.) Torque was 405 lbs/ft at 3,000 revolutions per minute (U.S.: 360 lbs/ft at 2,500), and compression ratio 8.8 to 1 (U.S.: 8 to 1). Acceleration was 7.4 seconds (U.S.: 8.9 seconds) from 0 to 100 kilometers (62 miles) per hour, and maximum speed was 225 kilometers (140 miles) per hour. The car had a wheelbase of 2,960 millimeters (116.5 inches) and the rear axle ratio was 2.65 to 1. The price in the United States for the 450 SEL 6.9 sedan at the time of introduction was $38,230. Production in 1975 was 474 units.

In 1976 the entire line of smaller sedans, from the 200 to the 280 E model, received new styled bodies. Several safety features were included. The 230/6 model was replaced by the new 250 model. That newly designed engine of 2,525 cubic centimeters had a four-bearing crankshaft with nine counterweights for smoother operation. Compression ratio was 8.7 to 1 and with the double down draft carburetor the engine developed 129 horsepower at 5,500 revolutions per minute.

The others which shared the 123 bodies were the 200 model which had the 1,987 cubic centimeter four-cylinder engine of 94 horsepower, the 230 model with the 2,307 cubic centimeter four-cylinder of 109 horsepower, the 250 model with the 2,525 cubic centimeter six-cylinder engine of 129 horsepower, the 280 model with the 2,746 cubic centimeter double overhead camshaft six-cylinder engine of 156 horsepower, and the 280 E with the K-jetronic fuel injection engine of 177 horsepower, and the diesel models 200 D, 220 D, 240 D, and 300 D.

The 280 S, 280 SE and SEL, and the 350 SE and SEL replaced the upper range of passenger cars, originally produced as the 250 S and SE, then the 280 S and SE, and 300 SEL, optional with a 3.5-liter engine. More than 383,000 of these cars had been built in the seven years.

The 280 line had the 2.8-liter double overhead camshaft six-cylinder engine of 160 horsepower for the carburetor version and 185 horsepower for the fuel-injection type. The 350 SE and SEL had the V-8 overhead valve engine of 3.5-liter displacement (3,499 cubic centimeters) developing 200 horsepower at 5,800 revolutions per minute with a 9.5 to 1 compression ratio. These engines were practically the same as previously,

but the oil could now be changed by sucking it through the dipstick pipe. A diagnostic socket was provided to quickly check the essentials of the engine operation and the hood could be opened wider for easier accessibility when servicing.

A synchronized four-speed transmission with floor shift was standard equipment, but a five-speed transmission with torque converter was available as optional extra on these models. The cars had a slightly longer wheelbase than before for improved comfort and road-holding. The front axle required no maintenance. All engines had a good torque; the 350 line 29.2 mkg at 4,000 revolutions per minute, the 280 S had 23 mkg, and the 280 SE and SEL had 24.3 mkg at 4,500 revolutions. Acceleration figures were 11.5 seconds for the 280 S, 10.5 seconds for the 280 SE and SEL, and 9.5 seconds for the 350 SE and SEL for the 0 to 100 kilometers (62 miles) per hour.

The 280 SL, 350 SL, and 450 SL models, two-seaters with sporty elegance and comfort, and their complementary coupe styles SLC, suitable for four to five persons, were virtually unchanged from the previous years. Stability of windshield pillars had been improved and their shape kept the side windows almost completely free of road dirt in bad weather. Rear lights had also been restyled for that purpose. These models had power steering, like all S-class cars. The 280 SL and SLC had the six-cylinder engine developing 185 horsepower, the 350 SL and SLC the eight-cylinder 200-horsepower engine, and the 450 SL and SLC had the eight-cylinder engine of 225 horsepower.

The larger sedans, 450 SE and SEL, remained unchanged from those introduced a few years before. The 6.9 sedan also was the same. And the two 600 limousine models were still available. The 6.3-liter engine developed 250 horsepower (300 SAE) and gave these luxuriously appointed sedans adequate power to cruise at fantastically high speeds in greatest comfort and safety. Acceleration was 9.7 seconds for the 0 to 100 kilometers per hour and maximum speed was 205 kilometers (127 miles) per hour for these 5,456- and 5,864-pound limousines.

In 1976 ten models were sold in the United States, although the company manufactured a total of twenty-seven different model cars, not includ-

The U.S. models, 450 SEL sedan, 450 SL roadster, and 450 SLC coupe, 1977

ing the large limousines, which were built only upon special order. The sale of the diesel-engined sedans was limited only by the production of these cars, although approximately 40 percent of all passenger cars sold by Daimler-Benz in this country were 240 D and 300 D models. With the enlarged fuel tank, these vehicles had a driving range of 638 and 576 miles, respectively, using the official Environmental Protection Agency figures.

A total of 380,348 passenger cars was manufactured in 1976. Of these, 297,250 were of the 200 to 280 E line and 73,098 of the S-class and SL and SLC models. During that year, 247,756 commercial vehicles were built, of which 193,204 units were produced in home factories and 54,552 in manufacturing plants abroad. In all offices and plants, 106,863 persons were employed by the company. Sales of the Daimler-Benz group were 23,503 million marks, an increase of 11.9 percent over the previous year. Exports amounted to 47.5 percent of production for the year 1976.

In late 1977 the horsepower output of the eight-cylinder engines for the 350 line of cars was given as 195 (DIN), and that of the 450 line engines as 217 (DIN). And a new coupe style was added to the existing models. Based on the W 123 sedan model, the coupe had a four-inch shorter wheelbase and was more elegantly outfitted. It was available with several different engine sizes: the four-cylinder 230 engine of 109 horsepower, the six-cylinder 280 engine of 156 horsepower, and the fuel-injection engine of 177 horsepower. In addition to these models, designated as 230 C, 280 C, and 280 CE, there was also the five-cylinder diesel-engined version for the United States market. This 300 CD coupe was priced, at the time of introduction, at $19,987, and the price of the 280 CE coupe was $20,610.

Greatly encouraged by the successful record run with the supercharged diesel engine, a modified installation was planned for a future production car by the engineers. It seemed merely a matter of timing. This was done for the Frankfurt Auto Show in 1977. One of the three new creations was the turbo-charged diesel sedan 300 SD. The 2,998 cubic centimeter turbo-charged diesel engine developed 115 horsepower (110 SAE) at 4,200 revolutions per minute, an increase of 44 percent in power. Torque was increased by 37 percent over the regular diesel engine. Fuel consumption was actually less, 10.6 liters per 100 kilometers (at 68 miles per hour). The 1,765-kilogram (3,883-pound) sedan had a maximum speed of 165 kilometers (103 miles) per hour. The elegant S-class 300 SD sedan was an economical, most comfortable car, the technician's answer to questions of energy conservation and environmental protection. It was created primarily for the American market.

Another new body style introduced at the show was the station wagon. This model, based on the lines of the regular 123 sedans, naturally had considerably more storage space. By folding down the rear seats, the flat area could be increased to a length of 1.78 meters, or a volume of 879 liters. Load-carrying ability was up to 700 kilograms. Special rails on the roof could carry racks for heavy loads. The T model station wagon was supplied with a choice of five different engines, the 230 of 109 horsepower, the 250 of 129 horsepower, the 280 E of 177 horsepower, and the two diesel engines, the 240 D and 300 D.

The third new model was the 450 SLC 5.0 coupe. This was a car for driving enthusiasts, offering high performance and comfort, and seemed suitable for rallies. The body was considerably lighter than the regular coupe, because the hood and rear deck were of light alloy. By using front and rear spoilers the wind resistance was reduced by 9 percent. The light metal engine (weighing 43 kilometers less) was a V-8 unit of 4,990 cubic centimeter displacement, developing 240 horsepower at 5,000 revolutions per minute. Torque was 41 mkg at 3,200 revolutions per minute. Compression ratio was 8.8 to 1. The car weighed 1,515 kilograms (3,330 pounds), and maximum speed was 225 kilometers (140 miles) per hour. It appeared doubtful that this limited production model (80 per month) would be available in the United States, at least in that form.

The 450 SLC 5.0 coupe with light alloy engine, shown in 1977

The station wagon, 240 TD, 300 TD, 230 T, 250 T, and 280 TE, shown in 1977

The turbo-charged 300 SD, shown in 1977

Mercedes-Benz 450 SEL 6.9 model, 1975

Fuel-injected engine of the high-performance 6.9 model, 1975

The five-cylinder turbo-charged diesel engine of the 300 SD, 1977

The 5-liter light alloy engine of 177 kw (240 DIN horsepower), 1977

The museum at the factory contains just about every model car and engine ever built

Model Details

Daimler passenger and racing car models before the merger of 1926

Year	Cylinders	Power	Description
1885	1 cyl	0.5 hp	Motorbicycle
1886	1 cyl	1.1 hp	Motor-carriage
1889	2 cyl	1.5 hp	Steelwheel car
1892	2 cyl	2.0 hp	Motor car
1893/99	4-6 cyl	2.0 hp	Vis-a-Vis; Phaeton; Victoria
1897/99	4-9 cyl	2 and 4 hp	with Phoenix engine, front mounted; Charette, Phaeton; Tonneau, Break
1899	4 cyl	23.0 hp	Racing car with Phoenix engine
1900	2 cyl	8.0 hp	Paul Daimler car; 2 and 4 seats
1900/01	4 cyl	35.0 hp	First Mercedes car
1900/01	4 cyl	35.0	First Mercedes racing car
1902/03	4 cyl	8/11, 12/16	Mercedes touring car
1902/06	4 cyl	18/22, 28/32, 40/45, 60/70	Mercedes-Simplex car
1903/04	4 cyl	60 and 90 hp	Mercedes-Simplex racing car
1904/05	4 cyl	80 and 100 hp	Mercedes racing car
1905	4 cyl	26/45, 31/55, 36/65	Mercedes touring car
1906	6 cyl	37/70	Mercedes touring car
1906	6 cyl	120 hp	Mercedes racing car
1907	6 cyl	39/80	Mercedes touring car
1908	4 cyl	130 hp	Grand Prix racing car
1908/13	4 cyl	8/18, 10/20, 14/35, 21/35, 22/40, 28/60	Mercedes shaft-driven car (poppet valve engine)
1910/13	4 cyl	10/30, 16/40, 16/45, 25/65	Mercedes-Knight car (sleeve valve engine)
1910/13	4 cyl	22/50, 28/60, 38/80, 37/90	Mercedes chain-driven car (poppet valve engine)
1914	6 cyl	28/90	Mercedes touring car
1914	4 cyl	115 hp	Grand Prix racing car
1916	4 cyl	16/50	Mercedes-Knight car
1919	4 cyl	10/35	2.6-liter touring car
1921/22	4 cyl	6/25/40 and 10/40/65	1.5-liter and 2.6-liter production car (with supercharger)
1924	4 cyl	120 hp	2-liter racing car with supercharger
1924	8 cyl	160 hp	2-liter racing car with supercharger
1924	6 cyl	15/70/100 and 24/100/140	4- and 6-liter touring car with supercharger

Benz passenger and racing car models before the merger of 1926

Year	Cylinders	Power	Description
1886	1 cyl	0.9 hp	Patent-Motor car; three-wheeled
1886/89	1 cyl	1.5 and 2.0 hp	Patent-Motor car; three-wheeled
1893/94	1 cyl	3.0 and 5.0 hp	Victoria, Vis-a-Vis; four-wheeled
1893/96	1 cyl	1.5 to 4.5 hp	Velo and Comfortable
1894/97	1 cyl	5.0 hp	Phaeton, Landau, hunting car, omnibus
1897/99	2 cyl	5, 8, 10, 12, 15	Dos-a-Dos, Mylord, Break
1899/1901	1 and 2 cyl	4, 5, 6, 9, 10	Duc, Ideal, Spider
1900/01	2 and 4 cyl	16, 25/35	Racing car
1901/02	1 and 2 cyl	5.0 and 8.0 hp	Elegant; front-engined
1902/03	2 cyl	16 and 20 hp	Phaeton, Tonneau
1903/04	2 cyl	8/10, 10/20, 12/14	Parcifal; front-engined, shaft driven
1903	4 cyl	60 hp	Racing car
1903/09	4 cyl	14/18, 16/20, 24, 18/28, 28/32, 24/45, 28/52	Phaeton, open or closed
1905/07	4 cyl	40, 50	Racing car (Herkomer Trophy)
1907	4 cyl	50, 60, 70/80	Racing car (Targa Florio, Semmering)
1908	4 cyl	150 hp	Racing car (Grand Prix, Semmering)
1908	4 cyl	25/35, 50/80, 75/105	Sports car (Prince Heinrich model)
1908/12	4 cyl	35/60, 10/18, 10/20, 20/35, 25/45	Phaeton, open or closed
1909/10	4 cyl	22/60, 28/80, 40/70	Sports Phaeton
1909	4 cyl	200 hp	Blitzen-Benz
1909/13	4 cyl	14/30, 29/60	Phaeton, open or closed, sports car, taxi
1911/13	4 cyl	8/18, 25/55, 18/45, 33/75, 39/100, 12/30	Runabout, Landaulet
1912/14	4 cyl	10/30, 16/40, 16/50, 28/100	Touring and sports car
1914/15	6 cyl	21/50, 25/65	Phaeton, open or closed
1918	4 cyl	6/18	Sports and racing car
1921/25	6 cyl	16/50	Sports and touring car
1918	6 cyl	27/70	Phaeton, Runabout
1922	6 cyl	80 hp	Tropfen racing car, rear-engined
1923	6 cyl	11/40	Phaeton, open or closed; Runabout

Daimler-Benz passenger and racing car models, 1926-1978

Year	Cylinders	Engine	Model
1926	6 cyl	2-liter, 8/38	Stuttgart 200
1926	6 cyl	3.1-liter, 12/55	Mannheim
1926	6 cyl	6.25-liter, 24/110/160	K sports car, with supercharger
1927	6 cyl	3.2-liter, 12/55	Mannheim 300
1927	6 cyl	6.8-liter, 26/120/180	S sports car, with supercharger
1928	6 cyl	2.6-liter, 10/50	Stuttgart 260
1928	6 cyl	3.5-liter, 14/70	Mannheim 350
1928	8 cyl	4.6-liter, 18/80	Nürnberg 460
1928	6 cyl	7.1-liter, 27/140/200	SS sports car, with supercharger
1928	6 cyl	7.1-liter, 27/170/225	SSK sports car, with supercharger
1929	6 cyl	3.7-liter, 15/75	Mannheim 370
1930	8 cyl	7.7-liter, 30/150/200	Grosser Mercedes, with or without supercharger
1931	6 cyl	1.7-liter, 7/32	170; first swing axle construction
1931	6 cyl	3.7-liter, 15/75	Mannheim 370 K (short) and 370S (sport)
1931	8 cyl	4.9-liter, 19/110	Nürnberg 500
1931	6 cyl	7.1-liter, 27/170/300	SSKL racing-sports car, with supercharger
1932	6 cyl	2-liter, 8/40	200, short or long
1933	6 cyl	2.9-liter, 11/68	290
1933	8 cyl	3.8-liter, 15/90/140	380 sport convertible with supercharger
1933	4 cyl	1.3-liter, 26 hp	130, first rear-engined car
1934	4 cyl	1.5-liter, 55 hp	150H, rear-engined sports car
1934	8 cyl	5-liter, 100/160	500K, sports car with supercharger
1934	8 cyl	3.36-liter, 354	750 kg formula racing car, with supercharger
1934	8 cyl	3.71-liter, 398	Record car (Gyon)
1935	4 cyl	1.7-liter, 38 hp	170H
1935	4 cyl	1.7-liter, 38 hp	170V
1935	4 cyl	2.6-liter, 45 hp	260D, first diesel passenger car
1935	8 cyl	3.99-liter, 430	750 kg formula racing car, with supercharger
1935	8 cyl	4.31-liter, 462	750 kg formula racing car, with supercharger
1936	6 cyl	2.3-liter, 55 hp	230 (box frame)
1936	8 cyl	5.4-liter, 115/180	540K sport convertible, with supercharger
1936	8 cyl	4.14-liter, 494	750 kg formula racing car, with supercharger
1936	12V cyl	4.98-liter, 540	Record car (Frankfurt-Darmstadt)
1937	6 cyl	3.2-liter, 78 hp	320
1937	4 cyl	2-liter, 50 hp	Sports car
1937	8 cyl	5.66-liter, 646	750 kg formula racing car, with supercharger
1938	8 cyl	7.7-liter, 155/230	Grosser-Mercedes with supercharger (swing axles)
1938	6 cyl	2.3-liter, 55 hp	230 (X-frame)
1938	6 cyl	3.4-liter, 78 hp	320
1938	12V cyl	5.57-liter, 736	Record car (Frankfurt) with 3-liter engine of 483 hp (Dessau)
1938	12V cyl	3-liter, 476	Formula racing car, 3 liter, with supercharger
1939	8V cyl	1.5-liter, 254	Racing car, 1.5-liter, with stage supercharger
1946	4 cyl	1.7-liter, 38 hp	170V
1949	4 cyl	1.7-liter, 52 hp	170S
1949	4 cyl	1.7-liter, 38 hp	170D
1950	4 cyl	1.8-liter, 45 hp	170Va
1950	4 cyl	1.8-liter, 40 hp	170Da
1951	6 cyl	2.2-liter, 80 hp	220
1951	6 cyl	3-liter, 115 hp	300
1952	6 cyl	3-liter, 150 hp	300S
1952	6 cyl	3-liter, 175 hp	300SL (carburetor)
1952	4 cyl	1.8-liter, 45 hp	170Vb
1952	4 cyl	1.8-liter, 40 hp	170Sb
1952	4 cyl	1.8-liter, 52 hp	170Db and 170DS
1953	4 cyl	1.8-liter, 45 hp	170S-V
1953	4 cyl	1.8-liter, 40 hp	170S-D
1953	4 cyl	1.8-liter, 52 hp	180 (side valve)
1953	4 cyl	1.8-liter, 40 hp	180D (from 1955, 43 hp)
1954	6 cyl	2.2-liter, 85 hp	220 coupe
1954	6 cyl	2.2-liter, 85 hp	220a
1954	6 cyl	3-liter, 125	300b

Year	Cylinders	Engine	Model
1954	6 cyl	3-liter, 215	300SL (fuel injection)
1954	8 cyl	2.5-liter, 280	Formula racing car, 2.5 liter, with fuel injection
1955	8 cyl	3-liter, 300	300SLR, with fuel injection
1955	4 cyl	1.9-liter, 105	190SL sports car
1955	6 cyl	3-liter, 125	300c/300c automatic
1955	6 cyl	3-liter, 175	300Sc, with fuel injection
1956	4 cyl	1.9-liter, 75 hp	190
1956	6 cyl	2.2-liter, 85	219 (from 1957, 90 hp)
1956	6 cyl	2.2-liter, 100	220S (from 1957, 106 hp)
1957	4 cyl	1.89-liter, 65 hp	180a (with overhead camshaft)
1957	6 cyl	3-liter, 160	300d, automatic transmission
1957	6 cyl	3-liter, 215	300 SL, roadster with fuel injection
1958	4 cyl	1.9-liter, 50 hp	190D
1958	6 cyl	2.2-liter, 115	220SE (fuel injection)
1959	4 cyl	1.8-liter, 68 hp	180b
1959	4 cyl	1.8-liter, 43 hp	180Db
1959	4 cyl	1.9-liter, 80 hp	190b
1959	4 cyl	1.9-liter, 50 hp	190Db
1959	6 cyl	2.2-liter, 95 hp	220b
1959	6 cyl	2.2-liter, 110	220Sb
1959	6 cyl	2.2-liter, 120	220SEb (fuel injection)
1961	4 cyl	1.89-liter, 68	180c
1961	4 cyl	1.99-liter, 48	180Dc
1961	4 cyl	1.9-liter, 80 hp	190c
1961	4 cyl	1.99-liter, 55 hp	190Dc
1961	6 cyl	2.2-liter, 120	220SEb/c (fuel injection)
1961	6 cyl	3-liter, 160	300SE (fuel injection — from 1964, 170 hp)
1963	6 cyl	2.3-liter, 150	230SL (fuel injection)
1963	8V cyl	6.3-liter, 250	600 Grosser Mercedes (fuel injection)
1965	4 cyl	2-liter, 95 hp	200
1965	4 cyl	2-liter, 55 hp	200D
1965	6 cyl	2.3-liter, 105	230
1965	6 cyl	2.3-liter, 120	230S
1965	6 cyl	2.5-liter, 130	250S
1965	6 cyl	2.5-liter, 150	250SE (fuel injection)
1965	6 cyl	3-liter, 170	300SEb (fuel injection)
1965	6 cyl	3-liter, 170	300SEL (fuel injection)
1967	6 cyl	2.5-liter, 150	250SL
1968	4 cyl	2-liter, 55 hp	200D
1968	4 cyl	2.2-liter, 60 hp	220D
1968	4 cyl	2-liter, 95 hp	200
1968	4 cyl	2.2-liter, 105	220
1968	6 cyl	2.3-liter, 120	230
1968	6 cyl	2.5-liter, 130	250
1968	6 cyl	2.8-liter, 140	280S
1968	6 cyl	2.8-liter, 160	280SE (fuel injection)
1968	6 cyl	2.8-liter, 160	280SE coupe and convertible (fuel injection)
1968	6 cyl	2.8-liter, 170	280SL (fuel injection)
1968	V8 cyl	6.3-liter, 250	300SEL 6.3 (fuel injection)
1968	6 cyl	2.5-liter, 130	250C coupe
1968	6 cyl	2.5-liter, 150	250CE coupe (fuel injection)
1969	V8 cyl	3.5-liter, 200	280SE 3.5 coupe and convertible (fuel injection)
1969	V8 cyl	3.5-liter, 200	300SEL 3.5 (fuel injection)
1970	V8 cyl	3.5-liter, 200	280SE/280SEL 3.5 (fuel injection)
1971	V8 cyl	3.5-liter, 200	350SL (fuel injection)
1971	V8 cyl	3.5-liter, 200	350SLC coupe (fuel injection)
1971	V8 cyl	4.5-liter, 225	280SE 4.5 (fuel injection)
1971	V8 cyl	4.5-liter, 225	280SEL 4.5 (fuel injection)
1971	V8 cyl	4.5-liter, 225	300SEL 4.5 (fuel injection)
1971	V8 cyl	4.5-liter, 225	450SL (fuel injection)
1972	6 cyl	2.8-liter, 160	280
1972	6 cyl	2.8-liter, 185	280E (fuel injection)
1972	6 cyl	2.8-liter, 160	280C coupe
1972	6 cyl	2.8-liter, 185	280CE coupe (fuel injection)
1972	6 cyl	2.8-liter, 160	280S
1972	6 cyl	2.8-liter, 185	280SE (fuel injection)
1972	V8 cyl	3.5-liter, 200	350SE (fuel injection)
1972	V8 cyl	4.5-liter, 225	450SLC (fuel injection)
1972	6 cyl	2.8-liter, 160	280S
1972	6 cyl	2.8-liter, 185	280SE (fuel injection)
1972	V8 cyl	3.5-liter, 200	350SE (fuel injection)
1973	4 cyl	2.3-liter, 110	230
1973	4 cyl	2.4-liter, 65 hp	240D
1974	6 cyl	2.8-liter, 185	280SEL (fuel injection)
1974	V8 cyl	3.5-liter, 200	350SEL (fuel injection)
1974	V8 cyl	4.5-liter, 225	450SE (fuel injection)

1974	V8 cyl	4.5-liter, 225	450 SEL (fuel injection)
1974	6 cyl	2.3-liter, 120	230
1974	5 cyl	3-liter, 80 hp	240 D 3.0 or 300 D
1974	6 cyl	2.8-liter, 185	280 SL (fuel injection)
1974	6 cyl	2.8-liter, 185	280 SLC (fuel injection)
1975	V8 cyl	6.9-liter, 286	450 SEL 6.9 (fuel injection)
1976	4 cyl	2-liter, 94 hp	200
1976	4 cyl	2.3-liter, 109	230
1976	6 cyl	2.5-liter, 129	250
1976	6 cyl	2.8-liter, 156	280
1976	6 cyl	2.8-liter, 177	280 E (fuel injection)
1977	4 cyl	2.3-liter, 109	230 C
1977	6 cyl	2.8-liter, 156	280 C
1977	6 cyl	2.8-liter, 177	280 CE (fuel injection)
1977	5 cyl	3-liter, 80 hp	300 CD
1978	5 cyl	3-liter, 115	300 SD (turbo-charged diesel)
1978	4 cyl	2.3-liter, 109	230 T station wagon
1978	6 cyl	2.5-liter, 129	250 T station wagon
1978	6 cyl	2.8-liter, 177	280 TE (fuel injection) station wagon
1978	4 cyl	2.4-liter, 65 hp	240 TD station wagon
1978	5 cyl	3-liter, 80 hp	300 TD station wagon
1978	V8 cyl	5 liter, 240	450 SLC 5.0 (fuel injection) coupe

Daimler called his first motorized vehicle (1889), which did not resemble a horse carriage, the Stahlradwagen (steel-wheel car). Benz named his first motor vehicle (1886) the Patent-Motorwagen (patent motor car), and his first four-wheeled car (1893) Victoria. The name Velo was derived from Velociped (bicycle). Such names as Phaeton, Landauer, Break, Tonneau, Vis-a-Vis, and others were taken from the carriage trade. To indicate the performance, the horsepower output was added later, as in "6 h.p. Spider."

From about 1902 the calculated rated output, called nominal output then, and the brake power were also given with the model designation, as in "14/18 h.p. Phaeton." After the introduction of the rating formula, the first number referred to the taxable horsepower and the second to the effective output, as in "10/30 Benz touring car." Because the authorities were not interested in the taxable rating of racing cars, the taxable rating was not stated. Vehicles with superchargers had three numbers: the taxable horsepower, the effective output without, and the maximum output with the supercharger.

The year of manufacture stated is the beginning of production, with racing cars the first time in competition. After the merger of Daimler and Benz (1926), the models were given special names, often indicating the plant where the cars were built, as Stuttgart, Nürnberg, Mannheim. From 1933 the taxable figure was omitted. The designation then was generally that of displacement, as "180" for the 1.8-liter engined car.

Diesel powered cars had the D added. H indicated a rear-engined model — H = Heck (rear-end). Other models were called DS = Diesel, Special model; S = Sport; SL = Sport, Leicht (light); SS = Super Sport; SSK = Super Sport Kurz (short); SSKL = Super Sport Kurz Leicht (light); SLR = Super Leicht Racing sports car. But later, and especially in passenger sedan models, the S meant Super. E = Einspritzungsmotor (fuel injection engine); SL = Sport Leicht (light); SLC = Sport Leicht Coupe. However, in SD the S means turbocharged, perhaps having thought of supercharged when making the distinct definition, because the T had already been used for the station wagon. Actually, the T stood for Touristik and Transport. The smaller letters (a, b, c) referred to the further development of those models, often the engines only.